The
Safe Hiring Audit

The Employer's Guide to Implementing a
Safe Hiring Program

By Lester S. Rosen, Esq.
With Michael Sankey

PO Box 27869
Tempe, AZ 85285
800.929.3811

www.brbpub.com

D0814988

The Safe Hiring Audit

The Employer's Guide to Implementing a Safe Hiring Program

©2008 First Edition

Written by: Lester S. Rosen, Esq. with Michael Sankey
Edited by: Kim Ensenberger
Cover Design by: Robin Fox & Associates

Publisher's Cataloging-in-Publication
(Provided by Quality Books, Inc.)

Rosen, Lester S.
    The safe hiring audit : the employer's guide to
implementing a safe hiring program / by Lester S. Rosen
; with Michael Sankey. -- 1st ed.
    p. cm.
    Includes index.
    ISBN-13: 978-1-889150-51-2
    ISBN-10: 1-889150-51-7

    1. Employee screening. 2. Employee selection.
3. Management audit.   I. Sankey, Michael L., 1949-
II. Title.

HF5549.5.E429R668 2008   658.3'112
                        QBI08-600143

All rights reserved. Printed in the United States of America. No part of this book may be used or reproduced in any form or by any means, or stored in a database or retrieval system without the prior written permission of the publisher, except in the case of brief quotations embodied in critical articles or reviews. Making copies of any part of this book for any purpose other than your personal use is a violation of U.S. copyright laws. Entering any of the contents into a computer for mailing list or database purposes is strictly prohibited unless written authorization is obtained from Facts on Demand Press.

The material in this book is presented for educational and informational purposes only and is not offered or intended as legal advice in any manner whatsoever. The materials should not be treated as a substitute for independent advice of counsel. All policies and actions with legal consequences should be reviewed by your legal counsel. Specific factual situations should also be discussed with your legal counsel. Where sample language is offered, it is only intended to illustrate a potential issue. A sample policy cannot address all specific concerns of a particular company and should not be relied on as legal advice.

Table of Contents

Chapter 3

Legal Compliance Issues 41

Chapter 4

The Application Process 77

Chapter 5

The Interview Process 93

Chapter 6

Checking Past Employment & Education Credentials 111

Chapter 7

Criminal Record Issues Important to Employers 137

Chapter 8

Limitations and Legal Use of Criminal Records 161

Chapter 9

Other Important Screening Tool for Employers   181

Chapter 10

Implementing the Screening Process   213

Chapter 11

Screening Essential Non-Employees   237

Screening Volunteers
Workers in the Home
Hiring Seasonal or Temporary Contract Personnel
About Hiring Juveniles
Summary and Best Practices

Appendix

Index

Introduction

Why Safe Hiring is So Important

This chapter discusses why safe hiring is so critical. For a business to engage in a true Safe Hiring Program, there must be buy-in at a number of levels. For example, hiring managers need to understand why an audit is important. A firm's CEO or CFO may need convincing.

The facts, figures, and examples in this chapter are meant to ensure that everyone involved in your business organization understands just what is at stake.

It's a sobering thought, but every time an employer hires anyone, there is the possibility that new hire can put him out of business. This person now has access to your assets, your clients, your co-workers, your money, your reputation, and even your very existence. If you make a bad-hiring decision, the results can be devastating.

Why? Because if a dangerous, unqualified, unfit, or dishonest candidate is placed in a job – and harm occurs – the employer risks a lawsuit for **negligent hiring**. Perhaps just as important, a bad-hiring decision can result in **loss of business** and **damage to a professional reputation** that may have been years in the making.

The following statistics are circulated by ADP, the payroll processing firm, from a 2003 Hiring Index Study compiled by its employment screening division—

- 30% of all business failures are due to employee theft and related forms of dishonesty
- The direct and indirect average cost of employee turnover is equal to 150% of the annual salary
- 51% of all resumes, applications, and references provided by applicants contain inaccurate information

Without knowing whom they are hiring, employers are playing Russian roulette with the future of their businesses every time they hire.

Even more difficult to measure are other *intangible costs* that also should be taken into consideration when calculating the long-term fallout from a bad-hiring decision—

- Lost customers or business causing damage to a firm's credibility
- Damage to employee morale
- Brand destruction
- Litigation

Yet many employers spend more time and effort choosing a copy machine or deciding between competing brands of laptops than they do in selecting employees.

Critical Issues That Employers Face

Even though everyone agrees that safe hiring and due diligence are missions critical for any business, there are still numerous employers who find safe hiring to be a challenge. Sadly, there are many employers who either do nothing when it comes to due diligence, or do way too little. Consider the following analysis of some of the key issues that employers must deal with when hiring.

Compliance With Hiring Laws

The laws associated with employment screening have sought to achieve a balance between privacy and due diligence. Although a number of laws limit, prohibit, or regulate obtaining and using background information, there is a great deal of information an employer is entitled to obtain and use in making the best hiring decisions. Certainly, all citizens have a reasonable expectation to privacy and a right to be treated fairly, yet, at the same time, an employer has the right to make diligent and reasonable job-related inquiries into a person's background so that the company, its employees, and the public are not placed at risk.

Therefore it is vital to keep the scope of reference checking and screening within specified legal boundaries. There are certain matters that are not valid predictors of job performance, and delving into them can be considered discriminatory. This can include information about religion or race, national origin, marital status, age, medical condition, and so forth. An employer cannot ask reference questions or obtain background information on those subject areas that cannot legally be raised in an interview situation with an applicant face-to-face.

There is No Instant Database That Gives All the Answers

In a perfect world, an employer needs only to go on the internet, put in an applicant's name and identity, and then up pops an instant thumps-up or thumbs-down result. Wow, with the click of a mouse, the employer knows if the person has a criminal record and if his or her credentials are accurate.

Unfortunately, there is no magic database in existence. There is no national credentials database where an employer can instantly confirm an applicant's past employment or education. There is no public record database where an employer can instantly find out if the applicant has a criminal record, a problematic driving record, or a job-related civil lawsuit.

Some employers have been given the legal authority to obtain government criminal records when filling positions involving security or access to groups at risk. In many states, for positions involving access to vulnerable patients or children, screeners for hospitals and school districts can submit applicant's fingerprints to be checked by the FBI or state authorities.

However, for most private employers, the challenge is more pressing because of the fact a criminal record check is not nearly as effective a tool as most employers might believe. Although certainly a criminal check is an essential part of any hiring program, it does not necessarily provide complete protection – there are more than 10,000 courthouses in 3,500+ jurisdictions in the U.S. Since employers cannot search every jurisdiction, there is always the possibility of missing a criminal record from a court not searched. The possibility of errors are compounded by the fact the searches are conducted by human beings who enter names in computers, scan listings of names, or engage in some other activity that ultimately depends upon human intervention. There is always the possibility of error. Even official government "rap sheets" are subject to possible errors.

There are privately assembled, multi-jurisdictional databases, but these, too, can lead to false negatives – that is, a person with a criminal record comes up clean

Confirming education credentials and past employment is equally labor intensive. Although some colleges and universities allow online record verifications and electronic transcripts, employers must still identify and individually go to each relevant school database. Past employers must be contacted, which is a process that presents its own difficulties.

There Are No Magical Tools That Find an "Honest" Person

In the wake of Enron, WorldCom and what appears to be a general collapse of corporate ethics and morality, more emphasis is now placed on the age-old question asked by Greek philosopher Diogenes, "How do you find an honest person?"

Part of the challenge in safe hiring is that by definition, employers are seeking an elusive quality. Ultimately, the ability to find an honest person depends on the correct use of a number of overlapping tools. These include 1) a number of objective fact-finding tools (pre-employment screening and reference checks); 2) tools used to convince applicants to be self-revealing (applications and interviews), and 3) to a subjective extent, instinct, and intuition. However, reliance only on instinct and intuition can be dangerous. Consider this fact— for every dishonest person ever hired, there was someone who sized up the person hired and concluded that this person would be good for the job.

There is no sure-fire test or method that will tell an employer if a particular person is an honest person.

It is Almost Impossible to Spot Liars at Interviews

Even if Diogenes had found an honest person, there is a body of modern evidence that suggests it is difficult for anyone, from ancient philosophers to modern-day employer, to use an interview to determine who is really who. Employers have a distinct challenge when it comes to spotting liars; industry statistics suggest that as many as 30% of all job applicants falsify information about their credentials, but trying to spot liars at interviews is, well, difficult, if not impossible.

There are lists of so-called "telltale signs" that a person is lying. For example, employers might observe if a person is avoiding eye contact, fidgeting, or hesitating before answering. Unfortunately, it can be a costly mistake for an interviewer to think lying can always be detected by such visual clues or by relying upon one's own instinct or intuition since some of the so-called "visual clues" can simply be a sign of nervousness about the interview, or stress, and not the intent to lie. In fact, accomplished liars are more dangerous because they can disguise themselves as truthful and sincere. An experienced liar will often show no visible signs.

The problem is further complicated because many people feel they can detect who is lying and who is not. Studies have demonstrated that most people are poor judges of when they are being told the truth and when they are being deceived. Paul Ekman, a psychology professor in the Department of Psychiatry at the University of California Medical School in San Francisco, is the author of 13 books, including *Telling Lies.*[1] Ekman has tested about 6,000 professionals trained to spot liars, including police officers, lawyers, judges, psychiatrists, and agents of the FBI, the CIA, and the Drug Enforcement Administration, to determine if they can tell if someone is lying. According to his research, most people are not very accurate in judging if a person is lying. The average accuracy in studies is rarely above 60%, while chance is 50%. Even among professional lie catchers, the ability to detect liars is not much better than 50%. In one study, custom agents who interviewed people at custom stations did not do any better than college students.

Another researcher at the same school, Dr. Maureen O'Sullivan, tested 13,000 people for the ability to detect deception. Using three different tests, only 31 subjects — nicknamed "wizards" — could usually tell whether a person was lying about an opinion, how someone is feeling, or about a crime.[2]

Some interviewees tell lies they have ingrained in their life story. They have created identities and legends of their own and, when they tell their stories, they are not fabricating on the spot. They put "it" on their resumes, talk about it and tell their friends about it. It becomes part of their personalities and personal histories because they have told it so often. It becomes second nature as they retell it again and again.

Employers, HR and security professionals should remember that as valuable as instinct may be, it does not substitute for factual verification of an applicant's credentials through background checks and other safe hiring techniques.

The Effects of Corporate Culture and Other Impediments

At some firms, efforts at safe hiring may be impeded by the simple fact that it historically has not been done. Pre-employment screening, reference checks, and criminal background checks are relatively new on the corporate scene. Although a recent study by the Society for Human Resource Management[3] suggests the use of screening tools is on the rise, there are some employers who are still reluctant to engage in background screening out of a concern that an applicant may find it insulting. There are even more reluctance to perform screening for higher-level positions, especially positions that have a C in the title such as CEO or CFO. The higher a person is in the organization, the more harm that person can do.

---

[1] Published by W.W. Norton, 2001.

[2] More information about these studies is available at www.paulekman.com.

[3] Issues common to this Study by the Society for Human Resource Management are discussed in throughout this book.

If Your Firm is Sued, Can You Show Due Diligence?

Every employer has a legal duty to exercise due diligence in hiring. Firms that fail to exercise due diligence in their hiring also have a litigation exposure. Employers can be sued for negligence if they hire someone who they knew, or in the exercise of reasonable care, should have known was dangerous, or unfit for that particular job.

If your firm is sued, the question before a jury is "Did your firm take appropriate steps in your hiring practices to protect the public, co-workers, or others at risk?"

A jury decides if an employer is negligent by using the mythical "reasonable person" standard. That standard leaves a great deal of latitude for a jury to decide that with a little more effort, an employer could have prevented the harm. Jurors are often employees themselves. They may be more likely to identify with an injured victim or family than an employer who was too lazy, cheap, or unconcerned to exercise due diligence procedures. Unless employers have a really good reason why the injury, sexual assault or other harm was not their fault, employers lose the majority of cases

So, for employers, here is the Big Question. If your firm is sued, can you demonstrate due diligence?

Of course, since an employer would not intentionally hire someone who was dangerous, unqualified or unfit, the question before the judge or jury is whether the employer reasonably should have known that the hiring decision was bad if he had only exercised a greater degree of care in screening the applicant.

In such a lawsuit, an employer would need to show, for example, whether credentials and education were verified, whether past employment was checked, and whether a criminal background check was done.

If an employer is sued, it may well be an uphill battle to win in court. The jury will hear evidence that about what the employer failed to do in the hiring process. And the attorney for the injured or dead employee would ask jury members, "Didn't the staffing professional not only have the resources and opportunity, but also the *duty* to screen the potential employee before approving his introduction into the workplace?"

In this scenario, it is not likely that the jury members will have much sympathy for an employer who does not exercise care in hiring.

What Can Employers Do?

There are defenses an employer can raise in a lawsuit for negligent hiring. In the real world, an employer cannot count on a defense being successful. It is much better not to get sued in the first place. For example, a defense that states due diligence would have cost too much, other firms do not do checks either, or the applicant lied and, therefore, the employer was also a victim of criminal behavior will not fly.

There are three defenses that have had some success—

1. Even if we had done a background check, there was nothing to find so there was no way to foresee a problem might that occur, or what would have been found was not related to the job

2. The injury that occurred was so unrelated to the job that the hiring decision did not cause the damage, or it was not foreseeable that any injury would occur. For example, if an employee with dangerous record makes friends with someone at work, and then assaults him off-premises at a function unrelated to the workplace, the employer can argue that the lack of due diligence was not connected to the injury.

3. One the other hand, since no background-checking program is perfect, a situation can occur where an employer, in fact, can show due diligence but the injury happened anyway. In that case, the employer's best defense is that he did conduct due diligence.

A key concept is that conducting due diligence does not mean that the employer was successful in avoiding every bad hire. It just means that the employer had systems in place reasonably deigned to avoid harm.

The Best Defense – A Safe Hiring Program

Due diligence and background checks go to the very heart of what makes a business successful – workers who are qualified and fit for the job. All relevant departments and personnel must be familiar with – and committed to – their company Safe Hiring Program.

If firms do not practice a Safe Hiring Program, then they can suffer what lawyers like to call the *Parade of Horribles*. These *Horribles* are bad things such as theft, fraud, economic losses, the intangible costs mentioned earlier, and issues that can lead to becoming a defendant in a lawsuit.

The Four Biggest Benefits Derived From a Safe Hiring Program

Employers do not have to sit back and wait to be victimized. By addressing workplace problems at their main source – **problem employees** – employers can substantially lessen risks to their businesses.

To prevent the hire of potentially problematic individuals, businesses are responsible for taking appropriate steps toward the development of policies and countermeasures before the hiring process begins. Properly implemented, a Safe Hiring Program helps employers in four key ways—

1. Deterrence

Making it clear that screening is part of the hiring process can deter potentially problematic applicants and discourage applicants with something to hide. An applicant with serious criminal convictions or falsified information on his resume is less likely to apply at a firm that announces pre-employment background checks are part of the hiring process. Do not become the employer of choice for people with problems when simply having a screening program can deter those problem applicants.

2. Encourage Honesty

The goal of a Safe Hiring Program is not to find only "perfect candidates." Many candidates who may have some blemish on their record may be still well-suited for employment. However, employers need to be fully informed when making a hiring decision. Having a Safe Hiring Program encourages applicants to be especially forthcoming in their interviews. Making it clear that background checks are part of the hiring process is strong motivation for applicants to reveal information about themselves they feel may be uncovered by a background check.

3. Fact-Finding

Although instincts play a large role in hiring, basing a decision on hard information is even better and safer. Effective screening obtains factual information about a candidate in order to supplement the impressions obtained from an interview. It is also a valuable tool for judging the accuracy of a candidate's resume. Facts limit uncertainty in the hiring process.

4. Due Diligence

Implementing a Safe Hiring Program helps employers practice due diligence in their hiring. Having this program is a powerful defense in the event of a lawsuit. The fact is that even the FBI and CIA cannot do perfect background checks, so a private employer cannot expect to get it right every time either. However, an employer can exercise logical due diligence on every hire. Thus, if a bad hire still is made, the employer can demonstrate they had reasonable procures in place.

Let us hope through luck or good fortune you have not *yet* encountered any *Horribles*. However, without a Safe Hiring Program, eventually a problem will occur.

A Key Partner for Employers: a Pre-employment Screening Company

A decision faced by employers is whether to perform the screening in-house or to outsource. Certainly there are some tasks an employer could perform in-house; however, the growing trend among profitable and efficient organizations is using a quality, pre-employment screening company. In today's world, background screening is not a commodity product – it is a service. A screening company is knowledgeable about the many complicated state and federal laws that govern background checking by employers.

Using a quality pre-employment screening company service is a critical step in a Safe Hiring Program and is essential for the safety and well-being of your company, your employees, and your customers.

Chapter 1

Introducing the Safe Hiring Program and Audit

Definition of a Safe Hiring Program

A Safe Hiring Program (SHP) is a series of policies, practices and procedures designed to minimize the probability of hiring dangerous, questionable, or unqualified candidates, while at the same time helping to identify those candidates who are capable, trustworthy, and best suited to the job requirements.

An SHP is part of the fabric of how a firm operates its businesses. The program—

- dictates the types of precautions to be taken and sets limits for eligibility for employment
- incorporates screening and selection procedures, clearly stating qualifiers and disqualifiers
- utilizes a series of overlapping tools, recognizing that no one tool is perfect, and
- recognizes that due diligence requires multiple approaches

Moreover, a Safe Hiring Program—

- maps out the events in the hiring process
- dictates policy in order to ensure all candidates are treated equally and fairly, and
- establishes legally defensible practices for dealing with undesirable or potentially problematic applicants

These practices are to be supported by documented procedures.

Yes, safe hiring is not something that occurs without some effort. Without an SHP, it is a statistical certainty that an employer will eventually hire someone with an unsuitable criminal record or false credentials, creating a very real possibility of a legal and financial nightmare.

The Key Components of a Safe Hiring Program

Given the enormous price tag of a bad-hiring decision, it is no surprise that all employers look to use various tools in hopes of boosting the effectiveness of the hiring process. The tools used include honesty and skills testing, behavior-based testing, group interview techniques, criminal records checks, and verification of previous employment.

Not one of these tools alone has proven 100% effective in weeding out bad candidates; each tool should be used in conjunction with your documented, overall SHP.

A **Safe Hiring Program** consists of five core areas—

Core Competencies	Key Components
1.Organizational Infrastructure	Have organizational commitment and structure to a Safe Hiring Program. The **S.A.F.E System**[4] sets in place the critical Policies, Practices and Procedures necessary for a Safe Hiring Program.
2. Initial Screening Practices	The **AIR Process** (for *Application, Interview* and *References*)[5] begins from the first job announcement or advertisement. It may also include an initial identification check.
3. In-Depth Screening Practices	Practices include a criminal record check and other tools described throughout the book.
4. Post-Hire Practices	Practices include a continuing commitment to a safe workplace even after an applicant has been hired.
5. Legal Compliance Practices	Practices include an awareness of the legal and regulatory environment surrounding safe hiring and compliance.

The above sounds well and good, but how does one start?

The first step is deciding to incorporate the elements of the S.A.F.E. System and the AIR Process into an overall Safe Hiring Program that is implemented on a company-wide basis.

---

[4] More about the S.A.F.E. System is presented in Chapter 2.
[5] AIR Process tools are analyzed in Chapters 4, 5, and 6.

The second step is to work with a reputable pre-employment screening agency to guide and ensure that your screening practices and legal compliance practices will stand up in court.

The Pre-Employment Screening Process

A key concept presented in this book is pre-employment screening or as it is sometimes called, employment screening. This process is also referred to as background checks. An SHP is *not* the same thing as a pre-employment screening because a pre-employment screening is *part* of an SHP.

In the broadest sense, the term pre-employment screening is shorthand for the process of assessing applicants for an employer's particular job or category of job. The background screen occurs when an employer or an outside professional firm assembles information such as criminal records, driving records, or credentials verifications on an applicant. The assessment is performed according to employer policies, based upon the nature of the job category and applicable laws, all designed to reveal fully qualified applicants.

These policies are implemented according to practices that are designed to reasonably separate those applicants who are qualified for the particular job from those who may not be qualified due to (1) lack of experience or credentials, or (2) other personal factors that may pose an unacceptable risk to the employer, other employees, or those using the employer's services.

Within an SHP, these practices are documented through procedures that methodically assemble standardized types of information concerning applicants.

Above all, the approach and assessment a firm takes to implement these pre-employment screening practices are integral to the success of a firm's SHP.

What Are These Tools and Procedures?

All of the elements involved in the screening process, including proper procedures, documentation, and related legal compliance issues, are examined in later chapters. Below is a partial list of these elements. Keep in mind that a few of these elements may be optional in your SHP—

- Civil Lawsuits, Judgments, Liens
- Credit Report
- Criminal History
- Education and Credentials Verification

- International Searches
- Motor Vehicle Report (driving record)
- Past Employment References
- Security Clearances
- Social Security Trace
- Vendor Databases

What Screening is Not

It is important to note that a background screen is not the same thing as an in-depth investigation of each applicant. The term investigation refers to a more focused look at each candidate and can include seeking to develop information unknown to the investigator. For example, in an investigation, the investigator may not know the past employers and schools and may have to locate that information. In a background screening, the employer is seeking to verify the past employment and school information given. In addition, an investigator may look for all property and assets owned by a subject, and this detailed approach is normally not appropriate for pre-employment screening.

Some firms believe that in order to show due diligence, they merely need to perform cursory background checks and criminal record searches at the lowest possible price. Some even feel that a $15 web-based background check is enough to ensure due diligence. This is a mistake. The ultimate purpose of an SHP is to get the best person for the job so that the company can prosper, and not get sued. A $15 background check will do neither.

Screening is not going to detect every potential problem of an applicant, and neither may an investigation. Given that a background check is performed on a number of applicants and that cost considerations are always present, even the best screening program can result in a "bad apple" getting through. However, using proper and legal employment screening in an SHP demonstrates that reasonable steps are taken to try to limit and discourage bad hires and to demonstrate due diligence by the company.

Issues for Small Employers

Because small businesses operate with fewer employees, a single bad hire can have a significant impact on small employers. Small businesses employ over 50% of all employees in the U.S. and yet it is amazing that many small businesses do not take meaningful precautions to know exactly whom they are hiring.

There are several reasons why small businesses may not perform background checks—

- Often small firms have the ability to hire people who are known to the firm. Also, firms operating in a small community often hire individuals recommended by current employees. Both instances help reduce a firm's risk of hiring a bad employee.

- Some firms are so busy growing they simply do not take time to re-organize their processes as they expand. For a firm to initiate components of a Safe Hiring Program, someone in management must recognize that safe hiring is a core business practice and take the initiative to make it happen.

- As firms get bigger, they hang onto methods that worked well when they were smaller. These methods often include *flying by the seat of the pants* hiring methods. As a firm matures, it should recognize that more methodical procedures are needed.

- As a small business gets bigger, it will eventually hire a human resources professional to handle the many tasks necessary to hire and maintain a large workforce. The number of tasks placed on a new HR position is immense, particularly if HR is a department of one. By the time a firm reaches 50 employees, an HR position probably is a necessity. Prior to that, someone who holds the position of "office manager" and/or "payroll" typically handles the HR functions.

- Safe hiring is focused on problem avoidance in the future. If a firm has not had a bad experience, then efforts at a Safe Hiring Program can seem like a waste of time and money. It is human nature to base future action on past experience; if a business has not had the issue arise, it's not a priority.

The good news is that even a small employer can implement a Safe Hiring Program at very low cost. Checking previous employment and education level or credentials using the AIR Process is not costly. The one step that may cost the small employer money is a criminal record search. An employer can either go the local courthouse or hire a screening firm that typically charges $20 or less to search per county.

A small business that hires negligently would be hard pressed to defend itself on the basis that it is too small to practice safe hiring. That defense has not proven successful. Although a small business may not be expected to perform at the same level as a Fortune 500 firm, the fact is that safe hiring can be performed at little or no cost. There is no reason why any small business has to hire blindly.

The 25-Step Safe Hiring Audit

The Safe Hiring Audit is an overall guide or blueprint that you can use to evaluate your firm's complete hiring practices and procedures. The goal of the Safe Hiring Audit is as a self-assessment tool of procedures found in the hiring process, and not an audit in the traditional sense of a financial audit. The audit is used to identify your present hiring program's strengths and weaknesses — to find areas that need improvement or where your compliance may be weak.

Each chapter to follow analyzes one or more of the 25 Safe Hiring Audit questions. Built-in to each chapter are **Best Practices**, **Procedures**, and **Reasons** that will help your organization to methodically review and improve, if necessary, your hiring program.

Using the Best Practices

The Best practices are adaptable for companies of all shapes and sizes. Of course, how to implement some of the Audit's *Best Practices* may work differently depending on the size of the firm. Also, firms that hire workers at a lower pay scale in high turnover industries may well need different practices then a firm hiring professionals with advanced degrees.

However the Audit is what all firms need; is a well thought out risk-management program that protects their business, as well as all of its stakeholders, including workers, customers, member of the public and owners. And in this way large organizations can ensure that hiring managers within different divisions and even different physical locations follow the same procedures.

Start with a Benchmark Exercise

One way to initially take the Audit is as an exercise to evaluate how your organization measures up in case you have to defend your firm's hiring practices in court or in a deposition before trial.[6]

---

[6] A deposition is a device used in a civil lawsuit where each side is allowed to question potential witnesses under oath. All information is recorded by a court reporter. This is part of what is called the "Discovery Process." In the discovery process, each side is allowed to discover facts that may be relevant to the case before the trial. A witness is put under oath by the court reporter and testifies as though the person was in court, but there is no judge or jury. Whatever a witness says is transcribed into a written booklet and can be referred to in court. There are other discovery devices as well, depending upon the jurisdiction (state or federal). For example, each side can send written questions to each other that must be answered. They are called "Interrogatories." Parties can also send a demand to each other requesting they

Trial attorneys often take a test drive to identify the fundamental thrust of case. A test drive can range from something as sophisticated as presenting their case to a mock jury to simply running the facts by non-lawyers to get their response. To determine how your firm may do in a negligent hiring lawsuit, let us create a hypothetical scenario and ask what you would tell a jury when called upon to defend your firm's safe hiring procedures. This test drive will establish a benchmark and you will be auditing your firm's hiring program.

Assume your organization hired an accounting clerk who falsified his credentials and later attacked and injured a co-worker during an argument over the clerk's numerous professional errors. The co-worker was hurt and cannot work, and consequently sues your firm for negligent hiring. Describe—

- What your firm did to exercise due diligence. To merely say you had a background screening firm do a check is not sufficient.

- What due diligence was exercised in selecting the background screening firm. Include pre-hire steps taken in the application, interview, and reference checking process before the background check.

After you have compiled and written your response to this exercise, take the Safe Hiring Audit that begins on the following page.

When performing the Audit, keep in mind the differences between policies, practices and procedures—

- A **Policy** is a general statement of a principle according to which a company performs business functions.

- A **Practice** is a general statement of the way the company implements a policy. Best practices support policy.

- A **Procedure** documents an established practice. Documentation is the KEY. In a lawsuit, documentation is a very critical factor. For example, it is not sufficient to simply have a training session. Can you document who attended, when, if they stayed for the entire time, what was taught, if there was any follow-up or testing of skills learned? Everything needs to be documented in writing.

A final hint: A firm cannot score high on this audit without documentation.

Note of caution: The Safe Hiring Audit is for educational purposes only. Do not create a document that could be construed as a

---

admit or deny certain items of information, called a "Request for Admission." Demands can also be made to provide documents, or to allow an inspection of premises.

company policy analysis; it could be used against your organization in court. If your organization decides to conduct a formal audit, then a best practice would be to have an attorney perform the audit so it would be protected by work product or attorney-client privilege.

Take the Audit

Below are the 25 questions used in the Safe Hiring Audit. Also indicated is the chapter where the applicable discussion and Best Practices are found for each question.

Grading

For each of the 25 steps that follow, measure your organization on a 0-4 scale.

0 = Doing nothing or out of compliance (equivalent to an F on a report card)

1 = Taking some steps but falling short of what an employer should do (D)

2 = Taking some measures but need to improve (C)

3 = Taking strong measures; have some but not all documentation (B)

4 = Your operation could be a model for other firms; all documentation is verified as legal (A)

Once your have answered all 25 questions, add the score. There are 100 possible points on a perfect Audit.

25-Step Safe Audit Questions	Score
1. Does your organization have written policies, practices, and procedures for safe hiring? (Chapter 2)	
2. Are the safe hiring policies, practices and procedures reviewed and updated every year? (Chapter 2)	
3. Are the organization's policies and procedures on safe hiring communicated effectively to the workforce and managers? (Chapter 2)	
4. Is there documented organizational responsibility for safe hiring with consequences of not following program spelled out?` (Chapter 2)	
5. Are tools and training in place to ensure hiring managers follow a Safe Hiring Program? (Chapter 2)	
6. Is a procedure in place to audit all of safe hiring practices? (Chapter 2)	

25-Step Safe Audit Questions	Score
7. Are all hiring policies and practices reviewed for legal compliance? (Chapter 3)	
8. Is the Fair Credit Reporting Act followed if third-party firms are involved in background screening? (Chapter 3)	
9. Are there procedures to place applicants on notice that your organization engages in best practices for hiring? (Chapter 4)	
10. Does the firm use an application form? (Chapter 4)	
11. Does the application form have all necessary and correct language? (Chapter 4)	
12. Are completed applications reviewed for potential red flags including employment gaps? (Chapter 4)	
13. Are the five critical questions used in a structured interview? (Chapter 5)	
14. Are interviewers trained in legal compliance? (Chapter 5)	
15. Does the firm check past employment? (Chapter 6)	
16. Does the firm check education credentials? (Chapter 6)	
17. Is the firm conducting an appropriate search for criminal records? (Chapter 7)	
18. Does the firm understand the appropriate uses and the limitations on criminal record databases? (Chapter 7)	
19. Is the firm's policy and procedures for the use of negative criminal information legal and compliant with federal and state laws? (Chapter 8)	
20. Does the firm use other screening tools and, if so, is the information used in accordance with safe hiring guidelines? (Chapter 9)	
21. Are the mechanics of your screening program documented? (Chapter 10)	
22. If screening is outsourced to a third-party firm, can the employer demonstrate due diligence and show procedures are being used per FCRA? (Chapter 10)	
23. Are procedures in place if a person with negative information is hired? (Chapter 10)	
24. Are procedures in place if employment is offered before a background check is completed? (Chapter 10)	
25. Does the organization have written policies, practices, and procedures for screening essential non-employees? (Chapter 11)	

Your Score

Conclusion— How Do Your Practices Measure Up?

After taking the Safe Hiring Audit and assessing your practices, an employer should begin a program of improving those areas where there is potential litigation exposure. If there are areas where your firm needs improvement, utilize the resources in this book.

If your overall score was less than 75, you have quite a bit of work to do.

Chapter 2

Setting Written Policies, Practices, and Procedures

To achieve a goal of hiring safe individuals qualified and fit for a position in your organization, it is important to review of your firm's written policies, practices, and procedures for safe hiring. Of course, if a firm does not have anything written, then a firm would fail this portion of the Audit.

Audit Question # 1:

Does your organization have written policies, practices, and procedures for safe hiring?

Audit Question # 2:

Are the safe hiring policies, practices, and procedures reviewed and updated every year?

Audit Question # 3:

Are the organization's policies and procedures on safe hiring communicated effectively to the workforce and managers?

Audit Question # 4:

Is there documented organizational responsibility for safe hiring with consequences of not following program spelled out?

Audit Question # 5:

Are tools and training in place to ensure hiring managers follow a Safe Hiring Program?

Audit Question # 6:

Is a procedure in place to audit all safe hiring practices?

Key Terms: Policies, Practices, Procedures

A significant foundation to the anatomy of a Safe Hiring Program is the documentation of a firm's policies, practices, and procedures. According to public records and screening expert Carl R. Ernst, policies, practice and procedures are defined as follows—

Policy

A policy is a general statement of a principle according to which a company performs business functions. A company does not need to maintain policies in order to operate. However, practices and procedures that exist without the underpinnings of a consistent policy are continually in jeopardy of being changed for the wrong reasons, with unintended legal consequences.

Practice

A practice is a general statement of the way the company implements a policy. Good practices support policy. To implement the policy statement example above, your company could establish a practice of validating the existence and currency of the registered entity on the public record.

Procedure

A procedure documents an established practice. Use of forms is one useful way procedures are documented. For a firm that has a practice of checking past court records for criminal records, the procedures would be the documentation on how it is done, as well as the documents showing it was done.

Policies, practices, and procedures that are not in writing are worthless. To the extent that policies, practices, and procedures are documented in writing, it is possible to independently verify whether employees are conforming to the practice, and therefore to the policy. The documentation makes it easy to perform reliable audits.

If policies and practices are not documented in writing, then the only documentation available is the actions of employees found on paper output, such as copies of filings, search requests and search reports, and vendor invoices.

In addition, it is also worthless having policies, practices, and procedures unless an employer can also demonstrate with documentation that there was training, implementation, and auditing to ensure that programs were followed.

The Elements of the S.A.F.E. System

As mentioned in the previous chapter, the S.A.F.E. System is the creative driving force behind a Safe Hiring Program (SHP).

This is what S.A.F.E. stands for—

S — Set-up an SHP that consists of documented policies, practices and procedures to be used throughout the organization to achieve safe hiring.

A — Acclimate and train all personnel involved with safe hiring responsibilities, especially hiring managers.

F — Facilitate/Implement the program.

E — Evaluate and audit the program by making sure that everyone responsible understands their compensation and advancement is judged in part by the attention they pay to the hiring process. Organizations typically accomplish those things that are measured, audited, and rewarded.

Let us take a look at each of these elements—

S – Set-up a Program of Policies and Procedures to be Used Throughout the Organization

This is done in four steps.

1. **Who is in charge:** For any program to succeed, someone in the organization must have both the responsibility and the authority to carry out the program. Unless someone is firmly accountable and holding others accountable, it is hard to succeed.

2. **Policies:** Have internal policies and procedures in place. A sample policy memorandum is contained at the end of this chapter.

3. **Set-up the elements for safe hiring:** The critical elements are the Application, Interview, and Reference Checking Process, also called the **AIR Process**. These are done within an organization, and are a matter of training and commitment. Typically it is not a line item in the budget.

4. **Criminal check:** Once an applicant has gone through the AIR Process, then a criminal check program can be conducted.

A – Acclimate/Train All Persons with Safe Hiring Responsibilities, Especially Hiring Managers

It is recommended that each hiring manager go through training. The program would include the importance of safe hiring and pre-employment screening, how to implement the AIR Process, and why it is personally a matter of importance to hiring mangers that due diligence be demonstrated in the hiring process. It is critical that all training be documented so that there is no question in the event of a lawsuit that there was adequate training. There should be documented organizational responsibility for safe hiring.

Safe Hiring Tip ➤ Providing a checklist is an effective way to communicate the organization's policies and procedures on safe hiring to the workforce and managers. A sample Safe Hiring Checklist appears in the Appendix.

F – Facilitate/Implement the Program

In order to facilitate the program, it is recommended that each hiring manager be provided with a Safe Hiring Checklist that goes into every applicant file. A sample checklist is attached at the end of this chapter. The elements on the checklist may vary for each firm. The checklist makes it easier for hiring mangers to follow the program since it creates a routine and provides a clear audit trail.

E – Evaluate and Audit the Program

As a general rule, members of an organization accomplish those things that are measured, audited, and rewarded. As a result, an SHP will be most effective if hiring managers clearly understand they will be audited periodically on how well they implement and follow the system. Otherwise, the hiring manager may just assume the SHP is just a flavor of the day from the central office and no one will follow-up. If regional and division managers routinely ask to see a number of files in order to ensure the Safe Hiring Checklists are in the file, then the hiring managers will quickly understand this is something they must do.

Compliance with the system must be part of the **evaluation** procedures for purposes of salary and promotion of a hiring manager or certain HR personnel. In turn, the regional managers must be held accountable by their supervisors who make sure they are checking. The audit trail must go to the top. Only in that way will every member of the firm understand that safe hiring is, in fact, a priority.

Place Language for Background Screening in the Employee Manual

An important first step when applying S.A.F.E. to your firm is an employee manual; it is one of the most effective ways to communicate general policies and procedures to employees. A well-written manual helps avoid misunderstandings about policies or benefits, helps avoid lawsuits and thereby enhances morale. Manuals also promote consistency of treatment and reduce the risk of charges of discrimination being made.

Many employers do not refer to pre-employment screening in their employee manuals, even when employers screen current employees for purposes of promotion, reassignment or retention. This is because there are no legal requirements that compel employers to do so. However, there is also no reason not to include mention in the employee handbook.

The following sample policy on employment screening is suggested language for an employee manual. The text shown below for the ABC Company can be modified as appropriate for firms that choose to include their employment screening policy in the employee handbook. Because no one handbook applies to all businesses or all situations, this language is a general suggestion.

And it's all on the Internet, right? No, not at all.

Sample Statement

ABC Company Written Policy on Employment Background Screening

To ensure that individuals who join this firm are well qualified and have a strong potential to be productive and successful — and to further ensure that this firm maintains a safe and productive work environment free of any form of violence, harassment, or misconduct — it is the policy of this company to perform pre-employment screening and credentials verification on applicants who are offered and have accepted an offer of employment. A pre-employment background check is a sound business practice that benefits everyone. It is not a reflection on a particular job applicant.

Offers of employment are conditional upon the firm's receipt of a pre-employment background screening investigation that is acceptable to the firm at the firm's sole discretion. Any applicant who refuses to sign a background screening release form will not be eligible for employment.

To ensure privacy, all pre-employment background screenings are conducted by a third party. All screenings are conducted in strict conformity with the federal Fair Credit Reporting Act (FCRA), the Americans with Disabilities Act (ADA), and state and federal anti-discrimination and privacy laws. All reports are kept strictly confidential, and are viewed only by individuals in this firm who have direct responsibility in the hiring process. All screening reports are kept and maintained separately from your personnel file. Under the FCRA, all background screenings are done only after a person has received a disclosure and has signed a release. In addition, you have certain legal rights to discover and to dispute or explain any information prepared by the third party background-screening agency. If the employer intends to deny employment wholly or partly because of information obtained in an pre-employment check conducted by the firm's Consumer Reporting Agency, then the applicant will first be provided with a copy of the background report, a statement of rights, and the name, address and phone number of the Consumer Reporting Agency to contact about the results of the check or to dispute its accuracy.

The firm also reserves the right to conduct a background screening anytime after the employee has been hired to determine eligibility for promotion, re-assignment, or retention in the same manner as described above.

Applicants also are expected to provide references from their former employers as well as educational reference information that can be used to verify academic accomplishments and records. Background checks may include verification of information provided on the completed application for employment, the applicant's resume, or on other forms used in the hiring process. Information to be verified includes, but is not limited to, Social Security Number and previous addresses. Employer may also conduct a reference check and verify the applicant's education and employment background as stated on the employment application or other documents listed above.

The background check also may include a criminal record check. If a conviction is discovered, then the firm will closely scrutinize the conviction in view of the policy of ensuring a safe and profitable workplace. A criminal conviction does not necessarily automatically bar an applicant from employment. Before an employment decision is made, a determination will be made whether the conviction is related to the position for which the individual is applying, or would present safety or security risks, taking into account the nature and gravity of the act, the nature of the position, and the age of the conviction.[7]

Additional checks such as a driving record or a credit report may be made on applicants for particular job categories if appropriate and job-related. Employment screening assessments to determine an applicant's job fit also may be required of all applicants for employment. Skills tests related to the demands of the job also may be required.

This firm relies upon the accuracy of information contained in the employment application as well as the accuracy of other data presented throughout the hiring process and employment, including any oral interviews. Any misrepresentations, falsifications, or material omissions in any of the information or data, no matter when discovered, may result in

---

[7] There is further language regarding the use of criminal records in Chapter 8, Limitations and Legal Use of Criminal Records.

the firm's exclusion of the individual from further consideration for employment or, if the person has been hired, termination of employment.

Use a Safe Hiring Statement

Issuing an internal polices and procedures company memo is an excellent example of how elements of an S.A.F.E. System are implemented.

This memo assumes the ABC Company is outsourcing the employment screening aspect of the SHP Program to a third party firm. However, if a company intends to perform those functions in-house, then the memo must be adjusted accordingly.

Sample Statement

ABC Company Safe Hiring Statement

To ensure that individuals who join this firm are well qualified and have a strong potential to be productive and successful, and to further ensure that this firm maintains a safe and productive work environment that is free from any form of violence, harassment or misconduct, it is the policy of this company to exercise appropriate practices to screen out applicants whose employment would be inconsistent with this policy.

These practices include certain procedures that occur prior to an offer being made, including adherence to the Application, Interview, and Reference checking (AIR Process) outlined below. In addition, this firm will perform pre-employment screening and credentials verification on applicants who are offered and have accepted an offer of employment. A pre-employment background check is a sound business practice that benefits everyone. The fact that a candidate is subject to a pre-employment screening is not a reflection on any particular applicant and is not a sign of mistrust or suspicion. All finalists are subject to this procedure. The success of our firm depends upon our people, and, although we operate in an environment of trust, our firm still must verify that all employees are both qualified and safe. All finalists for any position at this firm are subject to the same policy.

Therefore, offers of employment are conditioned upon the firm's receipt of a pre-employment background screening investigation that is acceptable to the firm at the firm's sole discretion.

All procedures will be reviewed by legal counsel to ensure they are in strict conformity with the federal Fair Credit Reporting Act (FCRA), the Americans with Disabilities Act (ADA), state and federal anti-discrimination and privacy laws, and all other applicable federal and state laws. All pre-employment background screenings are conducted by a third party to ensure privacy. All reports are kept strictly confidential, and are only viewed by individuals in this firm who have direct responsibility in the hiring process. All screening reports are kept and maintained separately from employee personnel files. Under the FCRA, all background screenings are done only after a person has signed a release and received a disclosure[8]

Document the Company's Policies

Another important communication statement is to outline the company's overall hiring procedures. The statement should indicate who will be responsible for the hiring program and what duties are required.

The following example contains specific considerations that should be spelled out, regardless of company size.

<u>Sample Statement</u>

ABC Company Policy: Overall Hiring Procedures

The Safe Hiring Program (SHP) will be coordinated by either the Human Resources Department or Security Department, hereinafter referred to as the Program Administrator.

The Program Administrator is responsible for implementation of procedures to ensure that all steps in the SHP are documented.

The Program Administrator is also in charge of implementing, training, and auditing adherence to this program, including periodic assessments to measure and evaluate the effectiveness of the program, review potential improvements, and to ensure continuing legal compliance.

The Program Administrator is also responsible for full documentation of the program, and maintaining ongoing documentation of the program's operation, as well as all training.

The Program Administrator will oversee training, keeping record of who participated, dates of attendance, and the training material as well as a monitoring of training's effectiveness.

The Program Administrator is also responsible for maintaining and updating his knowledge of the legal and practical aspects of safe hiring and background checks.

The Application and Interview Processes

Often, a company will process in-house the intake and review of applications, and will perform the needed interviews of job applicants. These procedures, part of the AIR Process as mentioned

---

[8] Additionally, the disclosure should include language about the impact of state laws if the employer operates in more than one state. Also, the impact of any union contract should also be considered.

in the last chapter, also should be documented in the form of a policy statement.

Chapters 4 and 5 fully explain how to implement and conduct best practices regarding the application and interview processes. Chapter 6 examines the necessary elements when performing reference checking. Each of these chapters contains examples of in-depth documented company policies for these processes. Rather than repeat the same text here, we will limit the statement below to an overall summary that would preceded these policies.

Sample Statement

ABC Company Policy for Application, Interview and Reference Checking

The following is a statement of best practices the firm will utilize in the application, interview, and reference checking stage of the hiring process. The Program Administrator is responsible for developing procedures for the implementation of these practices. These duties include—

- Developing forms that must be completed and placed in each applicant's file before the employment decision is made final.

- Training all persons with hiring responsibility in these procedures, and document the training.

- Institute and document procedures to ensure these practices are being followed.

[**Note**: See the appropriate chapter on Applications, Interviews, and References for the continuation of this subject.]

Establish a Safe Hiring Checklist

As mentioned, it is recommended that each hiring manager be provided with a Safe Hiring Checklist that goes into every applicant file. The checklist is an index of all the steps involved with hiring the applicant. Having a checklist illustrates two tasks that make life easier for hiring mangers:

1. **Creates a clear, concise routine**
2. **Provides a clear audit trail**

A sample Safe Hiring Checklist appears in the Appendix.

Chapter Summary

This Chapter provides information for **Audit Questions 1-6**.

Audit Question #1:   Does your organization have written policies, practices and procedures for safe hiring?

Best Practices #1:

- The company has written policies demonstrating a commitment to safe hiring found in employee manuals and/or operations manuals.
- The company's specific practices are documented.
- The company uses written forms and procedures.
- The company's commitment covers the extended workforce (temporary workforce or independent contractors) and vendors.

Audit Question #2:   Are the safe hiring policies, practices, and procedures reviewed and updated every year?

Best Practices #2:

- Written copies are maintained.
- Written documentation details dates and times that indicate how frequently policies and procedures are communicated.

Audit Question #3:   Are the organization's policies and procedures on safe hiring communicated effectively to the workforce and managers?

Best Practices #3:

- Written copies are maintained.
- Written documentation details dates and times that indicate how frequently policies and procedures are communicated.

Audit Question #4:   Is there documented organizational responsibility for safe hiring with consequences of not following program spelled out?

Best Practices #4:

- There is a position specifically responsible for safe-hiring practices; i.e. are safe hiring responsibilities are in someone's job description.

- If safe hiring is decentralized in hiring departments, there documented procedures in place across the organization, including procedures for training and audit of performance.
- There are documents consequences/penalties if the hiring manager or HR department, etc. fails to implement or follow the plan.

Audit Question #5: Are tools and training in place to ensure hiring managers follow an SHP?

Best Practices #5:

- A hiring checklist is used.
- Training is conducted on personnel involved with hiring. Documentation indicates the frequency of training and how training is monitored and measured.
- An identifiable person is responsible to analyze, implement, and evaluate the training program.

Audit Question #6: Is a procedure in place to audit all safe hiring practices?

Best Practices #6:

- Regional and division managers routinely ask to see a number of files in order to ensure the Safe Hiring Checklists are in the file.
- The audit trail must go to the top. Only in that way will every member of the firm understand that safe hiring is, in fact, a priority.

Chapter 3

Legal Compliance Issues

Due diligence and background checks go to the very heart of what makes a business successful – workers who are qualified and fit for the job. Employers must make sure that their efforts and background checks are compliant with federal and state regulations. This chapter examines these issues and educates employers on compliance issues.

Audit Question # 7:

Are all hiring policies and practices reviewed for legal compliance?

Audit Question # 8:

Is the Fair Credit Reporting Act followed if third-party firms are involved in background screening?

Understanding the FCRA is Very Important

When an employer uses a third party to help conduct a background check, there is a critical federal law the employer must be familiar with and follow. The law is called the **Fair Credit Reporting Act (FCRA)**. Even though the name of the law uses the term "Credit," the FCRA goes far beyond credit reports. The FCRA establishes specific requirements and rules for a pre-employment background report, called a **Consumer Report**, which is usually much broader in scope than just a credit report.

A Consumer Report can include a wide variety of obtained information concerning job applicants, such as criminal and civil records, driving records, civil lawsuits, reference checks, and any other information obtained by a Consumer Reporting Agency. Therefore, the FCRA fundamentally controls the information on applicants that is assembled, evaluated, or disseminated by certain third parties and used for employment purposes.

When first passed in 1970, the FCRA was primarily meant to promote confidentiality, privacy, accuracy, and relevancy regarding information gathered about consumers. The law was extensively amended in 1996, 1998, and 2003. The amendments substantially overhauled the use of Consumer Reports for employment purposes by providing greater protection to consumers.

FCRA Definitions — Important Terms Found in the FCRA

What is a Consumer Report? (FCRA Section 603(d))

A Consumer Report is a report prepared by a Consumer Reporting Agency that consists of any written or oral or other communication of any information pertaining to the applicant's or employee's credit worthiness, credit standing, credit capacity, character, general reputation, personal characteristics, or mode of living, if this information is used or expected to be used or collected for employment purposes.

What is an Investigative Consumer Report? (FCRA Section 603(e))

An **Investigative Consumer Report** is a special type of Consumer Report when the information is gathered through personal interviews (by phone calls or in person) of neighbors, friends, or associates of the employee or applicant reported on, or from other personal acquaintances or persons who may have knowledge about information bearing on the applicant's or employee's credit worthiness, credit standing, credit capacity, character, general reputation, personal characteristics, or mode of living, if this information is used or expected to be used or collected for employment purposes. The Investigative Consumer Report includes reference checks with former employers about job performance. However, a report would NOT be an Investigative Consumer Report if it were simply a verification of former employment limited to only factual matters such as the date started, date ended, salary, or job title. Once a reference checker asks about eligibility for rehire and job performance, then the report then becomes an Investigative Consumer Report.[9]

What is a Consumer Reporting Agency (CRA)? (FCRA Section 603(f))

A Consumer Reporting Agency, or CRA, is any person or entity which, for monetary fees, dues, or on a cooperative nonprofit basis, regularly engages in whole or in part in the practice of assembling or evaluating consumer credit information or other information on consumers for the purposes of furnishing reports to third parties. A CRA is often referred to as an employment or pre-employment screening company. Section 603F also includes private investigators who regularly engage in pre-employment inquiries.

What is Meant by Employment Purposes? (FCRA Section 603(h))

A report is prepared for employment purposes when the report is used for the purpose of evaluating an applicant or employee for employment, re-assignment, or retention. Under the FCRA, a Consumer Report for employment purposes is considered a "Permissible Purpose."

What is Meant by Adverse Action? (FCRA Section 603(k))

Adverse Action in relationship to employment means a denial of employment or any other decision for employment purposes that adversely affects any current or prospective employee.

The Good News and the Bad News About the FCRA

There is bad news and good news about the FCRA. The bad news is that the FCRA is a very complex and convoluted law that makes little sense if an employer sits down and tries to read it. Anyone wanting to read the law can go to the website for the Federal Trade Commission (FTC), the federal agency charged with administering

---

[9] Per FCRA Section 606(d)(4), if the information is adverse to the consumer's interest, the CRA must either obtain confirmation of the information from an additional source with independent knowledge or ensure the person interviewed is the best possible source of information.

the law. Web links to review the law are shown at the end of this chapter.

The good news is that there are only four basic steps an employer needs to know about the FCRA in order to begin an SHP while using an employment screening firm. These steps are explained in detail in the next section of this chapter.

Here is an important fact: the FCRA kicks in when a pre-employment background pre-screening is conducted by the CRA. Therefore, if an employer works with a professional pre-employment background firm, the employer should select the firm based in part upon the background firm's knowledge of the FCRA. A competent background firm should know how to fully comply with legal requirements of the FCRA, including preparation of all documents and forms needed for a fully compliant screening program.

Employers risk legal liability if the procedures utilized to check on applicants infringe on legally protected areas of privacy. By following the FCRA, an applicant's privacy rights are protected. For this reason, many legal experts advise employers to engage the services of an outside screening firm.

When engaging the services of a CRA, both the employer and the CRA must understand how critical it is to follow the FCRA. Failure to do so can result in substantial legal exposures, including fines, damages, punitive damages, and attorneys fees. Below is a brief summary of the substantial penalties involved for NOT following the FCRA.

FCRA Sec.	Type of Non-Compliance	Maximum Possible Penalties
616	Willful or reckless failure to comply with FCRA — applies to both employer and CRA	Attorney's fees / Punitive damages / $1,000 nominal damages even if no actual damages
617	Negligent non-compliance — applies to both employer & CRA	Actual damages/attorney's fees (no punitive damages or nominal damages)
619	Obtaining a report under false pretense — applies to both employer and CRA	Fine and two years prison
620	Unauthorized disclosure of consumer information by CRA officer or employee	Fine and two years prison
621	Administrative enforcement against CRAs engaged in a pattern of violations	Civil penalties

The FCRA in Four Easy Steps

To utilize the services of a CRA, you do not need to know all of the ins and outs of the FCRA. What is necessary for any employer is to understand the basic FCRA requirements in order to make sure that any supplier of hiring-related services is in compliance. Here are the four primary steps employers need to understand in order to make sure their program is in compliance—

Step 1— Employer Certification[10]

The FCRA created a unique self-policing system. Prior to receiving a Consumer Report (remember, that is shorthand for a background report), an employer must first certify to the CRA in writing the employer will follow all the steps set forth in the FCRA. The employer certifies it will do the following—

- Use the information for employment purposes only.
- Not use the information in violation of any federal or state equal opportunity law.
- Obtain all the necessary disclosures and consents as required by the FCRA (steps 2 and 3 below).
- Give the appropriate notices in the event an adverse action is taken against an applicant based in whole or in part on the contents of the Consumer Report (see step 3 below).
- Give the additional information required by law if an Investigative Consumer Report is needed.

These requirements are explained further in a FTC document titled Notice to Users of Consumer Reports. The FCRA requires a CRA to provide a copy of this document to every employer who requests a report. A copy of this notice is reprinted in the Appendix.

Step 2— Written Release and Disclosure

Before obtaining a Consumer Report from a CRA, the employer must obtain the applicant's written consent and also provide that applicant with a clear and conspicuous written disclosure that a background report may be requested. The disclosure must be provided in a separate, stand-alone document in order to prevent it from being buried in an employment application. The 1998 FCRA amendment clarified that the disclosure and the consent may be in the same document. However, the Federal Trade Commission, which enforces the FCRA, cautions that this form should not contain excessive information that may distract a consumer.

---

[10] See FCRA Sections 604 and 606. This also applies to Step 2 - Written Release and Disclosure, below. Some states may have additional requirements – see page 219 about CA.

As a general practice, the CRA will provide employers with all the forms needed for the Disclosure and Release. A special procedure is necessary when the employer requests a CRA to obtain employment references. When the CRA is merely verifying factual matters such as the dates of employment or salary, no special procedure is necessary. However, as mentioned previously, when the CRA asks for information on topics such as job performance, that falls into a special category of Consumer Report called an "Investigative Consumer Report." When an Investigative Consumer Report is used, there are some special procedures to follow—

- There must be a disclosure to the applicant that an Investigative Consumer Report is being requested, along with certain specified language. Unless it is contained in the initial disclosure, the consumer must receive this additional disclosure within three days after the request is made.

- The disclosure must tell the applicant he has a right to request additional information about the nature of the investigation.

- If the applicant makes a written request, then the employer has five days to respond with additional information and must provide a copy of a document prepared by the Federal Trade Commission called "Summary of Your Rights Under the Fair Credit Reporting Act," provided by the CRA.

As a practical matter, a CRA should handle all of these requirements for an employer as part of its services. Still, an employer should be aware there are legal issues involved in preparing a proper form. Not only is there required information that must be conveyed to applicants, but also wrong language or excessive language can put an employer at risk. There is also the issue on asking for date of birth, which is examined in the next two chapters about applications and interviews.

Another concern is if a release or disclosure form contains a release of liability meant to protect the employer, the furnisher of information sources, or the screening firm. A release can potentially be contrary to public policy by requiring an applicant to give up rights. A release can also violate the rule against excessive verbiage on a form, which could detract from a consumer's clear understanding of the documents signed. In response to this issue, some firms use separate release forms and disclosure forms, while only placing the release of liability language on the release form. A good idea for firms that utilize release of liability language on a form is to consider adding the phrase, "to the extent permitted by law" after the release language.

In 1998, Congress passed one exception to the FCRA rules concerning these various notices. The trucking industry has an exception allowing for telephonic or electronic communications from commercial drivers. The reason is that commercial drivers may be hired over the phone from truck stops, and there is not an opportunity to obtain a written release or give certain notices.

Where does an employer obtain these forms?

In order to utilize the services of a third party firm, the employer will need a certification form for the applicant to sign, along with an authorization and disclosure form. Yet, there are no industry-accepted or standardized forms in use. However, forms are available from a variety of sources. Nearly every background screening firm will provide forms. Part of selecting a screening firm is determining its ability to provide legally compliant forms. Also, law firms will sometimes provide forms to their business clients.

Step 3— Pre-Adverse Action Notice

When an employer receives a Consumer Report and intends not to hire the applicant based on the report, the applicant then has certain rights. If the adverse action is intended as a result of a Consumer Report, then the applicant is entitled to certain documents, see FCRA Section 604.

Before taking the adverse action, the employer must provide the following information to the applicant—

- A copy of the Consumer Report
- The FTC document "Summary of Your Rights Under the Fair Credit Reporting Act." This document is usually provided by the screening service.

The purpose is to give applicants the opportunity to see the report with the information being used against them. If the report is inaccurate or incomplete, applicants then have the opportunity to contact the CRA to dispute or explain what is in the report. Otherwise, applicants could be denied employment without knowing they were the victims of inaccurate or incomplete data.

Sample Statement

ABC Company Pre-Adverse Notice Letter

Dear Applicant,

A decision is currently pending concerning your application for employment at ABC Company. Enclosed for your information is a copy of the Consumer Report that you authorized in regard to your application for employment, together with a "Summary of Your Rights Under the Fair Credit Reporting Act."

> If there is any information that is inaccurate or incomplete, you should contact this office as soon as possible so an employment decision may be completed.
>
> Sincerely Yours,
>
> [List the CRA's name, address and phone number below, including toll-free numbers.]

As a practical matter, by the time an applicant is the subject of a Consumer Report, an employer has spent time, money, and effort in recruiting and hiring. Therefore, it is in the employer's best interest to give an applicant an opportunity to explain any adverse information before denying a job offer. If there was an error in the public records, giving the applicant the opportunity to explain or correct it could be to the employer's advantage.

The Reason Question

If there are other reasons for not hiring an applicant in addition to matters contained in a Consumer Report, the adverse action notification procedures still apply. Whether the intended decision was based in whole or in part on the Consumer Report, the applicant has a right to receive the report. In fact, these rights apply even if the information in the Consumer Report is not negative on its face. For example, an applicant may have a perfect payment record on his or her credit report, but an employer may be concerned the debt level is too high compared to the salary. The applicant still is entitled to a notice of pre-adverse action because it is possible the report is wrong about the applicant's outstanding debts. In a situation where the employer would have made an adverse decision regardless of the background report, following the adverse action procedures is still the best practice for legal protection.

The Time Question

A question that arises is how long an employer must wait before denying employment based upon information contained in a Consumer Report. The FCRA is silent on this point. However, many legal authorities advise that an employer should wait a "reasonable" period of time before making the final decision. This period should be the time needed for an applicant to receive and meaningfully review the report and make known to the employer or the CRA any inaccurate or incomplete information in the Consumer Report. A CRA should be able to assist employers in complying with these requirements. This does not mean an employer is required to hold the job open for a long period of time. After the first notice is given, and the applicant has had an appropriate opportunity to respond, an employer may either 1) wait until there has been a re-investigation, or 2) fill the position with another applicant.

As a practical matter, most employers find this provision of law does NOT impose any hardship or burden. While in rare situations an employer may question on how to proceed, the clear advantages of pre-employment screening far outweigh any complications that can theoretically arise from compliance.

Step 4— Notice must be given to an applicant after an adverse action[11]

If, after sending out the documents required in Step 3, the employer intends to make a final decision not to hire, the employer must take one more step. The employer must send the applicant a Notice of Adverse Action informing the job applicant that the employer has made a final decision, and must provide a copy of the FTC form "Summary of Your Rights Under the Fair Credit Reporting Act."

Many employers find it difficult to believe that Congress intended an applicant be notified twice, both before an adverse action and after. The law clearly requires two notices. This is also the interpretation of the FTC staff. The purpose is to give job applicants the maximum opportunity to correct any incomplete or inaccurate reports that could affect their chances of employment.

A special problem arises when an employer brings a worker on the premises before the background check is complete, only to later find the background report uncovers negative information that may have disqualified the person. An employer may be tempted to simply call the person in, hand them the report, a final paycheck, and both letters at the same time. However, this does not give the applicant a reasonable time to review, reflect, and respond to the report. If the background report was incomplete or incorrect, there is not a meaningful opportunity for the applicant to exercise his rights under the FCRA. The best procedure is to follow the FCRA by providing the worker with his report, a statement of rights, the first letter and an opportunity to offer any response. The second letter should be delayed until a reasonable time has passed for an applicant to respond. Although it is administratively more difficult than giving two letters at once, two letters at once may violate an applicant's rights.

---

[11] see FCRA sec. 615

<u>Sample Letter</u>

ABC Company Notice of Adverse Action Letter

Dear Applicant,

In reference to your application for employment, we regret to inform you that we are unable to further consider you for employment at this time. Our decision, in part, is the result of information obtained through the Consumer Reporting Agency identified below.

The Consumer Reporting Agency did not make the adverse decision, and is unable to explain why the decision was made.

You have the right to obtain within 60 days a free copy of your Consumer Report from the Consumer Reporting Agency as identified below and from any other consumer reporting agency which compiles and maintains files on consumers on a nationwide basis.

You have the right to contact the Consumer Reporting Agency listed below to dispute any information contained in the report that you believe may be inaccurate or incomplete. A copy of your rights under the Fair Credit Reporting Act is enclosed, entitled "Summary of Your Rights Under the Fair Credit Reporting Act."

Sincerely Yours,

[List the CRA's name, address and phone number below, including toll-free numbers.]

In the Appendix is a copy of the Summary of Rights that should be given to a job applicant any time an employer sends either a pre-adverse action or a post-adverse action letter.

Other Important FCRA Provisions

In addition to the four steps above, an employer may want to be familiar with other rules set out in the FCRA. Most of these rules govern what a CRA can and cannot do, but it is valuable for an employer to be aware of them especially when an employer selects a CRA. **If a CRA is not knowledgeable about these issues, look elsewhere.**

1. **A CRA must follow reasonable procedures concerning identity and proper use of information per FCRA 607(a).** Per the requirements of the FCRA, every CRA shall maintain reasonable procedures designed to avoid violations of section 605 (relating to what may be reported) and to limit the furnishing of Consumer Reports to the purposes listed under section 604. These procedures require that prospective users of the information identify themselves, certify the purposes for

which the information is sought, and certify that the information will be used for no other purpose. Every CRA is required to make a reasonable effort to verify the identity of a new prospective user and for the uses certified by a prospective user prior to furnishing the user a consumer report. No CRA may furnish a Consumer Report to any entity if it has reasonable grounds for believing that the Consumer Report will not be used for a purpose listed in section 604. Lesson— A CRA must know the client and the limitations on what can be reported. These rules are of particular importance in view of well-publicized incidents in 2005 of the theft of data from firms where criminals posed as legitimate users and were able to set-up accounts in order to steal personal information, using it to commit crimes.

2. **CRA must take measures to ensure accuracy of report (FCRA 607(b)).** Whenever a CRA prepares a Consumer Report, it shall follow reasonable procedures to assure maximum possible accuracy of the information concerning the individual about whom the report relates. Lesson— The CRA should have written procedures that are followed and enforced to ensure maximum accuracy.

3. **CRA must provide the employer with the FTC prepared summary, "Notice to Users of Consumer Reports: Obligations of Users under the FCRA."** See FCRA Sec. 607(d).12

4. **CRA must provide employer with FTC summary, "Summary of Your Rights," with every report.** See FCRA 604(b)(1)(B).13

5. **A CRA may only include certain items of information in a Consumer Report.** FCRA Section 605 specifically limits certain information—

    a. Bankruptcy cases older than 10 years, from the date of entry of the order for relief or the date of adjudication, as the case may be.[14]

    b. Civil suits, civil judgments, and records of arrest older than seven years from date of entry. Due to the 1998 FCRA amendment, this section now only refers to a seven-year limitation on arrests, but not criminal convictions. There are no limits under the federal FCRA for reporting criminal convictions although there are some state limits.

---

[12] A copy of the Notice is in the Appendix.
[13] A copy of the Summary is in the Appendix.
[14] See Chapter 9 for limitations on bankruptcy as related to employment.

    c. Paid tax liens older than seven years from date of payment.

    d. Accounts older than seven years are placed for collection or charged to profit and loss.

    e. Any other adverse item of information, other than records of convictions of crimes, which are older than seven years. Note that criminal convictions are excluded from the limitations, which leaves a seven-year limitation on using arrests without dispositions.

The FCRA, however, provides that these exceptions do not apply to an individual whose annual salary is reasonably expected to equal $75,000 a year or more.

6. **Rules concerning accuracy in reporting adverse public records.** If a CRA reports items of information as matters of public record but that are likely to have an adverse effect upon a consumer's ability to obtain employment, the CRA must maintain strict procedures designed to insure that whenever public record information that is likely to have an adverse effect on a consumer's ability to obtain employment is reported, it is complete and up-to-date. For purposes of this duty, items of public record relating to arrests, indictments, convictions, suits, tax liens, and outstanding judgments shall be considered up-to-date if the current public record status of the item at the time reported. See FCRA Section 613(a)(2). The duty to accurately report a criminal matter under FCRA section 613 is typically satisfied by a CRA sending a researcher directly to the courthouse and pulling any public record to insure it is accurate and up-to-date, and to also look for identifiers. See FCRA section 613(a)(2). However, the FCRA does provide an alternative procedure under FCRA section 613(a)(1). Instead of going to the courthouse, a CRA can notify the consumer of the fact that public record information is being reported by the CRA, together with the name and address of the person to whom such information is being reported.[15] However, in some states there is arguably the question: is this alternative procedure advisable? These states generally require that whenever a criminal matter is reported, reasonable procedures be followed such as double checking any database "hit" against the actual records at the courthouse. In California for example, a background firm can only report a criminal conviction or other matters of public record for employment purposes if "it is complete and up-to-date," which is defined as checking the

---

[15] see FCRA Section 613(a)(1)

status at the time the matter is reported.[16] Double checking a database "hit" at the courthouse certainly affords employees, applicants, and background firms the most protection and the highest degree of accuracy. The duty to deal with adverse information in a public record can have an important impact when using criminal record databases.[17]

7. **Re-investigation rule.** When a CRA prepares an Investigative Consumer Report, no adverse information in the Consumer Report (other than information which is a matter of public record) may be included in a subsequent Consumer Report unless such adverse information has been verified during the process of making such subsequent Consumer Report, or the adverse information was received within the three-month period preceding the date the subsequent report is furnished. See FCRA Section 614.[18]

8. **Disclosure rules.** Upon request, a CRA must disclose to a consumer what is in the consumer's file upon request, identify sources, identity everyone who procured a report for employment for the past two years, and comply with various rules, e.g. provide trained personnel who can explain to a consumer any information in the report. See FCRA Sections 609 and 610.

9. **Duty to investigate.** If an applicant contests what is in the report, the CRA has an obligation to investigate and determine accuracy within 30 days, and to take appropriate actions. The CRA must give notice to the report furnisher within five days. Various other duties are dependent upon results of re-investigation. See FCRA Sections 611 and 612. CRA must carefully follow a series of rules in terms of various notices and responses and have a FCRA compliance procedure in place.

10. **FACT Amendment.** On December 4, 2003 President Bush signed into law H.R. 2622, known as the Fair and Accurate Credit Transactions Act, (FACT). This amended the Fair Credit Reporting Act. This wide ranging law dealt with a number of topics such as identity theft, increased consumers access to their credit report, pre-emption of certain state financial laws by the federal law, and increasing the accuracy of credit reports. The new law allows consumers to receive a free credit report once a year from nationwide CRAs and to have access to their

---

[16] see California Civil Code section 1786.28(b)

[17] This is discussed in-depth in later chapters.

[18] This only applies to matters that are adverse on its face. Employment or education verification is not adverse on its face, even if it becomes adverse in the context of the application, such as the information shows an applicant lied about job history.

credit scores. The law also allows for fraud alerts to be placed in credit reports and to block credit reports.

For purposes of employment, these are some of the critical developments of FACT—

a. **Truncation of Social Security Number.** FCRA Section 609 was amended to allow consumers to request that the first five digits of his Social Security Number to be deleted from any to the consumer. The purpose is to help combat identity theft, since identity theft often occurs at the consumer's mailbox.

b. **Statute of limitations.** FCRA Section 618 sets the period of time that someone may sue for a violation of the FCRA. The statute of limitations has been extended from two years from the date of violation, to two years from the date of the discovery of the violation by the consumer, and up to five years from the date of the actual violation. CRAs should plan on keeping records for at least six years to allow time for the statutory period plus the normal delay time experienced in receiving notice of a lawsuit.

c. **Investigation of current employees.** Employers now have the ability to conduct third-party investigations of current employees without disclosure or having to first get written authorization.

Federal Lawsuit Demonstrates What Employers Should NOT Do

An opinion issued by the U.S. District Court in Northern District of Illinois in 2003 provides a case study on what an employer and screening firm should NOT do when it comes to safe hiring.

According to the allegations filed in the case, the plaintiff was contacted by a major hotel and offered a position. On his first day, he completed several forms, including an employment application where he truthfully stated he had no criminal record.

The application contained an authorization for a background check that the plaintiff did not initial. There was no indication in the court's opinion that any separate disclosure was signed as required by the FCRA.

After employment began, the major hotel hired a screening firm to do a background check. The screening firm mistakenly reported that the plaintiff had been convicted of a misdemeanor and served six months in jail. Neither the major hotel nor the background firm investigated the denial, and the plaintiff was terminated. According to the court opinion, the plaintiff, in fact, did NOT have a criminal conviction. To make matters worse, the plaintiff alleged that after he was fired the major hotel told third parties that he was fired because he lied on his application and spent time in jail. The plaintiff eventually found a new job, but at a substantially lower compensation.

Assuming all these facts were true, how many mistakes did the major hotel and the background firm make? Here are a few—

- Failed to provide a separate Disclosure for the background check under the FCRA.

- Failed to comply with the adverse action rules under the FCRA. If the consumer applicant had the chance to explain, it could all have been cleared up.

- Failed to re-investigate when told information was wrong.

Although the reasons for the mistaken criminal records are not clear, the question arises if reasonable procedures were used in obtaining the background data.

Even With FACT Act, Limitations Still Exist

First, the investigation cannot be made for the purpose of investigating a consumer's credit worthiness, credit standing, or credit capacity. A credit report is always covered by the FCRA. Secondly, the matter cannot be reported to an outside person or entity except for certain governmental agents and agencies.

Finally, there is still a procedure in place that must be followed if there are any adverse actions as a result of the investigation, such as termination or discipline. After taking any adverse action that was based in any part on the report, the employer must provide the consumer with a summary of the nature and substance of the investigation. However, there are limits on providing the source of the information.

State Laws Controlling CRA Activities

A number of states have their own rules and laws for regulating the background reports performed by CRAs. There may be situations where a CRA can legally report a criminal matter, but a specific state rule limits the employer's use of that same information. For example, under the FCRA and under many state laws, a CRA may report an arrest not resulting in a conviction. However, the employer may be under some separate state limitation on how the arrest is utilized. An employer needs to be aware that there are potentially separate state rules that control what a CRA can transmit to an employer, and separate state rules that control how the employer can use the information. Therefore, it is very important for employers to use a CRA that is fully familiar with the applicable state laws.

Subtle FCRA and State Law Differences

Differences between the FCRA and state laws can be very subtle. Here are examples that affect employers—

- In Massachusetts, the final adverse action letter must be in minimum 10-point type, sent within 10 days, with specified language.

- California, Minnesota, and Oklahoma have a "check the box" requirement where an applicant can check a box and is entitled to a copy of the report. In addition, California has two other possible boxes to check — one for credit reports and one for employers who do their own background reports.

Here are examples that affect CRAs—

- In New Jersey, a CRA must not only notify a consumer within five days that a dispute is considered frivolous (which is similar to FCRA 611), but also must state the reasons why.

- In New York, if an item of information is corrected or can no longer be verified, an agency must mail a corrected copy of the consumer's report to the consumer at no charge. A mailing is not required under FCRA § 611.

- In Texas, a CRA must mail a corrected copy to everyone who requested a Consumer Report in the past six months.

Same states are stricter— At least 20 states arguably have stricter state FCRA rules. These states are Arizona, California, Colorado, Georgia, Kansas, Kentucky, Louisiana, Maine, Maryland, Massachusetts, Minnesota, Montana, New Jersey, New Hampshire, New Mexico, New York, Oklahoma, Rhode Island, Texas, and Washington. Also, states law affecting screening can change anytime.

Examples of Different State Rules

The following list of states and state rules is not intended to be a comprehensive or definitive statement of current state laws. These examples are only illustrations of some of the differences found in some states. Of course, this list is subject to change without notice due to legislative action in a state.

- Special rules concerning the notice and initial disclosure— CA, MA, MN, NY, OK

- Rules for notice of Investigative Consumer Report (ICR) to consumers— CA, ME, MA, MN, NJ, NY

- Rules for Nature and Scope letter that is given to consumers if they request more information about an ICR— ME, NY

- Special rules for pre-adverse action and post-adverse action letters— GA, KS, LA, ME, MD, MA, MN, MT, NH, RI, WA

- Right of applicant to know if report requested— ME, NY

- Disclosures to consumer by agency— AZ, CA, CO, GA, ME, MD, NJ, RI

- Disputed accuracy rules— AZ, CO, MA, ME, MD, NJ, NY, RI, TX

- Rules on timing of notice for ICR— CA, ME, MA, MN, NJ, NY

- States that have separate rule just for credit reports where there is some complication about how and if the rules also apply to pre-employment reports— CA, NM, NV, RI

- States that prohibit the CRA from utilizing arrests not resulting in convictions. This is a separate set of rules where the CRA itself is under a state mandate (as opposed to employers being under the mandate). Examples include Kentucky, New Mexico, and New York.

- Several states that have a seven-year limitation on reporting criminal convictions and impose that state law directly on a CRA. Even though the federal FCRA was amended in 1998 to do away with the seven-year limitation on reporting criminal convictions, some states still have a version of a seven-year limitation law.

More About the Seven-Year Rule

According to Larry Henry and Derek Hinton, authors of *The Criminal Records Manual,*[19] the U.S. states that still restrict reporting of criminal information by a background firm to seven

---

[19] *The Criminal Records Manual* published 2008 by BRB Publications (Facts on Demand Press), Tempe, AZ www.brbpub.com

years are California, Colorado, Kansas, Maryland, Massachusetts, Montana, New Hampshire, New Mexico, New York, Texas, and Washington. However, Kansas, Maryland, Massachusetts, New Hampshire, and Washington waive the time limit if the applicant is reasonably expected to earn $20,000 or more annually. In New York, the exception is $25,000. In Colorado and Texas the amount is $75,000. With exceptions, California's rule is a prohibition on any conviction older then seven years.[20]

This leads to two immediate problems—

First, it is harder to create a workable national rule when some states have their own state-imposed limitation. So that there is no issue in determining applicable state law, as a matter of practical convenience some screening firms simply adopt the seven-year rule nationwide. This has some logic since cases older than seven years could potentially be stale under the Equal Employment Opportunity Commission (EEOC) standards. However, it can also lead to serious cases not being reported in states with no seven-year rule, and it can lead to situations where a CRA is aware that an applicant has a criminal conviction, but by law must keep it under wraps and sit on potentially important information.

The second problem is the question "When do the seven years begin to run?" The general rule is that the seven years begin to run from the date the consumer is free of physical custody, regardless of whether the person was on parole or probation. However, if the consumer violates probation or parole and went back into custody even for one day, the clock would arguably start to run all over again.[21]

Hiring Employees in Multiple States? Which State Law Applies?

A recurring issue for large firms with facilities in multiple states is 50-state legal compliance. As seen above, the rules for pre-employment background screening have become Balkanized, meaning many states have their own rules and regulations. This is similar to the early days of the railroads—one state had one type of rail, and the next state had a different rail, so at state borders things usually came to a halt. Compliance does become challenging for large employers trying to exercise due diligence across state

---

[20] Except in the event some other government regulation requires a criminal search to go back further.

[21] For a more detailed discussion, see: *The Safe Hiring Manual* by Lester S. Rosen (Facts on Demand Press) www.brbpub.com

lines, but challenging is not the same as impossible. Compliance just requires a little more work.

FACT Act, Pre-emption, and National Standards

As mentioned previously, the Fair and Accurate Credit Transaction Act (FACT) amended the FCRA. The primary thrust of FACT was to extend the FCRA federal pre-emption of conflicting state laws in the area of consumer credit. Congress and the financial industry were concerned that the FCRA allowed states to begin passing their own laws in 2004, undermining a uniform national credit reporting system. The FACT Act prevented that. The FACT ACT also increased identity theft protection, provided for free yearly credit reports, and changed the rules concerning investigation of current employees.

Although the FACT Act establishes that the FCRA takes priority over state laws when it comes to areas involving credit reporting, the inter-relationship between federal and state law is still complicated when it comes to employment issues.

FCRA section 625 (as amended in the 2003 FACT Act) provides that, in certain areas, state laws that existed prior to September 30, 1996 could prevail over the FCRA. Any state limit in effect on reporting criminal convictions prior to that date would be valid, although under federal FCRA rules there is no limit on how far back a background firm can go on reporting a criminal conviction.

For example, California had a seven-year limit in place prior to September 30, 1996 that did not allow criminal records to be reported beyond seven years unless the applicant made more than $30,000 a year. That was changed in 1998 to $75,000 a year and in 2002, California changed that limit to place a prohibition on reporting any convictions older then seven years regardless of salary.[22] The California law contains an exception if the Investigative Consumer Report is to be used by an employer who is explicitly required by a governmental regulatory agency to check for criminal convictions older than seven years when the employer is reviewing a consumer's qualification for employment.[23] An argument can be made that by changing the law, any California limitation is now null and void, and is pre-empted since the current law was not passed prior to September 30, 1996, and California now falls under the federal rules, which have no limit on reporting convictions. To date, no one has stepped forward as a guinea pig to test this theory. Similarly, Texas has a statute with a $75,000 limit that was

---

[22] see California Civil Code Section 1786.18
[23] see Civil Code 1786(b)(2)

effective September 1, 1997 that arguably has no force and effect under the FCRA.[24]

The Forms Issue

A major issue for multi-state employers is which form to use. A 50-state form would be a challenge due to the number of states with their own rules. If a form is written to accommodate all of the various state rules, one could argue such a form would be improper as it violates the FCRA mandate "...a clear and conspicuous disclosure has been made in writing to the consumer at any time before the report is procured or caused to be procured, in a document that consists solely of the disclosure."[25] Multi-state employers should work with CRAs that understand each of the separate state rules discussed above. This understanding should not only include forms, but also the different rights afforded to applicants at different stages of the process, as outlined in the previous sections.

Which State's Laws to Follow?

In order to give applicants all of their rights under state law, the next issue is which state's laws apply. Assume that a California resident is applying for a job in Ohio with a firm that is owned by a company in New York, and that a California screening firm does the background check. Both California and New York have a seven-year restriction on criminal records, but Ohio does not. Even though the applicant would likely move to Ohio if he gets the job, at the time of the search he is still a California resident. If the candidate has a criminal record in California older then seven years, can it be reported for a job in Ohio by a California screening firm? Can the candidate sue in California or New York for reporting a conviction that was too old under California and New York law, even though it would be permissible under the laws of Ohio?

So, what is the answer? Here is a very lawyerlike answer—*it depends.*

What does it depend upon? It depends upon some very complicated laws involving jurisdictions, and the issues surrounding which court will accept what type of lawsuit and from whom.

However, here is a rule of thumb—

The employer should first consider the law of the state where the employment is to occur. However, an employer or screening firm needs to understand where a consumer can possibly sue them, and

---

[24] see B & C Code Title 2, § 20.05

[25] see FCRA section (b)(2)

consider the laws of that state. If the laws are contradictory, then a choice must be made as to the state that would most likely have jurisdiction over a lawsuit.[26]

Does the FCRA Apply to Employers Who Perform Background Checks In-House?

Employers with an in-house security department may decide to avoid the requirements of the FCRA by conducting their own investigations. On its face, the FCRA only applies to third parties and not in-house resources. With that in mind, many employers believe that if internal security or Human Resources perform the background checks, the FCRA mandates are not applicable.

Unfortunately, these employers may still find that their actions inadvertently trigger the FCRA compliance rules.

For example, suppose an in-house security department hires a court retrieval service or an investigator merely to go to a courthouse to pull criminal records. According to an opinion letter by the FTC legal staff,[27] some court researching firms and private investigators can, in fact, be CRAs. If an employer happens to select a court researcher to obtain records, and the researcher happens to qualify as a CRA, then what the employer thought was an in-house report suddenly turns into a Consumer Report. At this point, even though the investigation started out as an internal security procedure, hiring a CRA can mean that all FCRA rules apply. This includes the need for written consent and disclosure and adverse action letters. Starting an in-house investigation without FCRA consent turns into an FCRA-covered investigation.

Similarly, an employer who directly accesses an online database to obtain information about an applicant may also invoke the FCRA. In general, there are two types of databases an employer may access. If an employer accesses a public records database maintained by courts or other public entities, then the employer is not going through a third party and the FCRA is probably not invoked.[28] However, if an employer utilizes a commercial database that compiles public records, the FCRA is arguably invoked. An example is an online criminal record service that compiles millions of criminal records from public sources. The FCRA may come into play in this situation because an employer is accessing information assembled by third parties that bears upon an individual's

---

[26] For employers who need more detailed information on this topic, see *The Safe Hiring Manual* by Lester S. Rosen

[27] see the Slyter letter dated June 12, 1998, at www.ftc.gov/os/statutes/fcra/slyter.htm

[28] additionally there may be state laws that apply

character, general reputation, personal characteristics, or mode of living as defined in the FCRA. In addition, some online commercial databases do not permit their data to be used for any FCRA-covered purpose, such as employment. These databases require a user to agree that the information can be used only as a source of "lead-generation" to conduct further investigation, such as going to the courthouse to confirm a criminal conviction. More information about the use of these databases is contained in Chapter 8.

What is the best advice for private employers who do in-house screening? Act as though the FCRA applies!

Conducting Internal Investigations

A policy least likely to trigger the FCRA is for an internal security department to obtain only records that any member of the general public can obtain, and to use only its own internal employees to obtain the records. An example of the latter is a company sending its own employees to a courthouse to obtain criminal records.

A best practice to avoid legal complications is for internal security to conduct its program within the framework of the FCRA. Additionally, if the employer operates per the FCRA, the applicant would have the right to first review the report before any decision was finalized and to clarify any mistakes. If corporate security does not follow the FCRA, and the applicant is erroneously denied employment without a pre-adverse action letter and the opportunity to be heard, then the employer could be held liable for illegal employment practices if the rejected applicant pursues legal recourse.

When considering whether to conduct internal investigations, companies also must consider pertinent state laws. There are two sets of laws any employer must consider. The first set is the myriad of labor laws that apply to all information obtained by employers, regardless of who obtains it. Examples of discrimination rules discussed in later in this chapter.

The second set of laws to consider is state FCRA-type laws. If an employer accidentally triggers the federal FCRA, the employer may be sued under state law as well.

In addition, there is a new trend aimed at applying FCRA-type protections to applicants who are screened in-house. Many privacy advocates consider the fact that internal investigations are not regulated as a loophole in the FCRA. Here is the issue: suppose an employer utilizes a screening firm and operates under the FCRA. If negative information is found, the applicant has a right to receive an adverse action letter and has the opportunity to review and respond before the action is made final. However, if an employer conducts the investigation, the employer does have to follow the FCRA procedures. This includes the adverse action sections, since the FCRA only applies to outside agencies. An employer can simply deny employment and never tell the applicant. The problem is that there have been documented cases of employers getting the information wrong and the applicant never knowing why he did nor get the job, or there were errors in the public records.

The Story of Mr. Lewis

In a lawsuit filed by Scott Lewis in Ohio, Mr. Lewis alleged that he suddenly lost his current job and had severe difficulty getting a new job. He could not figure out why suddenly no one wanted to talk to him. He reported that on one occasion, he called the employer back after believing he had a good interview and was told he was an unsavory character and if he contacted the employer again the employer would contact the police.

According to the case allegations—

"Plaintiff states that, after months of searching for employment with no success, he engaged a private investigator to determine the reason for his repeated rejections. The investigator conducted a criminal background check on Plaintiff, which, according to Lewis, produced a record consisting of various felony convictions, including a 1996 murder conviction, all of which properly belong to Timothy Lockhart. Plaintiff contends that whomever entered Mr. Lockhart's arrest data entered the last four digits of his telephone number as the last four digits of his Social Security Number. This error resulted in Mr. Lockhart's information being entered under Plaintiff's Social Security Number. Thus, any third party who did a search using Plaintiff's Social Security Number would retrieve Mr. Lockhart's criminal history."
— Lewis v. OPEN, 190 F.Supp. 2d 1049 (S.D. Ohio, 2002)

The problem, according to Mr. Lewis, was that private employers accessed a private database in Ohio and obtained information about applicants. If the information was erroneous, as it was in this situation, the applicant would never know because private employers had no FCRA duty to give the applicant a copy of the report or a chance to explain.

Essentially, a person could be "blackballed" and never know it.

Partly in response to the facts in the Lewis matter, California passed the nation's first law that attempted to regulate in-house employer investigations. Effective in 2002, the law required that information about public records obtained by an employer, even without the use of an outside agency, must be provided to an applicant, unless that applicant waived the right. California employers are required to follow a series of steps when they do an in-house investigation that gives FCRA type protection, including adverse action notices if public record is obtained and used adversely.[29]

Sources of Information About the FCRA

The FTC's home page for the FCRA is at www.ftc.gov/os/statutes/fcrajump.shtm. The text of the FCRA is available online at www.ftc.gov/os/statutes/031224fcra.pdf.

Following the 1997 amendments, the FTC staff wrote letters in response to questions that were published online. The staff letters are online. These letters do not carry the force of law, but they are persuasive. They may eventually form the basis of any commentary published by the FTC.[30]

Commentary for FCRA prior to amendments effective 1997 can be found in 16 CFR Ch. 1(1-1-97 edition). Future FTC commentaries on the FCRA are likely.

FCRA required documents also are found on the FTC website and in the Appendix. These are—

a. General Summary of Consumer Rights

b. Notice of Furnisher Responsibilities

c. Notice of User Responsibilities

Federal and State Discrimination Laws

Federal and state anti-discrimination laws make it clear that decisions based on prohibited criteria are illegal. These criteria include race, color, national origin, religion, ancestry, medical condition, age, marital status, sex, or exercise of family care or medical leaves. These are prohibited criteria because they are not valid predictors of job performance or bona fide occupational qualifications (BFOQ). In the past, prohibited criteria have been found to cause unfair treatment and discrimination. This type of discrimination is called "disparate treatment." A person is being

---

[29] see CA Civil Code section 1786.53

[30] see www.ftc.gov/os/statutes/fcra/index.htm

prejudged based upon membership in a group or status instead of what he can accomplish as an individual. The word prejudice simply means to prejudge a person based upon the color of the person's skin, country of origin, sex, or some other criteria that has nothing to do with job performance.

The situation becomes complicated because information that appears neutral on its face can be utilized in a discriminatory way. This is called "disparate impact" and occurs when employer selection processes that appear fair on the surface actually result in a screening out of identifiable groups from employment. For example, credit reports and criminal records are perfectly legal for employers to obtain provided the methods used comply with various state and federal rules. However, the use of credit reports or criminal records can have a discriminatory impact if they are used in such a way that results in a disparate impact upon certain groups. The considerations surrounding the use of criminal records and discrimination are discussed in Chapter 8.

Employers do need to have a basic understanding of the statutes, cases, and regulations on both the federal and state levels that affect how any employer can legally collect and utilize personal information about job applicants in order to make hiring decisions.

Federal Discrimination Laws

There are a number of federal laws that prohibit discrimination in employment. The EEOC enforces these laws at the federal level. The EEOC also provides oversight and coordination of all federal equal employment opportunity regulations, practices, and policies. According to the EEOC website at www.eeoc.gov, these are the primary federal laws that prohibit job discrimination—

- **Title VII of the Civil Rights Act of 1964 (Title VII)**, which prohibits employment discrimination based on race, color, religion, sex, or national origin; see www.eeoc.gov/policy/vii.html

- **Equal Pay Act of 1963 (EPA)**, which protects men and women who perform substantially equal work in the same establishment from sex-based wage discrimination; see www.eeoc.gov/policy/epa.html

- **Age Discrimination in Employment Act of 1967 (ADEA)**, which protects individuals who are 40 years of age or older; see www.eeoc.gov/policy/adea.html

- **Title I and Title V of the Americans with Disabilities Act of 1990 (ADA)**, which prohibit employment discrimination against qualified individuals with disabilities in the private

sector, and in state and local governments; see
www.eeoc.gov/policy/ada.html

- **Sections 501 and 505 of the Rehabilitation Act of 1973**,
  which prohibit discrimination against qualified individuals
  with disabilities who work in the federal government; see
  www.eeoc.gov/policy/rehab.html
- **Civil Rights Act of 1991**, which (among other things)
  provides monetary damages in cases of intentional
  employment discrimination; see
  www.eeoc.gov/policy/cra91.html

The federal laws only affect those employers above a certain size.
For example, the Civil Rights and the Americans with Disabilities
Acts cover employers with 15 or more employees based upon the
number of employees during each working day of 20 or more
calendar weeks of the current or preceding calendar year. However,
the Age Discrimination Act utilizes 20 employees as the threshold.
As a practical matter, even small employers who believe they fall
below the federal limits are well advised to take these federal laws
into consideration. First, it can be complicated to determine how
many employees a small firm has for purposes of determining if the
law applies. All employees including part-time and temporary
workers are counted. An employer may not count "independent
contractors," but the possibility exists that the contractors may be
counted if, in fact, they are really engaged in an employment- type
relationship, regardless of how the employer chooses to compensate
them. If an employer has two or more separate businesses, there
are circumstances where the businesses will be counted as one for
purpose of determining the employee count.

The rules about counting employees to determine if a firm is large
enough to meet the threshold for application of federal civil rights
laws also can be very complex. In addition, there are states where
state laws can be in effect even if a federal law technically does not
apply, as discussed below. More importantly, if a small employer
engages in any conduct that would have been a violation of federal
law if they were larger, an aggrieved applicant or employee still may
be able to go to court stating an alternative cause of action, such as
intentional infliction of emotional distress.

The Civil Rights Act and the Americans with Disabilities Act are
probably the two most well known laws that apply to discriminatory
hiring practices. These laws prohibit any non-job-related inquiry,
either verbal or through the use of an application form, which
directly or indirectly limits a person's employment opportunities
because of race, color, religion, national origin, ancestry, medical
condition, disability (including AIDS), marital status, sex (including

pregnancy), age (40+), exercise of family care leave, or leave for an employee's own serious health condition.

These laws generally prohibit any type of questions of applicants that—

- Identifies a person on a basis covered by the Act; or,
- Results in the disproportionate screening out of members of a protected group; or,
- Is not a valid predictor (not a job-related inquiry) of potential successful job performance.

More About the Americans with Disabilities Act (ADA)

This federal law regulates hiring of Americans with disabilities and has broad implications. In terms of background screenings, an employer may not use or obtain any information that violates the rights afforded under this law. The most obvious impact of the law relates to medical records, disabilities, and workers' compensation records. Screening firms may provide worker compensation records, but only under the strict procedures mandated by the Americans with Disabilities Act (ADA).

One occasion where the ADA (and similar state laws) may raise a concern is for criminal convictions involving drugs or alcohol. Under the ADA, an employer cannot discriminate on the basis that an applicant is an alcoholic or a former drug user. However, the ADA and similar state laws do not protect a person who is currently using drugs or abusing alcohol. Where a person is otherwise qualified for a position, and the background screening reveals a drug or alcohol conviction, an employer should carefully review the totality of the circumstances involved before denying employment on that basis. Certainly, the current use of illegal drugs is not protected. The decision also may depend upon the position in question. For driving positions, for example, an employer may certainly evaluate driving-related convictions more seriously.

State and Local Discrimination Laws

To add to the complexity for employers, a number of states and local jurisdictions have their own rules governing discrimination. The federal EEOC website at www.eeoc.gov indicates more than 100 state and local Fair Employment Practice Agencies, or FEPAs. Most states have their own Civil Rights Acts, as well as an agency within state government that enforces these state laws. State laws can vary from the federal rules in terms of the size of the employer covered and what constitutes a violation.

Even local jurisdictions and cities can regulate employers. For example, the City and County of San Francisco have the San

Francisco Human Rights Commission that can investigate and mediate complaints of discrimination for employees of any San Francisco employer, regardless of size.

Here is where it gets even more complicated for employers—they are generally subject to the most stringent discrimination laws in their jurisdictions. For example, even though the federal Civil Rights Act limits jurisdiction to employers with 15 or more employees, a California employer is subject to the California Fair Employment and Housing Act (FEHA) that has jurisdiction starting at five employees. Other states apply the discrimination laws to all employers. Most states have websites for the agency that enforces civil rights and fair employment practices law. For example, see the site for the state of Michigan at www.michigan.gov/mdcr/. To access data concerning civil rights and discrimination laws for each state, see the CCH Business Owners Toolkit at:

www.toolkit.com/small_business_guide/sbg.aspx?nid=P05_0160.

How to Avoid Previous Names and Marital Status Discrimination

One of the areas where the discrimination laws have an effect on safe hiring is the use of previous names in a criminal search. The issue arises because past names are a necessary identifying piece of information. For example, when searching for criminal records, researchers base the search on the last name. However, if an applicant at one time was known by a different name, a complete criminal search must be conducted under BOTH names. The most typical situation where an applicant has a previous name is in the case of a woman who marries and changes her name.

The problem is that by referring to a name as a maiden name, an applicant potentially is being identified on the basis of her marital status or sex, which can be a violation of federal and state discrimination laws. In California for example, asking for an applicant's maiden name has been specifically labeled as an unacceptable question by the California Department of Fair Employment and Housing, the California agency charged with enforcing the California civil rights laws. Consequently, a previous name search should not be referred to as a "maiden name" search, since that clearly indicates that an employer is obtaining information on martial status, which is a prohibited basis upon which to make an employment decision. That is why any application or consent for background screening should always include the phrase "previous name" instead of "maiden name."

Is this an example of a distinction without a difference, or political correctness going too far? No. Marital status has been a traditional basis for a woman to be the subject of discrimination. The fact is that whether a man or woman is married is simply not a valid basis to predict job performance. However, the reality has been that a woman applicant who is married may be the subject of discrimination based on a belief that she may leave the job to have a family. By phrasing it as a "previous name," the same information is obtained for purposes of a background check, but the application information is facially neutral. In addition, a female applicant is not discouraged from applying based upon an apprehension that by asking for a "maiden name," there is a likelihood of discrimination.

How to Avoid Age Discrimination

Using the Date of Birth Information on the Job Application

As you will learn in the next two chapters, information tending to reveal age should not be requested on an application form or during an oral interview. Asking for date of birth tends to deter older applicants from applying. If the application material contains date of birth information, the inference is that a firm may be methodically denying consideration of older workers.

Asking for date of birth or age during the selection process could violate the Federal Age Discrimination Act of 1967 and various state equivalent acts even though there is not an absolute prohibition against asking for it, which is a common misconception among employers. In fact, the EEOC has specifically ruled that asking for date of birth or age is not automatically a violation of the act. However, the EEOC ruling indicated that any such request would be closely scrutinized to ensure that the request has a permissible purpose. The EEOC also indicated that the reason for asking for date of birth should be clearly disclosed so that older applicants are not deterred from applying.[31]

According to the EEOC website at www.eeoc.gov/types/age.html —

"Pre-Employment Inquiries

The ADEA (Age Discrimination in Employment Act) does not specifically prohibit an employer from asking an applicant's age or date of birth. However, because such inquiries may deter older workers from applying for employment or may otherwise indicate possible intent to discriminate based on age, requests for age information will be closely scrutinized to

---

[31] see 29 Code of Federal Regulations Part 1625

make sure that the inquiry was made for a lawful purpose, rather than for a purpose prohibited by the ADEA."

Many states have rules that prohibit an employer, either directly or through an agent, from seeking or receiving information that reveals date of birth and age before an offer is made. For example, the California Pre-employment Inquiry Guidelines by the California Department of Fair Employment and Housing (DFEH) lists specific age questions that cannot be asked.

Using the Date of Birth Information for Background Checks

Special problems for back checking are faced when an applicant's date of birth is not available. When researching court records, the date of birth is probably the most important factor needed to identify an individual since many court records do not contain Social Security Numbers. In fact, in some jurisdictions, a criminal search cannot be conducted without a date of birth. It is also needed in many states in order to obtain a driving record, thus the date of birth is key piece of identifying data on Department of Motor Vehicle records.

If a firm does screening in-house, then the firm may consider performing all screening and obtaining information post-offer. This provides maximum protection since there can be no inference that age played a role in the decision to hire or not hire.

If an employer outsources background screening, the screening firm will normally need date of birth to perform the service.

There are several options an employer can take in this situation. First, consider outsourcing to a screening firm only post-offer. If a conditional offer of employment is made that depends upon a background screening report, then asking for the date of birth post-offer is probably safe. The downside however, is that it is an administrative burden for most employers to coordinate giving offers, collecting the date of birth, and then transmitting it to a screening firm. Most employers have a practice of requiring all applicants to fill out a consent form for the background screening firm at the same time the original application is filled out, and the screening firm's forms will typically need date of birth information.

Another possible route is to only request the date of birth information on the screening firm's form, and not on any employer form. Furthermore, the applicant release forms should not be made available to the person or persons with hiring authority so as to avoid any suggestion that age information was used in any step of the hiring process. Most employment screening companies recommend that employers keep the screening forms and reports separate from the employee's personnel file or application papers.

In addition, to further protect the employer, the form used for the screening company can have such additional language as—

- The information requested on the screening firm's form is for screening and verification of information only and has no role in the selection process.
- All federal and state rights are respected in the employer's screening process.
- The year of birth is optional on the form.
- The information is used for identification only and that without such information the screening process may be delayed.

Another option is an employer can require a screening firm to take steps to remove all references to age and date of birth in its reports so that employers will not receive age information.

Another option some employers have used is to set-up a system that communicates the date of birth directly to the screening firm so the data is never in the employer's possession. This can be done by establishing a special "800" phone number the applicants call to leave their date of birth, or with a tear-off form that the applicant mails in. One downside to these types of workarounds is they will likely delay screening reports because of the extra steps involved.

Another option is to have someone in the office such as a receptionist physically separate the screening firm's form from the application so there is no question that a decision maker has not viewed the date of birth before the applications are reviewed. Also new are online options where an applicant can supply the date of birth as part of the application process, but only the screening firm will be able to see it.

Most employers choose the option of asking applicants to place date of birth on the screening company forms. For questions about a form's legality, employers should consult their legal counsel, seek advice from their attorney, or contact the appropriate local or state authority or federal EEOC office.

Safe Hiring Programs and Privacy Laws

Another major area of legal concern for employers is privacy. Employers have a legal duty to respect the privacy of applicants and employees in a variety of areas, such as privacy limitation when it comes to what information an employer can obtain, how to protect the data, who else can see the data, and the rights of applicants and employees to discover what data has been obtained. With news media revelations in 2005 of large-scale theft of data from firms that store large amounts of personal and identifiable data, maintaining privacy has become a very critical concern.

The subject matter of workplace privacy is very broad, and spans a whole range of issues from electronic monitoring of email, searches of personal belongings and physical surveillance to regulating workplace behavior and dress codes, off the job conduct, and the protection and dissemination of confidential information. For purposes of this book, the concern is focused on gathering, utilizing, and protecting information necessary for hiring and retention decisions.

The right to privacy is guaranteed to every American citizen by the U.S. Constitution. Although the federal constitutional protections do not extend to private employers dealing with job applicants and employees, most states have passed privacy legislation that recognizes a right to privacy to employees of private employers. Many states have passed privacy laws that cover specific situations, such as states that do not allow consideration or regulation by an employer of various forms of "off-duty" conduct.

There is a "common law" right to privacy in employment matters as well. A common law right means a legal right created by precedents set by court cases, instead of laws created by a legislative body. Common law rights include—

- The right to avoid public disclosure of private information.
- The right to be protected from false or misleading statements being made in public.
- Unreasonable intrusion into private affairs, either physically (such as a polygraph test) or otherwise invading an area of personal privacy.
- Infliction of emotional distress by outrageous conduct.

A Good Safe Hiring Program Will Not Invade Privacy

There is no reason why a well-designed SHP should violate any statutory or common right to privacy. The processes outlined in this book are NOT intended to pry into an applicant's private life, turn employers into "big brothers" or turn hiring managers or HR professionals into the "hiring police." In fact, the type of information employers obtain is job-related information about how people conduct themselves in their "public" lives — an area of their life that is visible to the public. For example, where a person has worked or attended school are generally not confidential matters. Anyone who was interested could see where the applicant was working or studying. Those activities are done in the open. In addition, if a person has a criminal record, that too is a matter of pubic record. An SHP does not invade a zone of privacy that a reasonable person would feel unduly invades those areas that society generally keeps private and confidential. The one tool that comes closest to butting up against a reasonable expectation of privacy would be credit reports, which are discussed in Chapter 9.

In addition, all of the Safe Hiring techniques recommended in this book are done with an applicant's expressed consent. As outlined in the next chapter on applications, a conscientious employer will require each applicant to consent and authorize in writing a background screening. If pre-employment background screening is outsourced to a background screening firm then pursuant to the FCRA there must be written authorization and disclosure.[32]

Of course, just because information may not be private does not mean it is not confidential. If an employer locates a criminal record, efforts must be made to limit that information to just those in the company with a need to know for purposes of making a hiring decision. Personal identifiable information such as a Social Security Number is confidential and must be safeguarded. The right to privacy extends to how information obtained in a SHP is stored in order to protect against unauthorized viewing or theft. Another consideration is computer security when applicant data is transmitted or stored over a network. Maintaining confidentiality and security is a critical employment screening task.

As mentioned throughout this book, employers who engage in a SHP do not find that good applicants feel their privacy rights are being violated provided there are safeguards and assurances in place that the information will be kept confidential and used for legal purposes. Honest candidates understand that background screening is a sound business practice that helps all concerned. Job applicants want to work with qualified and safe co-workers in a profitable, professional environment.

Privacy and Performing Background Checks In-house

When conducting pre-employment investigations, an employer essentially has two choices. The employer can either conduct the investigation in-house or outsource to a third party.

One advantage of outsourcing background screening is that screening companies must abide by the FCRA, which is the gold standard of privacy. Under the FCRA, all background screening is done with the applicant's written authorization as well as a disclosure of rights. There are limits to what may be obtained, and for what reasons, and who can access the information. There are also rules about maximum accuracy and re-investigation. By

---

[32] An exception is for truck drivers, and even then there still must be verbal authorization.

following the FCRA, employers have less concern that an applicant can allege a violation of privacy since everything is done pursuant to federal law at the onset.

However, if an employer performs in-house applicant screening, then the employer no longer has the protection of the FCRA. In this situation, the employer's actions are governed by privacy law considerations. As a result, the employer needs to have an in-depth understanding of the privacy law framework within his jurisdiction or at the location where the job is being performed.

Safe Hiring Tip ➤ Essentially, an employer who does in-house screening or investigations must be aware of the general balancing test that attempts to reconcile the employer's need to have certain information with the privacy rights of job applicants and current employees. While it is not unlawful for an employer to conduct his own background checks, and considering the promulgation of more laws intended to preserve individual rights to privacy, employers can be at risk when performing screening in-house. To minimize risk, firms that do their own screening should act as though the FCRA applied.

For an applicant or current employee to allege a violation of a privacy right, generally the person must show that his reasonable expectation of privacy was seriously invaded by the employer.

In analyzing an invasion of privacy claim in an employment context, courts will first look to see if the employer invaded an employee's or applicant's protected privacy rights. If the employer's action did intrude upon privacy rights, then the court will examine—

1. Did the employer's action further a legitimate and socially beneficial aim?

2. If so, did the purposes to be achieved outweigh any resulting invasion of privacy?

3. Was there a less intrusive alternative that could have accomplished the same aim without invading privacy?

California has led the nation in issues involving employee privacy. A leading case is *Hill v. National Collegiate Athletic Association*, 7 Ca. 4th 1 (1994). In the Hill case, the issue was whether a college athletic association could require student athletes to sign consent forms for drug tests. The California Supreme Court ruled that the drug testing requirement was an invasion of privacy in that drug testing required an intrusion into bodily integrity. The court further held that the NCAA failed to show that the particular program it proposed furthered the intended goal, that the benefits did not outweigh the intrusion of rights, and there were less intrusive means to accomplish the goal.

There are other privacy matters that are not a matter of balance but have been made illegal directly by statute. For example, in 1988, the U.S. Congress enacted the Employee Polygraph Protection Act.[33] This act severely limits the ability of most private employers from using a polygraph or lie detector test for job applicants or current employees who are being investigated. Although there are some narrow exceptions, as a practical matter this law ended the use of lie detectors.

The Disturbing Trends of Data Sent Overseas and Use of Home Operators

A developing trend among some U.S. firms is to send Personal and Identifiable Information (PII) data abroad to call centers and data centers in order to take advantage of low-cost foreign labor. Privacy advocates are concerned when these U.S. firms send sensitive information such as medical records, and Social Security Numbers beyond the privacy protections of the U.S.

In California for example, bills have been introduced in the past requiring firms to disclose to consumers if their personal data is sent overseas, or to ban the practice all together. In Washington D.C., efforts have been made to make regulatory agencies take action to protect privacy rights from being harmed by this overseas outsourcing of data. Even for international verification of employment or education, employers should carefully monitor if and how PII is sent outside of the U.S. If a background firm performs international verifications, the employer should determine how PII is protected. A suggested practice is to only share personal information with the foreign employer or school directly, and not send personal information to an unregulated agent outside the U.S.

An employer should also carefully consider utilizing a background firm that uses home-based operators to make employment and education verification calls. Not only would that raise quality issues, but does an employer really want the applicant's personal data such as date of birth or Social Security Number spread out on kitchen tables and dorms rooms across America.

Discrimination and Privacy — Conclusion

Legal limits and privacy/confidentiality are two important concepts presented in this chapter that will be revisited throughout this book and are intertwined with an SHP.

---

[33] Employee Polygraph Protection Act, 29 U.S.C. Sections 2001-2009

There are legal limits on what an employer can and cannot find out about applicants. The primary law that affects this issue is equal employment opportunity laws on the federal, state and sometimes even the local level. The basic rule is that an employer can ask an applicant either directly on an application or interview – or find out indirectly through a past employment reference check – anything that is—

1. A valid predictor of job performance.

2. Not barred specifically by an equal employment law, such as questions concerning race, ethnicity, religion, age, or sex.

3. Not prohibited due to a disparate impact even though neutral on its face, such as the use of arrest records.

4. Not prohibited by a specific statute, such as the prohibition on lie-detector machines.

5. Not prohibited due to illegal procedures, such as failure to follow the FCRA.

The role of privacy rights and confidentiality is the second key point in a Safe Hiring Program. An employer who follows the FCRA should not run afoul of privacy rights.

Chapter Summary

This Chapter provides information for **Audit Questions 7-8**.

Audit Question #7: Are all hiring policies and practices reviewed for legal compliance?

Best Practices #7:

- Discrimination rules set by the EEOC and states' equivalent discrimination rules are followed by the firm.

- ADA and state equivalent ADA laws are followed by the firm.

- Privacy protection and defamation-avoidance procedures are in place.

Audit Question #8: Is the Fair Credit Reporting Act (FCRA) followed if third-party firms are involved in background screening?

Best Practices #8:

- The firm is knowledgeable and complies with Sections 616, 617, 619, 629, and 621 of the FCRA.

- The firm is knowledgeable and complies with state equivalent FCRA laws.

Chapter 4

The Application Process

Use of a job description and an employment application form is considered a best practice.

Applications ensure uniformity, include all needed information that is obtained, prevent employers from having impermissible information, and provide employers with a place for applicants to sign certain necessary statements.

Audit Question # 9:

Are there procedures to place applicants on notice that your organization engages in best practices for hiring?

Audit Question # 10:

Does the firm use an application form?

Audit Question # 11:

Does the application form have all necessary and correct language?

Audit Question # 12:

Are completed applications reviewed for potential red flags including employment gaps?

The Application Process Starts BEFORE the Application Is Filled Out

When does the application process start? From the point of view of a Safe Hiring Program, it starts before applications are printed or given out. It really starts when the job is first created.

Using the Job Description

For several important reasons, an employer first needs to create a job description. A job description that clearly defines the essential function of the job and core competence not only helps identify and select the right candidate during recruitment, but also provides **legal protection** for claims of discrimination or compliance with the ADA. Also, it is essential to have a job description if a criminal record is disclosed or discovered. This helps insure the employer is consistent with the requirements of the EEOC, as discussed in the previous chapter.

A job description should clearly indicate the education and experience levels required of candidates. If a candidate misleads an employer about knowledge, skills, or experience, then the fact that the requirements were clearly set forth in the job description will assist the employer in the event there is a rejection or termination. An employer can always take the position that dishonesty on an application is grounds for termination. However, the employer's position is buttressed when it is clear from a well-written job description there were certain requirements for the position, that the job description was provided to the applicant, and the applicant misled the employer about his or her qualifications.

Managers' job descriptions are also a critical consideration. Does part of the written job description indicate a manager's duty to "record, report, and address issues of workplace misconduct such as acts of workplace violence, or harassment, or drug abuse?" Placing these duties in the written job description of supervisors serves to re-enforce their role in workplace safety.

Numerous resources and websites, as well as commercially available software, can assist an employer in preparing job descriptions. A useful site with a job description writer is found at www.acinet.org/acinet/jobwriter/default.aspx. Employers also may use the job descriptions formulated by the National Academy of Science, Committee on Occupational Classification and Analysis. This organization created the Dictionary of Occupational Titles or

DOT.[34] See www.wave.net/upg/immigration/dot_index.html for an online dictionary of jobs.

Inform the Applicant about the Background Check

As part of any recruitment effort, the employer is well-advised to place applicants on notice that the firm practices safe hiring with background checks. The goal is to get maximum advantage from safe hiring by discouraging applicants to hide something when applying. Employers can place a phrase in the job announcement, bulletin, classified advertisement, or Internet site that indicates the firm requires background checks.

The most likely effect is that applicants with something to hide will go down the block. Let a competitor be the employer of choice for people with problems. Announcing a company background check policy does not keep good applicants from employers no more then security checkpoints at airports stop people from flying.

Using the Application Form as a Hiring Tool

One of the most critical safe hiring tools is the application process. Done correctly, the application process protects the employer. Although it seems obvious, the most important aspect of the application process is to use a proper job application form. Consider it a best practice. A professionally reviewed, pre-printed job application should allow the employer to legally obtain the necessary information to begin the hiring process. Applications ensure uniformity and that all needed information is obtained. Also, applications protect employers from having impermissible information a resume may contain. The application provides employers with a place for applicants to sign necessary statements that are part of the hiring process.

As a rule of thumb, resumes are not always complete or clear. If an employer insists upon using resumes, then the employer is well-advised to always use a standardized application form as well. Learn more about using resumes later in this chapter.

Revealing Negative Information

Negative information honestly disclosed and explained on an application or in an interview may very well have no effect, especially if the applicant otherwise has an excellent and verified work history. However, when an applicant has failed to honestly disclose negative information such as the existence of a criminal

---

[34] This DOT is not to be confused with the Department of Transportation and DOT drug testing.

conviction, then the employer's concern turns to the lack of honesty involved. If the applicant is dishonest and negative information is first revealed by a background check, then the failure to hire may be justified. That is why it is important to have broad language in the application to cover all relevant offenses.

Establish Who Is Responsible For Applications and Application Review

As mentioned in Chapter 1, the AIR Process (Application, Interview, and Reference Checking) is a critical part of an SHP. Any firm, large or small, must have a designated administrator responsible for developing procedures for the implementation of the application process. These duties include—

1. Developing forms that must be completed and placed in each applicant's file before the employment decision is made final.

2. Training and documenting the training for all persons with hiring responsibility in the procedures used to review applications.

3. Institute and document procedures to ensure these practices are being followed.

The Reasons Why Employers Should Not Rely on Resumes

Some employers still hire based primarily upon a resume. This is a major mistake. For an applicant, a resume is a marketing tool. In a resume, an applicant picks and chooses whatever information he or she wants to share. Many job hunters use a resume writing service, and while there is nothing wrong with using a service to prepare a professional looking resume, the service typically will attempt to enhance the applicant's experience. The service's goal is to get the applicant to the interview stage.

Employers, however, need facts in order to make hiring decisions.

Resumes May Have Information an Employer Should Not Have

For some reason, job applicants often feel compelled to reveal things about themselves that an employer does not need or legally should not know. Resumes often reveal volunteer affiliations, hobbies, interests or memberships in groups that reveal such prohibited information as race, religion, ethnicity, sexual orientation, or age. For example, a resume may reveal a person does volunteer time with a church, or belongs to a group that is clearly associated with a particular race or nationality. The problem is the EEOC and equivalent sets of individual state's rules prohibit an employer from obtaining or using such information. An applicant cannot volunteer irrelevant information an employer should not possess. Having this information in the form of a resume in the employer's file is not a good practice in the event the employer is ever the subject of civil litigation or a government investigation into his hiring practices.

Resumes May Not Have Information an Employer Needs

As mentioned previously, resumes may amplify facts and experience. At the same time, resumes may not give an employer all the information needed to make an informed hiring decision. With a proper application, an applicant cannot skip over jobs he or she rather not mention. An application can allow an employer to spot unexplained employment gaps. Also, job applicants typically do not self-reveal their criminal records in a resume.

Bottom Line: Because employment applications provide legal and practical advantages, some firms astutely reject resumes and may return them to applicants. Jobseekers are told they must fill out the company-approved application only.

10 Critical Items Every Application Needs

It is much easier for an employer to prescreen candidates using a standardized application. An employer trying to screen a large number of resumes can more easily compare applicants.

Ten critical things need to be addressed in every application as part of an SHP—

1. The application needs to clearly state that "there will be a background check" or "a background check will be performed." A well-worded application form discourages applicants with something to hide, and encourages applicants to be open and honest.

2. There should be the broadest possible language asking about convictions and pending criminal cases. This is covered in detail later in this chapter.

3. All applications should have this language: "The information provided by the applicant is true and correct, and that any misstatements or omission of material facts in the application or the hiring process may result in discontinuing of the hiring process or termination of employment, no matter when discovered." This is critical when an applicant is not truthful about a criminal conviction.

4. The form should clarify that "a criminal conviction is not automatic grounds for rejection." As discussed in later chapters, it could be a form of discrimination to automatically reject an applicant because of a criminal record. The keyword is automatically. Without the statement that there is no automatic rejection, an applicant may be deterred from applying in the first place out of fear of being automatically rejected upon honestly answering the question. The chilling effect on an applicant could be a form of discrimination in itself, which is why this additional language is necessary. Conversely, if a person has lied about a criminal violation, then dishonesty may become the basis for disqualification.

5. The application form should indicate the applicant consents to "pre-employment background screening, including verifying educational and professional credentials, past employment, and court records." Such a release may discourage an applicant with something to hide, or encourage an applicant to be forthcoming in an interview. If an employer uses an outside service to perform a pre-employment screening, the federal FCRA requires there must be a consent and disclosure form separate from the application.

6. The consent portion on any release form used for a background check must indicate the release is "valid for future screening for retention, promotion, or reassignment (unless revoked in writing)." This is helpful, for example, when an employer needs to conduct a post-employment investigation into allegations of sexual harassment or other workplace problems.

7. The application form must ask for ALL employment for the past 5-10 years. This is critical. A standardized application form makes it easier to spot unexplained gaps in employment. That is an important step in the hiring process and a critical part of exercising due diligence. Even if an employer hires a background company to perform a pre-employment criminal check, records can be missed because there is no national criminal record resource available for use by private employers. Criminal checks must be done in each county where the applicant has lived, worked, or attended school. If a person has an uninterrupted job history, an employer may have more confidence that the applicant has not been in serious trouble over the years.

8. The form should ask about addresses for the last 7-10 years. This helps in determining the scope of any criminal record search.

9. The form should allow the applicant to indicate whether the current employer may be contacted for a reference.

10. Finally, an employer can cover other standard matters. Examples include: the organization's "at will" policy; the employer is "a non-discriminatory employer;" uses mandatory arbitration in disputes; and requires that applicants provide original documents to verify their identity and right to work in the U.S.

An Example of an Application Language Law

A good example of #4 above is an Illinois law that was passed in 2004. The Illinois law requires employers to modify their employment applications to "contain specific language which states that the applicant is not obligated to disclose sealed or expunged records of conviction or arrest." This law also bars employers from asking "if an applicant has had records expunged or sealed." 20 ILCS 2630/12 (2004).

The Critical Areas and Questions Applications Must Avoid

Federal and state laws prohibit any non job-related inquiry, either verbal or through the use of an application form, which directly or indirectly limits a person's employment opportunities because of race, color, religion, national origin, ancestry, medical condition, disability (including AIDS), marital status, sex (including pregnancy), age (40+), exercise of family care leave, or leave for an employee's own serious health condition. There are other areas that an employer may go into, but with limits, such as criminal records.

Employers want to avoid application questions and interview questions that directly identify a person as a member of a protected group. However, even questions that appear neutral on their face can be illegal if the question results in a disproportionate screening of members of a protected group or is not a valid predictor of job performance. Examples include application questions about arrests.[35]

---

[35] Arrests are discussed in detail in later chapters on criminal investigations and criminal records.

Safe Hiring Tip ➤ As a rule of thumb, an employer cannot ask anything in an application that an employer cannot ask in a face-to-face personal interview. In the next chapter, there is an in-depth chart listing questions that are prohibited when conducting an interview. These same rules apply to applications.

---

10 Sure Signs of a Lawsuit Waiting to Happen

After going through the process of preparing an effective application and utilizing it instead of a resume, many employers make the fatal mistake of not reading the application carefully. This is a major mistake. Employee lawsuits often catch employers by surprise. Another way employers are bitten by their applications is when, upon closer examination, the employee's application shows that the employer could have reasonably predicted they were hiring a lawsuit just waiting to happen.

By looking for the following ten danger signals, an employer can avoid hiring a problem employee in the first place—

1. **Applicant does not sign application.** An applicant with something to hide may purposely not sign the application form so the applicant later cannot be accused of falsification.

2. **Applicant does not sign consent for background screening.** When a firm uses an outside agency to perform screening, federal law requires a separate disclosure and signed consent from the applicant. A background consent form protects employers in two ways: 1) it discourages applicants with something to hide and 2) encourages candid interviews. If a candidate fails to sign the consent, it is not a good sign.

3. **Applicant leaves criminal questions blank.** An applicant with a past problem may simply skip the questions about criminal records. Every employment application should ask, in the broadest possible terms allowed by law, if the applicant has a criminal record. Most jurisdictions only permit questions about convictions and pending cases. A criminal record can be either a felony or a misdemeanor; employers make a big mistake if they only ask about felonies since misdemeanors can be extremely serious too. Although employment may not be denied automatically because of a criminal conviction, an employer may consider the

nature and gravity of the offense, the nature of the job, and the age of the offense when evaluating whether there is a sound business reason not to employ someone with a criminal record. If an applicant lies about a criminal record, then the false application may be the reason to deny employment.

4. **Applicant self-reports a criminal violation.** Just because an applicant self-reports an offense does not eliminate the possibility other offenses exist, or the applicant may report it in a misleading way to lessen its seriousness. An employer is well-advised to check it out.

5. **Applicant fails to explain gaps in employment history.** There can be many reasons for a gap in employment. For example, an applicant may have been ill, gone back to school, or had difficulty finding a new job. However, if an applicant cannot account for the past 7-10 years, that can be a red flag. It could potentially mean he was in custody for a criminal offense. It is also important to know where a person has been because of the way criminal records are maintained in the U.S. Contrary to popular belief, there is not a national criminal database available to most employers. Searches must be conducted at each relevant courthouse, and there are more than 10,000 courthouses in the U.S. However, if an employer knows where an applicant has been, it increases the accuracy of a criminal search, and decreases the possibility that an applicant has served time for a serious offense. If there is an unexplained gap, an employer may not know where to search and can miss a criminal record.

6. **Explanations for employment gaps or reasons for leaving past jobs do not make sense.** If there were employment gaps reported by the applicant, do the reasons for the gaps make sense? A careful review of this section of the application is needed and anything that does not make sense must to be cleared up in the interview.

7. **Applicant fails to give sufficient information to identify a past employer for reference checks.** If an applicant does not give enough details about past employers, that can be a sign of trouble. Verifying past employment is a critical and important tool for safe hiring. Some employers make a costly mistake by not

checking past employment because past employers historically tend not to give detailed information. However, even if a reference check only reveals dates of employment and job titles, this critical information eliminates employment gaps. In addition, documenting the fact that an effort was made will demonstrate due diligence.

8. **Applicant fails to explain reason for leaving past jobs.** Past job performance can be an important predictor of future success.

9. **Applicant fails to indicate or cannot recall the name of a former supervisor.** Another red flag. Past supervisors are important in order to conduct past employment checks.

10. **Excessive cross-outs and changes.** This can be an indication that an applicant is making it up as he goes along.

The first four points above are sometimes referred to as the "**honest criminal syndrome.**" A person may have had a criminal record in the past and does not want to be dishonest about it. On the other hand, the person may not want to be fully revealing either. That is why it is so critical to look at the application's criminal question carefully to ensure it is filled out. Self-reported offenses should be looked at extra carefully. For example, an applicant self-reported that he stole some beer from a store. He neglected to mention it was stolen at the point of a gun, which is robbery, a much more serious offense. Another applicant reported he was stopped by police when he was younger and some recreational drugs he had were found under the car seat. A review of the court records revealed it was actually two pounds of cocaine — which is a lot of recreation.

Importance of Analyzing the Employment Gap

Red Flag #6 above is the first time we see the term "unexplained gaps in employment history." This is an important consideration for employers. However, gaps are not just discovered at the application stage; the interview process and past employment checks are also concerned with employment gaps. This underscores a critical point about safe hiring—that a good program will have overlapping tools. No one practice or procedure all by itself will insulate an employer from a bad-hiring decision. The use of multiple tools however increases an employer's chance of avoiding the bad hire. That is why we will return to the topic of "unexplained employment gaps" again in other chapters.

Review the Form with the Applicant

One way to avoid making these mistakes is to go through the application with the jobseeker, checking to be certain that the applicant filled out the forms completely. Rehash the question with the applicant if he has shown questionable answers. The process is not intended to necessarily ensure accuracy, but to determine with certainty that the applicant stands behind what he has stated on the application form.

How Lack of Follow Through Leads to Negligent Hiring

The author testified as an expert witness in a case where a school district hired a teacher who had been convicted in another state of a felony charge – sex with a minor. The offense made the person ineligible to teach. On the employment application, where it asked if the applicant had ever been convicted of a crime, the applicant put a slash mark in between the Yes and the No. The school district has a policy of reviewing the application with the applicant to clarify what the applicant meant. A school district employee asked the applicant which box he meant to check, and the applicant then clearly indicated "Yes." Unfortunately, after being on notice there was a criminal offense in the applicant's background, the school district failed to follow through and investigate the offense. After the applicant was hired, he was accused of inappropriate behavior with female students at the school. Under legal scrutiny, the failure to follow through after being put on notice of a past crime was found to be negligent hiring.

Applications and the Disclosure of Criminal Records

One of the most effective uses of an effective application form is to enable an employer to directly ask an applicant if he or she has a criminal record. Unfortunately, many employers use language in their applications that either is too narrow, too broad, or too ambiguous. Each of these mistakes can put an employer in difficulty. Let us review this language in detail—

Too Narrow

An example of a question that is too narrow is to ask only about felonies and not misdemeanors (of course, ask only in those states that permit the use of misdemeanors for making hiring decisions). Misdemeanors can be very serious. Under California law, for example, most employers would want to know if an applicant had a conviction for offenses such as fighting with a police officer, illegal possession of weapons, spousal abuse or child abuse, commercial burglary, assault and many other offenses. Yet in California, these can all be misdemeanors. Many serious offenses are plea-bargained down to misdemeanor offenses as well. Without the proper language, an applicant can honestly answer he has not been convicted of a felony even though there may be serious misdemeanor convictions an employer *needs* to know about.

Too Broad

On the other hand, some employers ask questions that are so broad that it improperly covers matters that are protected. There are a number of limitations under state and federal law concerning what an employer may legally ask about or "discover" concerning an applicant's or employee's criminal record. In fact, it can be a misdemeanor in California for an employer to knowingly violate some of these rules. Furthermore, if an applicant is placed in a position where he is forced to reveal information about himself that he is legally entitled not to disclose, an employer can actually be sued for "defamation by compelled self-publication" — in some states. In other words, if forced to say something defamatory about himself, an applicant may be able to file a lawsuit against the employer for defamation.

Too Ambiguous

The third mistake is to ask an applicant, "Have you ever been convicted of a felony or serious misdemeanor?" or "Have you ever been convicted of a crime of violence?" or a similar question that calls for an opinion. The problem occurs when an applicant is called upon to make a judgment about his own offense. For example, if a misdemeanor is serious, this can call for a very complex legal and factual determination on which lawyers, and even judges, could disagree. By asking a question that is ambiguous and leaves waffle room, an applicant can argue that in his mind the offense was not serious and a "no" answer was truthful. That is why a question cannot contain any ambiguity.

At times an applicant is simply confused by court proceedings and may not understand the results or what they mean.

Be Aware of State Laws

Chapter 9 indicates a number of states with additional limitations regarding disclosure of criminal records. For example, let's look at some of the limitations in California. Although not every state has rules as restrictive as California, employers in all states should be careful to ensure that their applications are legally compliant.

- An employer may NOT ask about arrests or detentions that did not result in a conviction.

- An employer may only consider convictions or pending cases.

- There are certain limitations on misdemeanors, crimes that have been sealed or otherwise expunged, cases where a person participated in pre-trial diversion, or certain minor marijuana convictions.

- An employer should NOT automatically deny employment due to a criminal conviction, but should consider the nature and gravity of the offense, whether it is job related, and when it occurred.

Below are examples of language that a California employer should consider using. Again, keep in mind that every state has its own rules, and an employer should check with an attorney in regards to state law.

Have you ever been convicted for a crime? (Exclude convictions for marijuana-related offenses for personal use more than two years old; convictions that have been sealed, expunged or legally eradicated, and misdemeanor convictions for which probation was completed and the case was dismissed)
Yes_____ No___

An alternative wording that avoids the problems associated with certain minor convictions—

Have you ever been convicted of a felony, or a misdemeanor involving any violent act, use or possession of a weapon or act of dishonesty for which the record has not been sealed or expunged?

If yes, please briefly describe the nature of the crime(s), the date and place of conviction and the legal disposition of the case.

This company will not deny employment to any applicant solely because the person has been convicted of a crime. The company however, may consider the nature, date and circumstances of the offense as well as whether the offense is relevant to the duties of the position applied for.

Are you currently out on bail, the subject of a current warrant for arrest, or released on your own recognizance pending trial? Yes ___ No ___

As mentioned previously, it is normally recommended the application contain language saying "the conviction of a crime will not automatically result in a denial of employment." Automatic disqualification could be a violation of state and federal discrimination laws. However, an employer may deny employment if the employer can establish a business-related reason for the refusal to hire. See the previous chapter for a detailed discussion on discrimination laws and safe hiring.

Where to Find a Good Application Form

Application forms are available from a number of sources.

- The local or state Chamber of Commerce may have forms available.
- A firm's business or labor attorney will normally have a new employee package available with an application form
- Human resources consultants and HR organizations may have forms.
- Office supply stores sell basic business forms including application forms.
- Books about running a business are available from local book stores and may have sample forms.
- There are firms that specialize in selling employment-related forms and products on the Internet.
- Many firms design their own employment forms to reflect the particular needs of their firm or industry.

One word of caution – many states have unique rules regarding what can and cannot be on an application. Some of these rules concern what an employer may ask about past criminal convictions. It is beyond the scope of this book to review the requirements for all 50 states; however, an employer is well advised to consult with a labor attorney for every state he hires within to review the legality of his application forms.

Chapter Summary

This Chapter provides information for **Audit Questions 9-12**.

Audit Question #9: Are there procedures to place applicants on notice that your organization engages in best practices for hiring?

Best Practices #9:

- There is a notice in the job announcement, bulletin, classified advertisement, Internet site, etc. that the firm performs background checks.

Audit Question #10: Does the firm use an application form?

Best Practices #10:

- The firm uses application forms, not resumes, as the primary tool for to insure uniformity in the hiring process.

Audit Question #11: Does the application form have all necessary and correct language?

Best Practices #11:

- The application requires applicant to provide all necessary information, prevents employer having impermissible information, and gives places where applicants sign certain statements.

- The application specifically asks if a person has been convicted or has pending charges. It uses the broadest legal language for both felonies and misdemeanors.

- In applicable states the applications acknowledges some limitation or controls on the use of misdemeanor records.

- The application contains a statement that a fraudulent statement or material omissions by the applicant are grounds to terminate the process, or employment, no matter when discovered.

Audit Question #12: Are completed applications reviewed for potential red flags including employment gaps?

Best Practices #12

- Applications are reviewed for the following—
  - Does not sign application
  - Does not sign release

- o Leaves criminal questions blank – the honest criminal syndrome
- o Applicant self-reports offense
- o Fails to identify past employers
- o Fails to identify past supervisors
- o Fails to explain why left past jobs
- o Excessive cross-outs and changes
- o Unexplained employment gaps

- It is critical to verify employment to determine where a person has been **even if you only get dates and job title**.

Chapter 5

The Interview Process

An essential part of a Safe Hiring Program is to question applicants carefully about their knowledge, skills, abilities, and experience. Part of the interview is designed to determine if the applicant will be a good fit, taking into account the work environment and the team the person will work with.

Interviews must be conducted in a manner that not only assures the employer of finding the best candidate for the position, but also is legal and does not put the employer in harm's way.

Audit Question # 13:

What five critical questions are used in a structured interview?

Audit Question # 14:

Are interviewers trained in legal compliance?

The Importance of Interviews

The interview is the first opportunity for an employer to meet face-to-face with applicants who may literally and figuratively hold the keys to future business success in their hands. An employer practicing safe hiring during the interview process must take steps to protect the workforce as well as ensure that the best and most qualified candidates are hired.

An interview is typically accomplished using a written set of questions selected ahead of time by the employer and provided to the hiring managers conducting the interviews. There are literally thousands of potential interview questions that can be asked. An employer needs to review all potential questions and select a set of questions that would be the most useful for selecting the best employees. That does not mean that everyone is always asked the exact same question. Different positions may require that certain portions of an interview require customized questions. Questions also can depend upon the particular industry, the needs of the firm, and the position being filled. If a supplemental question set is used that is position-specific, the interview should assure all similarly situated candidates have the same question set.

When using an SHP, an interview should accomplish three goals—

- **Reinforce the message already communicated in company application forms and job announcements — the firm practices safe hiring.** Conveying this message to the applicant will encourage honesty and discourage bad applicants. All applicants need to clearly understand that the employer has an SHP.

- **Allow for the transfer of information from the applicant to the employer.** The interview is when an employer has an opportunity to fill in any gaps. Also, the employer has a chance to ask the additional penetrating questions if the candidate seems to have attempted to conceal or lie about unfavorable information.

- **Permit an assessment of the candidate.** The interview provides the employer an opportunity to assess the knowledge, skills, and abilities of the applicant in person. However, keep in mind that good candidates can come across poorly, and bad candidates can come across well. The assessment is just one of many tools used in the calculus of a hiring decision.

Given these three goals, how does an organization ensure that positive results happen? This chapter examines the needed tools.

Advantages of a Structured Interview

A structured interview is when the interviewer has a standard set of questions that are asked of all candidates and are used "across" an organization. Structured interview questions are usually pre-printed on forms.

The advantages for an employer using a structured interview are significant. First, it ensures uniformity and equal opportunity for all candidates in the interview process and protects against claims of discrimination or disparate treatment.

Second, it helps to keep hiring managers on track by using legally defensible questions. By giving interviewers a script to follow, it helps an employer's efforts at training interviewers not to ask prohibited questions. A discussion and chart of permissible and impermissible questions is presented later in this chapter.

Third, and most critical from the aspect of an SHP, the structured interview ensures the employer that certain essential "integrity questions" are asked of all candidates.

The process does not mean that interviewers are simply clerical robots, going through the motions and recording responses in a rote fashion. Penetrating follow-up questions and keen observations of the applicants are still critical to make sure all required areas are covered.

Behavior-Based Questions Should be Used

Interview techniques where the applicant is merely told to "tell me about yourself" have not proved altogether effective. In order to obtain more insight, employers may ask hypothetical questions such as "what would you do if...." The "if" could be anything ranging from working with difficult people to completing assignments under deadlines. However, using the "if method" does not necessarily tell how the person actually did in the past.

Behavior-based interviewing is one of the newest and most effective methods for establishing if a person is a good fit for both the job and the organization. In a behavior-based interview, a person is asked to accurately describe real situations he has encountered and what he did to resolve the issue or problem. The method is based on the concept that the most accurate predictor of how a candidate will perform in the future is how he performed in the past in a similar situation. The question could be about a time when a person faced a typical workforce problem. This type of interview question may typically start with the phrase, "Tell me about a time when...."

There are numerous books, resources, and websites that offer suggestions on behavior-based interview questions. Here are sample questions to demonstrate the format—

- Tell me about a time when you had to coordinate several different people to achieve a goal. What were the challenges involved, and how did you overcome them?

- Tell me about the most difficult business-related decisions you have had to make in the past six months. Describe the situation and what made it difficult. How did you resolve it?

- Give me an example of when you had to work with someone who was very difficult to get along with, and how you handled that situation.

The Integrity Interview

Organizations that hire people for extremely sensitive or high-risk positions can conduct a full integrity interview" to determine if a person is a good fit. Also, the same questions can be used to help detect if there is any reason NOT to hire the person.

Integrity questions are used to explore the following—

- Does the applicant really have the knowledge, skills, abilities, and experience as claimed?

- Is the applicant really who he says he is?

- Has the applicant left any material out of the application process?

- Has the applicant misstated any qualifications in the application process?

- Is there any reason to think the applicant's moral rudder is not set straight? (In other words, is the applicant an honest person?)

A good interviewer creates a comfortable and professional environment but also stresses the need for complete honesty. Consider the following specific questions—

"It is not unusual to exaggerate in an application or resume. However, we need complete and accurate information concerning certain areas."

"Is there anything in your employment application that you want to change or correct? This is the time."

"If we checked with your former employers, would any of them report that you were asked to leave?"

If the interviewer wished to cover potential security issues such as criminal record or drug and alcohol use, then this question could be asked—

"If we were to check court records, would we find any convictions or outstanding warrants?"

Safe Hiring Tip ➤ One way to accomplish an integrity interview is to retain the services of a professional interviewer from outside your office. This professional can conduct an in-depth interview covering a full employment history and also address security concerns such as terminations, drug and alcohol use, and criminal record. In the case of a large firm, the interview could be completed by another person within the organization such as personnel in security or loss prevention departments.

Use Open-Ended Questions and Follow-Up Questions

A proven technique of an integrity interview is the use of open-ended and follow-up questions and not to rely upon information given beforehand.

Let us say the interviewer starts with questions about a person's job history. If the interviewer does not have a resume or application, every question is open-ended, meaning the applicant supplies all the information and no part of the answer is suggested by the question. This is the opposite of a leading question where the question itself suggests an answer.

For example, if an interviewer says, "I see you left Acme Industries due to a lay-off." That is a leading question. It suggests the answer, allowing the applicant to merely expand on that theme. An example of an open-ended question is "How long was your employment with Acme?" or "Why did that employment end?"

It is critical to ask follow-up questions when the answers do not make sense. If an applicant says something illogical, the interviewer should not hesitate to ask the applicant to review the answer. Sometimes it helps to ask the same question in a different way. For example, ask the applicant to describe in detail what occurred leading up to or after the event. If the applicant is making something up, that may be obvious. If an applicant gives a non-answer or an answer that is too fast and too pat, then a follow-up question would be helpful. For example, if an applicant says, "We already covered that," the interviewer, simply says, "I must have missed it. Can we review that again?"

As a practical matter, company managers and HR professionals are not expected to give every applicant the third degree. **However, interviewers should be trained so they are not so glued to the questioning process that they do not pay attention to the manner in which answers are given.**

Using a Preliminary Phone Screen

Another helpful hiring tool is a preliminary telephone screen. After an employer has initially reviewed and selected a possible list of candidates, performing a telephone screen will help narrow the list even further and save an employer valuable time. A phone screen is accomplished by calling each potential candidate and asking the same list of questions. If the candidate appears to meet the initial criteria, then an interview can be immediately scheduled. If a message is left and the applicant does not call back, then that applicant can be eliminated from consideration.

The 5 Questions That Should Be Asked In Every Interview

To help hiring managers have a better understanding of a candidate, and to weed out those who are unacceptable risks, it can be very effective to empower interviewers with some key standard questions. There are five suggested, critical interview questions related to an SHP that every employer or hiring manager **should be trained** to ask.

Asking these five standard questions has several advantages. They allow for a consistent process, so that all applicants are subjected to the same questions. Also, this creates a more comfortable environment for the interviewers since they do not have to memorize questions because the questions are written out for them. If the questions on safe hiring issues feel uncomfortable, then the interviewer can simply indicate that these questions are asked of everyone and they are required due to standard company policy.

Of course, an employer would not want to get the interview off on the wrong foot with questions aimed at past criminal conduct or negative employment experiences. However, every interview does have a "housekeeping" portion where standard questions are asked. That would be a good time for the following five questions.

1. *Our firm has a standard policy of conducting background checks on all hires before an offer is made or finalized. You have already signed a release form. Do you have any concerns about that?*

   This is a general question about screening. Since the applicant has signed a release form, there is a powerful incentive to be honest and reveal any issues.

2. *We also check for criminal convictions for all finalists. Do you have any concerns about that?*

This question goes from the general to the specific. Be sure to ask the question in a form that is legally permissible in your state. It is important NOT to ask a question that is so broadly worded that it may lead to an applicant revealing more information than allowed by law. Again, make sure the applicant understands that he has signed a release and this process is standard company policy.

3. **When we talk to your past employers, what do you think they will say?**

   Note the questions states: "When we contact your past employers..." indicating that they will be contacted. This general question again provides a powerful incentive to be very accurate.

4. **Will your past employers tell us that there were any issues with tardiness, meeting job requirements, etc.?**

   This question goes again to a specific area. Ask detailed questions about matters that are expressly relevant to the job opening.

5. **Tell me about any unexplained gaps in your employment history.**

   If there are any unexplained employment gaps, it is imperative to ask about them.

Since applicants have signed consent forms and believe the firm is doing checks, applicants will have a powerful incentive to be truthful. These questions are the equivalent of a "New Age" lie detector test. Employers can no longer administer actual lie detector tests and probably would not want to even if they could. However, these questions serve a valuable function by providing a strong motivation for applicants to be self-revealing. It also takes advantage of the natural human trait to want to have some control over what others say about you. If an applicant believes a future employer may hear negative information from a past employer, the applicant may want to be able to set the record straight before the future employer has the chance to hear negative information from someone else.

Good applicants will shrug the questions off and applicants with something to hide may reveal vital information. Applicants with something to hide may react in a number of different ways. Some applicants may tough it out during the first question. However, the questions are designed to go from the general to the specific. By the second question, an applicant may well begin to express concerns or react in some way that raises a red flag. An applicant may object to the questions by asking if the questions invade his privacy rights. If an applicant raises such an objection, then simply indicate that these are standard job-related questions asked of all applicants.

Why Are Employment Gaps So Important?

We first discussed employment gaps in the last chapter. The interview process also helps employers detect unexplained gaps that may be relevant to employment. An employer related the following story that illustrates why this is an important concept.

The Ideal Applicant

The applicant was just perfect for the computer job. He had all of the right qualifications. During the interview, the interviewer asked the usual questions. While taking a last look at the resume, the interviewer happened to notice a two-year gap in the employment and education history. Out of curiosity, the interviewer asked about the gap.

The applicant explained that he had decided to go back to go school and retrain so he could join the computer age. The interviewer was merely curious about the classes because he wanted to find some good classes for other employees. *Where was it?* Oh, it was a state-sponsored job-retraining program. *Where was the program based?*

With just a few questions it finally came out. The so-called computer school where the courses were taken was actually classes offered at a state prison. Of course, the applicant did have a perfect attendance record.

This story illustrates two key points—

1. Look at the resume or application for unexplained gaps.
2. Use the interview to ask the applicant about any gaps.

Actually, the criminal record by itself would *not* have disqualified the computer technician. The real problem was that the job the applicant interviewed for required a person to go inside state prisons to fix computers – and prisons may not care to have former inmates come back in a professional capacity.

Training the Interviewer: The Questions Not to Ask – and Why

As mentioned at the outset of this chapter, a true SHP means the job interview process must be conducted in a legal manner. Just as there are troublesome, improper areas or questions to be avoided on an employment application, the same is true for job interviews. If certain questions are asked, or if questions are asked in a certain way, an employer can be exposed to a variety of discrimination charges and lawsuits.

Rod Fliegel, an attorney and shareholder with Littler Mendelson, P.C., has graciously supplied us with the following chart, an excellent guide to use for protecting an SHP's application and interview processes.[36]

It is critical that the person in the firm who performs interviews is thoroughly knowledgeable about this chart or a similar set of guidelines, and in the manner that questions may be asked.

Pre-Employment Inquiry Guidelines Chart

	You May Ask:	Do <u>Not</u> Ask:
Name	"Have you ever used another name?" "Is any additional information necessary to enable a check on your work and education record such as a name change, nickname, or use of an assumed name? If yes, please explain."	"What is your maiden name?"
Address/ Residence	"Can you be reached at this address?" "Can you be reached at these telephone numbers?"	"Do you own your home or rent?" "Do you live with your spouse?" "With whom do you live?"
Age	"If hired, can you show proof of age?" "Are you over eighteen years of age?"	Any questions that tend to identify applicants over 40, e.g., birthdates, dates of attendance or completion of elementary or high school.

---

[36] Rod Fliegel has extensive experience defending national and local employers in state, federal and administrative litigation, including high-stakes class actions. He has special compliance and litigation expertise concerning the intersection of the federal and state background check laws. The chart was adopted from "Employment Inquiries," California Department of Fair Employment & Housing

	You May Ask:	Do Not Ask:
Citizenship	"Are you able, after employment, to present authorization to work in the United States?" If this questions is asked, it should be asked of all applicants and not only of those with accents or who otherwise appear to have non-USA origins in order not to discriminate based on national origin, language, etc.	"Are you a United States citizen?" (Note: In very limited circumstances involving national security, citizenship could be a qualification for employment.) Any questions about birthplace of applicant or applicant's parents, spouse, or other relatives. Any questions about requirements to produce naturalization or alien registration papers prior to a decision to hire.
Color or Race		Any questions concerning race or color of skin, eyes, hair, etc. Any requirement to provide a photograph.
Credit Report		Any report that indicates information otherwise unlawful to ask such as marital status, age, residency, birthplace, and so on. "Have you ever had a bankruptcy?"
Criminal Records	You may ask applicants about misdemeanor or felony convictions except for those that have been sealed, expunged, or eradicated by statute, or convictions for certain marijuana-related offenses over two years old. You may ask whether the applicant has charges pending and awaiting trial. Tell the applicant that a Yes answer will not necessarily be disqualifying.	Questions about arrests. Certain states have restrictions employers must follow. Law enforcement and certain state agencies, school districts, businesses and other organizations that have a direct responsibility for the supervision, care or treatment of children, mentally ill or disabled persons, or other vulnerable adults, may have more latitude to make inquiries.

	You May Ask:	Do Not Ask:
Disability or AIDS or Medical Condition	"Are you currently able to perform the essential duties of the job for which you are applying?" "Are you able to perform [specific task]?" If the disability is obvious, or disclosed, you may ask about accommodations that would enable the applicant/employee to perform the essential duties of the job. Statement that an offer may be made contingent on passing a physical exam.	"Are you disabled?" "How much sick time or medical leave did you use at your last job?" "Have you ever been hospitalized?" "Have you ever been treated by a psychologist or psychiatrist?" "Are you taking any prescription medications? If not, have you?" "Have you ever had treatment for drug or alcohol use or any other addiction?" Any questions about health or medical conditions. An employer may not make any medical inquiry or conduct any medical examination prior to making a conditional offer of employment. In California, post-offer, pre-employment medical examinations also must be job-related and consistent with business necessity. Any questions about an applicant's prior workers' compensation history.
Education	"Are you presently enrolled or do you intend to enroll in school?" "What subjects did you excel in at school?" "Did you participate in extracurricular activities that relate to the job you are seeking with us? In what ways?" "What did you select as your major?" "Did you work an outside job while attending school? Doing what? What did you like/dislike about your part-time job during school?" "Are you interested in continuing your education? Why? When? Where?" "Did your education prepare you for the job you are seeking with us? In what ways?"	Any questions about dates of schooling. Privacy-related education issues— "Who paid for your educational expenses while you were in school?" "Did you go to school on a scholarship?" "Do you still owe on student loans taken out during school?" "When did you graduate from high school?"

	You May Ask:	Do **Not** Ask:
Experience, Skills, and Activities	Questions about special skills or knowledge; when the applicant last used skills that are related to the position; and activities that have provided the applicant with experience, training, or skills that relate to the position for which the applicant is applying.	"Does your physical condition make you less skilled?" "When did you acquire that skill?"
Family	Name and address of parent or guardian if applicant is a minor.	Questions that elicit any information on marital status. "How many children do you have? How old are they?" "Who takes care of your children while you are working?" "Do your children go to day care?" "What does your husband think about your working outside the home?" "What does your spouse do?" "What is your spouse's salary?"
Marital Status, Sexual Orientation	"Please state the names of any relatives already employed by our organization." Employers may state the company policy regarding work assignment of employees who are related.	"Is it Mrs. or Miss?" "Are you single? …Married? …Divorced? …Separated? …Engaged? …Widowed?" "Do you have a domestic partner?" Any questions that elicit information related to marital status or sexual orientation.
Military Service	"Have you served in the U.S. military?" "Did your military service and training provide you with skills you could put to use in this job?	"Have you served in the military of a foreign country?" "What type of discharge did you receive from the U.S. military service?" "When was your discharge from military service?" "Can you provide discharge papers?"
National Origin	You may state that, after hire, verification of the legal right to work in the United States will be required in order to comply with the Federal Immigration Reform and Control Act of 1986.	Any questions regarding nationality, lineage, ancestry, national origin, descent or parentage of applicant or his/her parents or spouse. "Where were you born?" "What is the origin of your name?" "What is your mother tongue?" "What country do your ancestors come from?" Any questions on how the applicant acquired the ability to read, write, or speak a foreign language.

	You May Ask:	Do Not Ask:
Notify In Case Of Emergency	"Whom should we contact in case of an emergency?"	Name, address and/or relationship of relative in case of accident or emergency.
Organiza-tions	"What organizations do you participate in that relate to the job for which you are applying? Please omit any organization that is not job-related or any organization that indicates your race, religious creed, color, national origin, ancestry, disability, medical condition, marital status, sex, sexual orientation, or age."	"List all organizations, clubs, societies, and lodges to which you belong."
Photographs	For identification purposes, ask for a photograph after hiring.	Ask applicant to submit a photograph whether mandatory or optional before hiring. Any questions about physical characteristics such as height or weight. Any applicant to submit to videotaping of the interview.
Pregnancy	"How long to you plan to stay on the job?" "Are you currently able to perform the essential duties of the job for which you are applying?"	"Are you pregnant?" "When was your most recent pregnancy terminated?" "Do you plan to become pregnant?" Any questions about pregnancy and related medical conditions. Any questions about child bearing or birth control.
Prior Employment	"How did you overcome problems you faced there?" "Which problems frustrated you the most?" "Of the jobs indicated on your application, which did you enjoy the most, and why?" "What were your reasons for leaving your last job?" "Have you ever been discharged from any position? If so, for what reason?"	"How many sick days did you have at your old job?" "Did you file any types of claims?"

	You May Ask:	**Do <u>Not</u> Ask:**
References	"By whom were you referred for a position here?"	Questions on the applicant's former employer or persons given as references that elicit information about the applicant's race, color, religious creed, national origin, ancestry, physical or mental disability, medical condition, sex, marital status, sexual orientation, or age.
Religion or Creed	You may make a statement about the regular days, hours and shifts that are required by the job.	"What is your religion?" "What church do you go to?" "What are your religious holidays?" "Does your religion prevent you from working weekends or holidays?"
Sexual Orientation		"Are you a homosexual?" "Do you have a domestic partner?" "What are your views of same-sex partner relations and benefits?"

Additional Integrity Questions – That are Legal to Ask

Below are additional questions that can be legally used during an in-depth integrity interview.

- Tell me every job you have had in the past 10 years, including start and end date, salary, job title when started and ended and supervisor, including names, addresses, and telephone numbers.
- Are there any falsifications on your application?
- Did you leave any jobs off your application?
- How will your previous employers describe your attendance? …Excellent? …O.K.? …Poor?
- How many days have you missed in the last year?
- How many verbal/written reprimands for your attendance did you receive in the past 2 years?
- How many days of tardiness were recorded in your personnel file in the last year / job?   Why?
- How many disciplinary actions in the past 3 years?

- Where have you been suspended? Why?

- Where have you been fired or asked to resign? Why?

- Will any of your previous employers say they let you go or fired you?

- Where will you receive your best evaluation? The worst evaluation?

- Where have you suspected or had knowledge of co-workers or supervisors stealing?

- What have you taken?

- What will be found when your criminal record is checked? Note: convictions will not necessarily disqualify any applicant from employment.

- What does your current driving record show in the way of violations?

- Describe your best work related qualities

- What is the worst thing any former employer will say about you?

- Whom do you know at the place of employment you are applying at?

- When was the last time in possession of illegal drugs?

- Currently, or within the past six months, what is your use of any controlled substance? ...Marijuana? ...Cocaine? ...Speed? ...PCP? ...LSD? ...Hashish? ...Other?

- What is your current use of alcohol?

- Has the use of alcohol ever interfered with your work?

- To what extent do you gamble? Has gambling ever been a problem for you?

- Have you ever been the subject of, or a witness in, any type of investigation at work?

Train Interviewers to Spot Red Flag Behavior

An interviewer should be trained to spot red flags that indicate when further questions may be needed. Many of these tip-offs are non-verbal in nature. Of course, a perfectly honest and capable candidate may exhibit these red flags, while a practiced liar may not exhibit any at all! Therefore, this standard list of non-verbal clues is certainly not to be used as a basis for a hiring decision, but could be used as a basis to ask more questions.

The list below is by no means complete, since many additional behaviors could be added.

- Non-responsive answers such as answering a question other than the question asked
- Answering your question with a question or repeating your question
- Answers do not make sense or are inconsistent
- Becoming defensive inappropriately
- Breaking eye contact
- Clearing throat, stuttering, voice changing pitch, speed, or volume
- Shifting body position or defensive body language such as crossing arms, shrugging shoulders
- Hesitation before answering
- Inability to remember dates and details
- Loss of previous cooperative behavior
- Making excuses before asked
- Nervous hand movements such as wringing or tightly gripping hands, repeated fluttering, brushing of lint, or moving documents
- Not remembering something when applicant has remembered other events in detail
- Protesting too much that they made the choice to leave a company

Chapter Summary

This Chapter provides information for **Audit Questions 13-14**.

Audit Question #13: What five critical questions are used in a structured Interview?

Best Practices #13:

- Since the applicant has signed a consent form and believes the firm is doing background checks, there is a powerful incentive to be truthful.
    - ○ "We do background checks on everyone we make an offer to. Do you have any concerns you would like to discuss?" (Good applicants will shrug this question off.)
    - ○ "We also check for criminal convictions for all finalists. Any concerns about that?"

(Make sure question reflects what employer may legally ask in your state)

o "We contact all past employers. What will they say?"

o "Will past employer tell us…?" e.g., applicant was tardy, did not perform well, etc.
(Questions must be on job-related issues only)

o Where gaps in the employment history are not explained, it is critical to ask, "Can you please tell us what you were doing during the periods between employments that you listed."

Audit Question #14: Are interviewers trained in legal compliance?

Best Practices #14:

- All interviewers are trained to—

  o Question all applicants in a similar fashion

  o Not ask illegal questions, i.e., questions that are discriminatory or prohibited by law

  o Respond when an applicant volunteers impermissible information

  o Not to respond when an applicant volunteers impermissible information and not to make any notes about it

  o Not to make statements to an applicant such as promises about the job

  o Not mark or make notes on resume

- The interviewer's training and audit results are documented

Chapter 6

Checking Past Employment and Education

Past employment verification is a key component in a Safe Hiring program. To protecting your workplace from someone who is unsafe, unfit or unqualified.

Verification of educational credentials is also an important part of an employer's decision-making process in hiring. Educational achievement tells an employer a great deal about an applicant's ability, qualifications, and motivation.

Audit Question # 15:

Does the firm check past employment?

Audit Question # 16:

Does the firm check education credentials and achievements?

Trust, but Verify

Checking references is part of the **AIR Process** mentioned in Chapter 1. Ideally, these checks provide specifics about past job performance and education are likely predictors of future success.

The first part of this chapter examines how to implement past employment checks as part of a Safe Hiring Program. The second portion examines how to implement education and credential verifications as part of an SHP.

Legal and Effective Past Employment Checks

Key Terms

First, let us differentiate some important terms—

- **Verification** of past employment refers to verifying factual data such as start date, end date, and job title.

- A **Reference Check** of past employment means obtaining qualitative information about the person's performance such as how well the person did, where improvements are needed, or if the person would be rehired.

- Often, larger firms provide verifications through a Human Resources, staffing or payroll departments, or through someone else who does not actually know the applicant but is familiar with the firm. The verifier has the applicant's history of dates of employment and job titles. A reference, by comparison, is typically given by someone who actually knew the applicant, such as a former supervisor. This type of reference check is referred to as a **Supervisor Reference**.

- A **Personal Reference** comes from someone who is familiar with the applicant in a context other than employment.

More About Checking Personal References

Most employers consider that personal references are friends of the applicant and that they will not relate anything negative about the applicant. Checking personal references, although certainly not as important as checking with someone who knows the applicant in a work situation, are nonetheless useful. Many of the procedures and techniques regarding past employment checks taught in this chapter are also applicable when checking personal references.

If you do check personal references, below are several specific criteria concerns to keep in mind—

- Determine the value of the reference by asking how the person knows the applicant and in what capacity did they meet.
- Ask only job-related questions. Do not ask a question that could support a discrimination claim or an invasion of privacy.
- If the applicant has lived in the same geographical area for a number of years, consider it is red flag if none of the references are local.

Even if All You Get Are Name, Rank, and Serial Number, Verification Checks Are Critical

Some employers make the costly error of not checking references. They know many organizations have policies against giving out detailed information about current or former employees. Thus, some employers assume the effort is worthless because all they will get is "name, rank, and serial number," if anything at all.

However, here is the critical point—

Even if all you get is verification of dates of employment and job titles, past employer phone calls are still vital for safe hiring.

Why is this so important? There are actually five essential reasons why an SHP requires calling past employers regardless of whether the past employer limits the information to start date, end date, and job title.

1. Allows an Employer to Demonstrate Due Diligence

This is a critical point—if something goes wrong, an employer needs to be able to convince a jury that the employer made reasonable efforts, given the situation, to engage in safe hiring. Documentation for each person hired shows that an employer took reasonable steps by contacting past employers to confirm job information and to ask questions. This is powerful evidence an employer was not negligent. As stated before, an employer is not expected to be 100% successful in hiring. No one is. Any employer is expected to act in good faith and to take diligent efforts to hire safe and qualified people. This cannot be done without demonstrating that the employer made the effort, which means documenting that he picked up the phone and tried.

What constitutes a reasonable effort? Taking reasonable care means attempting to obtain employer references and documenting those attempts. To a degree, the level of reasonable inquiry depends upon the nature of the job and the risk to third parties. A higher standard of care may be required for hiring an executive than a food service worker. Regardless, every employer has a legal obligation to exercise appropriate care in the selection and retention of employees. The law does not require that an employer be successful in obtaining references. It is clear that an employer must at least try.

2. Eliminates Unexplained Employment Gaps

As covered in previous chapters, an employment gap may be indicative of a red flag. The issue is not whether a person has gaps in his or her employment, but whether any gaps are unexplained. Not everyone has an uninterrupted employment history. Employment gaps can have very reasonable explanations, such as time off to go to school, for a sabbatical, or for personal and family reasons. Sometimes it can take time for a person to find a new job.

But gaps can indicate negative things too, such as a prison or jail stay. By eliminating any gap in employment over the past 5-10 years, it lessens the possibility the applicant spent time in custody for a significant criminal offense. Of course, finding no gaps does not completely eliminate the possibility an applicant spent time in jail for some lesser offense. In many jurisdictions, a person convicted of a misdemeanor, such as a DUI, can fulfill a jail sentence in alternative ways – community service program, weekend custody, a "bracelet program," etc.

The importance of looking for unexplained gaps is underscored by the requirements imposed by the Federal Aviation Administration (FAA). When jobs fall under its authority, such as at airports and airlines, everyone hired must have a complete, validated 10-year history. If there is a gap, then the gap must be explained.

3. Indicates Where to Search for Criminal Records

Since there is no national database of criminal records that private employers can legally access, criminal record searches must be conducted at each relevant courthouse. As mentioned, there are more than 10,000 courthouses covering some 3,500+ state and federal jurisdictions. When an employer knows where an applicant has been, then knowing where to look increases the accuracy of a criminal search. If an employer does not know where to search, then he can easily miss a court where an applicant had a significant criminal act, and thereby inadvertently hire a person with a serious, undisclosed criminal record. Details are discussed in the next two chapters.

4. Allows an Employer to Hire Based Upon Facts and Not Only Instinct

The "warm body theory" of hiring is not part of an SHP. Although the use of instinct is valuable in the hiring process, there is simply no substitute for factual verifications. Given the statistics that up to one-third of all resumes contain material falsehoods, the need to verify statements in a resume or application is critical. Just knowing with certainty that the applicant did, in fact, have the job and position as claimed goes a long way toward a solid hiring decision.

5. Potential Employer May Receive Valuable Information

Many employers assume that when they call a past employer they will get a "No comment," or "We do not give references." However, there is a significant percentage of time when both a verification and reference is possible. Sometimes this occurs when a firm has not been strongly counseled by its employment attorney not to give a reference. The overwhelming numbers of employers in the U.S. are small employers who may not have been trained by a lawyer not to give references. Also, the previous employer may feel morally obliged to give references. Successful reference calls also can occur when the person calling has excellent communication skills, is professional, and is able to start some dialogue. There are many HR and security professionals who have developed the ability to obtain references, even from the most reluctant sources. Techniques on how to obtain references are given later in this chapter.

How Far Back Should Reference Checks Go?

How far back should one go when checking previous employers? The answer can depend upon the applicant's relevant work history, the sensitivity of the position, and the availability of information. Some applicants may have had only one employer in the past 10 years. Others may have had a large number. If a person is an hourly worker, then it is possible the person has held numerous past jobs. A young worker may not have a work history to check.

As a general guideline, employers should go back a minimum of five years, although 7-10 is much better. If the employer is in an industry where there is a great deal of turnover, then it may not be practical to go back even five years, if the five-year span represents a large number of previous employers.

Safe Hiring Tip ➤ Employers should utilize a rule of reason, but also must be internally consistent so that all similarly situated applicants are treated in a similar fashion. If an employer goes back five years for an administrative assistant, then all candidates who have reached the stage where references are conducted should also have their references checked going back five years.

Who Should Make the Past Employment Calls?

There are three different entities that can do past employment checks—

1. The Actual Hiring Manager
2. Human Resource Personnel
3. A Background Screening Firm

Here are the pros and cons of each group—

Hiring Manager

Advantages: The manager knows the job and knows what talents and skills are needed. Also, the hiring manager is the person who has to live with the decision. For sensitive or critical positions, the manager may want to receive input directly from previous employers. Even if the previous employer has a "no comment" policy, there still may be an advantage in talking personally to the previous employer and attempting to glean what information is available "between the lines."

Disadvantages: There is much less control over the process in terms of whether the hiring manager is asking legal questions, or treating candidates in a similar fashion. In addition, many hiring managers may be tempted to make fewer calls, and may settle for just one completed call before making a decision. Hiring managers may not be as concerned about the need to establish a full employment history or look for employment gaps. Although these drawbacks can be lessened with written procedures, training, and auditing of hiring files, they are still sources of concern.

Human Resources

Advantages: Any reference check done by HR more than likely will be done thoroughly, properly, and legally with proper documentation and consistency.

Disadvantages: The HR department does not know the job requirements nearly as well as the hiring manager. In addition, even for a firm with a fully staffed HR department, employment reference checking is a time-consuming task. The difficulty with performing employment reference checks in-house is not the time the actual interview takes; it is the constant interruptions of returned phone calls throughout the day, tracking the progress of each candidate, and making repeated attempts when there is not a callback. It can also take time to locate former employers and phone numbers as well.

Background Checking Firm

Advantages: Since a background firm can be counted on to methodically contact all past employers, a firm knows that nothing will fall through the cracks. In addition, the fees charged by screening firms are typically very modest.

Disadvantages: A verifier employed by a screening firm typically knows little about the employer or the job. Screening firms often do employment checks in high volume and are unlikely to ask in-depth, pertinent questions. In addition, given the prices charged by screening firms, the verifiers are not HR professionals, but rather have skills that are closer to a professional call center.

Who Makes the Call? — Conclusion

One way to answer this answer is to recognize the difference in how the reference checks are used. Many organizations encourage the hiring manager to make whatever employment checks are needed to help decide if the person is a good fit — to form an opinion as to whether or not to make a job offer in the first place. Of course, an SHP will make sure a hiring manager is trained, so that only legal and permissible questions are asked.

In order to make sure nothing falls through the cracks, HR or a background screening firm may be called upon to do a check, just to make sure all the bases have been covered. The worst that can happen is some former employer may be called twice — once by the hiring manager and again by HR or a background screening firm.

Using Safe Hiring Procedures in a Quality Reference Checking System

Regardless of who does the reference checking and verifications, an effective reference checking system must be in place. All aspects of the system must be documented and all personnel using the system must be trained. A system indicates who has been called, the status of each call, and who else needs to be called. Here are eight important steps that the background screening companies use. A successful, in-house system of reference checking is possible if the employer incorporates these steps into a documented system to obtaining past references. Use of this system is worth its weight in gold should an employer ever be called upon to demonstrate due diligence in court.

1. Start with a Worksheet

Have a prepared Past Employment Worksheet for each candidate. Fill in the name and contact information for each past employer as well as any standard reference questions. Use the Past Employer Worksheet to track all phone calls, including who was called, and all the results. Even if the reference attempt was unsuccessful, a completed worksheet showing each call — including the date, time, phone number, person called, and the result — is the best possible proof that an employer exercised due diligence.

In advance, it is helpful to place on the sheet any essential information reported by the applicant during an interview or on the application. In this way, the reference checker can note what a past employer reports, providing an easy-to-read side-by-side comparison.

Makes sure any specific job-related questions relevant to the knowledge, skill, and abilities related to a particular position are on the sheet.

Using a Past Employer Worksheet insures you are asking the same questions for similarly situated candidates. A critical function of reference-checking in an SHP is to treat all candidates fairly. Treat similarly situated candidates the same way! A sample *Employment Verification and Reference Worksheet* is found in the Appendix.

2. Independently Confirm the Phone Number for a Past Employer

To avoid the possibility of a fake reference,[37] it is recommended that a verifier independently locate the past employer's phone number by use of an Internet service or local phone book. Any legitimate firm will have a listed phone number. Here are some websites where employer phone numbers can be located—

- www.infousa.com
- www.city-yellowpages.com
- www.switchboard.com
- www.superpages.com
- www.infospace.com
- www.411.com

In addition, verifiers can also "Google" the past employer by running the name on the Internet search engine at www.google.com.

---

[37] It may not happen very often, but there are situations where an applicant has set up a fake reference on a resume by providing a friend's telephone number, with the friend standing by to answer, posing as a past employer to give a glowing and professorial reference. Fake references can be set up using a voicemail service belonging to a supposed reference with a friend later returning the call posing as a past supervisor.

There may be times when a firm is not listed. That can happen if the firm has moved, merged, changed names, or gone out of business. In that situation, talk further with the applicant to find someone who can verify an employment.

Of course, a verifier must also use good judgment. If the phone is not answered in a professional manner, or there are the sounds of traffic and children in the background, then something is not right.

Finally, if there is any suspicion of a set-up or fake reference, it may be necessary to verify if the person giving the reference was, in fact, employed by the past employer. That may even require, in some situations, calling HR or payroll to make sure the person the verifier is talking with was in fact employed there.

3. Be careful when contacting an applicant's current employer

A current employer should NOT be contacted unless the applicant specifically gives permission. The reason is there are some employers who, upon learning a current employee is looking to leave, will immediately take steps to terminate the employee. This is especially true for positions of greater responsibility where the applicant may have access to customer lists or trade secrets. If such a hasty departure is caused by a phone call by the prospective new employer, and the job offer does not come through, then the applicant is left without a job and free to contemplate whether they should visit a lawyer.

In order to avoid this, here is a simple two-step program—

- On the application, in large letters, make sure there is a box someplace asking an applicant "May we contact your current employer?"

- Do NOT call the current employer unless the applicant has clearly marked the "Yes" Box. If the applicant failed to check either box, then do not call until that is clarified. Anything other than a clear indication of YES can create problems.

If the employer still needs to verify current employment, there are three options to incorporate into the system—

a. Ask the applicant for the name of a past supervisor or co-worker who is no longer working with the applicant at the current place of employment. Again, if there is any question about the authenticity of the supplied name, the employer can call and verify the ex-employee did in fact work at the current workplace.

b. Ask the applicant to bring in W-2s (or 1099s) for each year of work, or at least the full past year.

c. Wait until after the employee is hired before calling the past employer, providing the new hire is subject to a written offer letter that clearly states "continued employment is conditional upon a background screening report that is satisfactory to the employer." Once the new employee comes on broad there can be a final phone call. By making current employment part of the written offer letter, an applicant has a powerful incentive to be accurate about his current employment situation, since any false or misleading statements or omissions will have serious consequences. It is also important to say the screening report must be "satisfactory to the employer" in order to avoid a debate with an applicant/new hire about what is or is not a good screening report.

4. Use Reference Questions that are 100% Legal

Remember the same standards apply to reference checking that apply to interview questions. That is, all questions must be specifically job-related. Never ask any question of a reference that you would not ask the candidate face-to-face. Focus on skills and accomplishments as well as performance issues that apply specifically to your job opening, such as the ability to meet deadlines or to work well with others on a team project. See the chapter on interviews for a list of questions that can and cannot be asked of an applicant in an interview. Again, these questions are also applicable when interviewing a past employer.

5. Correctly Using the "Eligible for Rehire" Question

A standard reference question is asking if the previous employer would rehire the applicant, or whether the applicant is eligible for rehire. Even firms with a "name, rank, and serial number" policy are comfortable with answering this question. In reality, the past employer is being asked the ultimate question, which is... "Knowing what you know about the person," and assuming you are also a highly trained, competent and motivated HR manager... "would you want the person back?"

However, there are several problems with the "Eligible For Rehire" question. First, if firms have a no reference policy, then they are technically violating their policy if they answer. They are essentially giving a qualitative evaluation of the person. If they answer "No," that potentially could be construed as a form of defamation.

Second, a real issue with the question is the answer is often meaningless. Suppose a past employer is called and asked about "eligible for rehire" and the past employer says, "Yes." What does that mean? It could mean that technically the person is "eligible" to be rehired because there is no notation on the personnel file that indicates there is a prohibition against accepting that application. However, in truth, that past employer would never consider rehiring that person, he just won't say so.

Conversely, a "No" answer could mean the particular employer has a policy against rehiring anyone who left, even though the applicant was the best worker he could ever hope for.

The wording of the question that is most helpful is the following: "Knowing what you know about Mr. Smith, if you were in a position to rehire him for the same job he left, would you want him back?"

In order to interpret that answer, the verifier must understand the assumptions being made. He is assuming that the person who is giving the answer has a similar interest to the new employer and is capable of making a meaningful judgment. In other words, in order to give the answer meaning, the verifier has to make assumptions about the knowledge and judgment of the person giving the information.

If an HR professional, who the verifier happens to know, is giving the information and the verifier has respect for the experience and judgment of the HR professional, then the answer is extremely valuable. If the verifier is talking to a stranger, then it is really a judgment call as to the value of the information.

It really comes down to the old rule – information from a trusted source is the best information.

6. Send a Fax Request if Voice Messages are Ignored

If the verifier has left numerous voicemail with no response, it becomes less likely the past employer intends to respond. Assuming the verifier has verified that the reference person is not away on a leave or vacation, and it is the right person, the verifier still needs a way to get through (or at least demonstration the intent). The next best thing is to send a fax request. A piece of paper demands attention; people feel they need to do something with a piece of paper but they can ignore voicemail. A fax to a former employer can also include the information to be verified, along with a return fax number, of course.

A faxed request shows a due diligence effort to get the information. The fax to the past employer should be maintained in the file as proof of the efforts made.

Another technique is to mail a written request. This technique is only effective for verification of factual information.

7. Document When Calling Other Sources, Such as Former Co-Workers or Supplied References

Depending on the importance of the position and the time and resources available, the verifier may attempt to talk with a professional reference the applicant has supplied. This is known as a *supplied reference*.

Another technique is to ask a supplied reference for another person who may know the applicant. This is known as talking with a *developed reference* – a source of information the verifier has developed on his own, without input from the candidate.

Talking to a developed reference can be a very valuable source of information. The verifier can get information from someone who was not told in advance he would be contacted, which increases the probability of a truly spontaneous and non-rehearsed conversation leading to additional insights about the candidate.

8. How to Handle Other Non-Contact Issues

A previous employer may not be available for a past employment check if the former employer is out of business, bankrupt, moved, merged, or cannot be located. If so, there are several ways to go about verification, of course documenting for each step.

If a firm has merged or been acquired and no one can locate the personnel records, a verifier has several options. As described earlier, you can contact the applicant to locate a former co-worker or supervisor or to request a copy of a W-2 or 1099. To help confirm employment, an employer can also "Google" the applicant or use www.zoominfo.com to see if there are any references on the Internet.

If a past employer says there is no record, then a verifier needs to go one step further. Before jumping to the conclusion the applicant has lied, a verifier should dig deeper. There can be reasonable explanations for apparent discrepancies. An applicant may have worked at the previous company as a temporary worker, under contract, or was actually employed by a third-party employer organization.

Many companies utilize the services of a Professional Employer Organization (PEO) to act as the employer of record although the work is performed at the company workplace under the company's direction and control. In these situations, the previous company's records will show that no such person worked there, though the facility was the physical location where the applicant worked. Since the applicant physically worked at the firm's premises, the applicant may well report that business as the employer. The applicant may not be certain who actually issued the check.

It is also important to ask the employer to double check his records under the applicant's Social Security Number and any other names the applicant may have used.

Safe Hiring Tip ➤ Some employers utilize an outsourced service called The Work Number for Everyone found at www.talx.com. An employer or background firm attempting to verify past employment pays a fee to access a computerized, phone-message service that gives basic employment data about the applicant. If there is concern about the accuracy of data about an individual applicant, TALX provides an email address for questions.

Suggestions on How to Deal with Requests for References

Employers who are concerned about obtaining references will undoubtedly find themselves in the position of being asked for references. Employers and HR professionals have responded in various ways.

Many firms have a rigid policy of not giving any information beyond the basics, such as start and stop date and job titles. Requests for references are often referred to payroll or accounting departments. That gives the maximum legal protection because it limits situations where a manger may give a reference against company policy.

A number of large firms have signed up for a "900 number" telephone service where employment verifications are conducted by a computerized voice only. Other firms are willing to indicate only that a person is eligible for rehire. However, some companies are concerned that even stating an employee is not eligible for rehiring could cause legal exposure.

One possible solution is to follow the old adage that unless you have something nice to say about someone, then do not say anything at all. Some companies have a policy of only giving reference information when they can do so without reservation. The downside is that an ex-employee can complain that by implication of a no response, he is receiving a negative reference.

Companies that would like to give negative information often do so **"between the lines."** One example is to suggest the new potential employer ask their applicant to send a release-of-performance appraisal files because "that would make interesting reading." That implies enough to raise a red flag.

Keep in mind there is no such thing as comments **"off the record."** If litigation should ever occur, and an HR staff member is asked to give a deposition under oath, there is no privilege not to reveal information given "off the record."

Other companies, as a matter of their own corporate philosophy, are willing to disclose negative information as well as positive information in order to protect other employers and the public. In those situations, it is important to take steps to document the sources of the information, and document to whom it is given.

The Following Safe Hiring Guidelines Should be Considered When Giving Reference Information

- A firm should have a written policy and procedure for giving references.
- All information should go through a central source. This gives a firm consistency and reduces the chances that a manager may give out information that is contrary to company policy.[38]
- Clearly document who is requesting the information and for what purpose. Former employees have been known to have friends or paid "reference checkers" contact previous employers. Also document exactly what is provided.
- Clearly document who in the company is giving the information because this can be important in order to trace who-exactly-said-what in a reference check. Keep in mind that staff members may leave a company and, without a written record of a staffer's account, an employer may not be able to defend his reference actions.
- If the information requested goes beyond dates and job title, a company may ask for a copy of a written release. This also provides some protection against defamation lawsuits.
- If an ex-employee has filed a discrimination charge or lawsuit against the company, then no information should be given beyond job dates and job title without contacting your legal department.

If the employer intends to give negative information, the following may be helpful—

- Remember that employees most often seek the advice of an attorney when there are surprises. Imagine an applicant's

---

[38] As a practical matter, many organizations understand that even though there may be such a policy, there is in reality a practice of individual managers giving information. When that is the case, an alternative policy is to allow managers to do so under a strict program where there are procedures, training, and consequences for failing to follow procedures.

surprise when he hears for the first time from some new potential employer that he is getting a negative reference from a past employer. If negative references may be an issue, what the past employer intends to say should be handled and documented at the time the employee leaves during the exit interview.

- Disclose only factual information. Make sure everything has been documented. For example, if the former employee was convicted of a crime, a past employer can simply report the public record. A past employer's evaluations of the employee can be a good source of information. The employee has already seen the performance evaluations and, in most cases, signed them.

- Avoid conclusions and give facts instead. For example, avoid saying a former employee "had a bad attitude." Instead, convey facts showing a failure to get along with team members. Let the facts speak for themselves.

- Include favorable facts about the employee. That demonstrates an employer is even handed.

- Make sure the personnel file is factually correct. That is something HR may do when an employee leaves.

In the event the former employee has a pending claim against the company for any reason (e.g. workers' compensation, lawsuit), an employer should strictly limit any comment to only the basic data such as start date, end date, and job title.

Safe Hiring Tip ➤ There is another reason to be very careful about giving references. There are a number of firms that offer private references checking services on behalf of job applicants who want to find out if a past employer is giving a negative reference. In fact, there is one firm that hires court reporters to call past employers on behalf of job applicants. The court reporters transcribe the conversation exactly as it occurs. In many states a tape recording would be illegal, but a court always accepts a court reporter's transcript as accurate. The court reporter calls a past employer and tells him that he is doing an employment reference. He just doesn't happen to mention that it is on behalf of the past employee fishing for material for a defamation lawsuit.

Education and Credentials Verifications

Educational achievement tells an employer a great deal about an applicant's ability, qualifications, and motivation. Many employers feel that educational qualifications are a critical factor in predicting success on the job. For many positions, education is a prerequisite in terms of subject matter knowledge or for obtaining the appropriate license for the position. Confirming diplomas, degrees, or certificates, along with dates of attendance, verifies applicants' education and skills as an indication of their ability to do the job. Confirmation also supports their honesty by substantiating claims made on an application.

However, education and credential information is often misstated. In fact there are a number of studies found on the web that have examined resumes and application forms and documented that as many as 30% of all job applicants falsify information about their educational backgrounds. The falsifications can include outright fabrications such as making up degrees from legitimate schools the applicant never attended or valueless degrees from diploma mills. Candidates often turn their months or weeks of attendance into an AA degree, or claim a BA or an advanced degree, even if they did not complete the course work or fulfill all graduation requirements.

The incidence of fraud underscores the need to do research on the educational qualifications of candidates. To the employer, the value of diplomas, degrees, or certificates also depends upon the quality of the degree-granting institution. The issue of accreditation is important for employers attempting to determine if a degree translate into knowledge, skills, or experience that will be of benefit in the workplace.

What to Verify

There are four primary pieces of information to verify on an applicant's education –

1. The school attended does exist.
2. The school is accredited by an approved accrediting body.
3. The subject attended the school during the time period claimed.
4. A degree was actually granted to the subject as claimed.

If the position involves proof of course-taking, then–

5. The student's completed courses of study for any degree are granted are shown on an official copy of his school transcripts.

Employers have two methods to verify education. First, employers can call the school themselves. The alternative is to outsource the process to a third-party firm, typically an employment screening firm.[39]

For employers who verify education in-house, the first step is to locate the school. Schools normally verify information through the registrar's office. Schools and universities often can be located through directory assistance or by using an Internet search engine.

Searching accreditation resources is perhaps the best way to find a post-secondary institution. A school's accreditation must be issued by an organization – accreditor body – that has been **recognized** by the U.S. Department of Education (USDE) and/or the Council for Higher Education Accreditation (CHEA). To be "recognized" means that an accrediting body must meet the quality standards of at least one of these two respective organizations. Schools may operate without accreditation, as long as a state grants the authority to operate. The schools that operate without accreditation *and* without authority are generally known as "diploma mills."

Both CHEA and the USDE provide online search capabilities to find accrediting bodies and schools. See www.ope.ed.gov/accreditation or www.chea.org/search/default.asp.

The Accrediting Bodies

Generally, accrediting entities are of two types:

1. Regional associations
2. Specialized accreditors

Specialized accreditors focus on **topics** – religion (ABET), teaching (NCATE), or health, social work, music, etc.

Regional Accrediting Associations

Regional associations focus on a school's overall programs. For most U.S. institutions with liberal arts programs, one of the six following regional associations of colleges and schools takes primary accrediting responsibility for the entire school. The list below includes the name of the accrediting association, web address, the phone number, and the list of the states or territories covered by the association. These are excellent resources. How to find and use these associations should be included on the documented instructions for performing these verifications. All provide web look-ups of the institutions they accredit.

---

[39] At an increasing number of colleges and universities, students may access their information online, directly from the school's computerized database. Access is password protected, and the student's ID or username is required.

1. **MSACHE** (or **MSA**)   Middle States Association of Colleges and Schools, 215-662-5606, www.msche.org. DE, DC, MD, NJ, NY, PA, Puerto Rico, Virgin Islands

2. **NEACHE** (or **NEASC CIHE**)   New England Association of Schools and Colleges, 781-271-0022, www.neasc.org. CT, ME, MA, NH, RI, VT. The New England Association of Schools and Colleges Commission on Technical and Career Institutions is a separate entity within NEACHE.

3. **NCACHE** (or simply **NCAC** or **NCA**)   North Central Association of Colleges and Schools, 800-621-7440, www.ncahigherlearningcommission.org.   AZ, AR, CO, IL, IN, IA, KS, MI, MN, MO, NE, NM, ND, OH, OK, SD, WV, WI, WY

4. **NWCCU** (or **NASC**)   Northwest Commission on Colleges and Universities, 425-558-4224, www.nwccu.org. AK, ID, MT, NV, OR, UT, WA

5. **SACSCC** (or **SACS**)   Southern Association of Colleges and Schools, 800-248-7701, 404-679-4500, www.sacs.org. AL, FL, GA, KY, LA, MS, NC, SC, TN, TX, VA

6. **WASC** (erroneously known as WACS)   Western Association of Schools and Colleges: Senior College Commission 510-748-9001, www.wascweb.org. CA, HI, territories of Guam, American Samoa, Federated States of Micronesia, Republic of Palau, Commonwealth of the Northern Marianas Islands, the Pacific Basin, and East Asia, and areas of the Pacific and East Asia where American/International schools or colleges may apply to it for service. WASC-JR is separate entity within WASC for accrediting junior colleges.

Specialized Accrediters

Colleges and universities wish to emphasize their accreditations. Many provide a convenient hot link to their *"Accreditations"* webpage. Usually one of the six regional accreditors appears first (if applicable), followed by a list of specific-topic accreditors. The list of specialized accreditors clues you in on the types of programs the school offers. For instance, NCATE indicates an accredited program for teachers. AVMA indicates veterinary medicine. A list of accreditation acronyms is found at www.aspa-usa.org/resources/acronyms.html.

Using Safe Hiring Procedures in a Quality Education/Credentials Checking System

This verification service is provided by most background screening companies, but a successful, in-house system of reference checking is possible if the employer incorporates certain steps into a documented system. And just as with checking past employment, there are guidelines to follow when performing education and credential checks under an SHP.

Track and Record Calls

A simple system is all that is needed. Using of a worksheet or a copy a printout from the software or IT platform of the applications is advised. The worksheet should indicate when a call is made to a school and status if not completed. For large companies who employ staff personnel to place calls, as opposed to a hiring or HR manager, it is not advised to use the employment application as the work document. The reason is there may be confidential information (prior wages, work history, etc.) that should be cloaked from non-management personnel.

Be Aware What Information can Legally Be Obtained

Under the federal Family Educational Rights and Privacy Act (FERPA) – if a school has received funds from an applicable program from the U.S. Department of Education – there are limits to what student information a school may make available to an employer. Schools cannot provide confidential information such as actual grade point average. A school will normally provide dates of attendance and degrees and honors awarded. If an employer has a need to obtain the actual listing of course work and grade point average, then a signed release is required. For employment purposes, many employers simply want to verify dates of attendance and any degree awarded, but some employers will ask the applicant to contact the school and obtain the transcript, which typically requires the applicant to contact the school to obtain the appropriate record access procedures. Schools normally charge a fee for a transcript; a well-prepared job applicant may already have a transcript copy in hand.

How to Handle Typical Verification Problems

There are some practical issues an employer may experience when verifying past education. For each situation, the worksheet should document what names were searched and when calls were placed.

Name of Institution

The popular name for a school may not match the "official" name which can be confusing when searching for a school. A person may report that he or she went to school at Michigan— the actual school name is the University of Michigan, which means looking up the school name under "U" for university rather than "M" for Michigan.

Also, given the number of schools in the U.S., there can be name matches. For example, there are Gateway Community Colleges in both New Haven, Connecticut and in Phoenix, Arizona.

Different Campuses

Many state university systems have a number of campuses. The employer must be certain to call the right division or campus. For some state systems, there may be a central Registrar's office for the entire system. In other cases, each campus maintains its own records.

Use of Fax Numbers

Some schools, but not all, allow an employer to fax a form asking for the information. A blank request form may be found online on the Registrar's webpage, or a "forms" page.[40] Employers ask for results to be returned by fax, though some schools will not fax back the results unless it is to a local number or toll-free number, or they only mail back the results.

Verifying Through NSLC or degreechk.com

Nearly 25% of schools have outsourced verification duties to a third-party vendor. There are two primary vendors that are under contract with higher education schools to provide verification services on behalf of schools. This outsourcing ostensibly takes the task out of the hands of cost-conscious registrar offices. Fees are involved and requesters must generally provide the subject's signed release. By far the largest vendor is the National Student Loan Clearinghouse (NSLC), 703-742-4200, fax- 703-318-4058, in Herndon, VA, www.nslc.org. Another verification provider with a shorter list of participating schools is Credentials Inc. at Northfield, IL 60093, 847-716-3000, www.degreechk.com.

Both vendors also provide a transcript copy service, though their transcript participating school lists are substantially smaller then their bread-and-butter service – verifications.

---

[40] The online or CD version of BRB Publication's *National Directory to College and University Student Records* gives registrar offices access information, see www.brbpub.com.

If Falsification is a Possibility

There are occasions when it may appear the person has falsified a credential. This can occur when a school apparently has no record of the applicant attending. In that situation, the employer must ask the school to search records under the Social Security Number to guard against an error caused by a variation in name. Many institutions of higher learning have different campuses, or different colleges that may maintain different records, so the employer needs to double check to be certain he is calling the right school and the right campus. One screening firm reported that a major university did not verify an applicant with the first name "Thomas." It turned out that in his college days, "Thomas" went by "Tommy," and that the university recorded by exact name only. Under the name "Tommy," the applicant had the degree claimed.

If an employer suspects a phony academic credential, a good practice is to give the applicant a reasonable opportunity to prove his claim. Jumping the gun can lead to a perfectly qualified applicant being wrongfully eliminated from consideration.

Watch for "Genuine" Fake Diplomas

With statistics showing that resume fraud is a significant issue, employers must be very cautious about accepting a physical diploma as proof of a degree. When presented with a physical diploma or transcript, employers should fax a copy to the school to confirm its authenticity. Most background firms can tell stories of faxing copies of degrees, supplied by the applicant, to high schools and colleges only to be told the degree is a fake.

Go to any search engine and run keywords such as "fake diploma" and anyone can instantly "graduate" from nearly any school in America with a very handsome and authentic-looking diploma suitable for hanging.

One such website advertises that it creates, "very realistic diplomas/transcripts. These diplomas/transcripts are extremely high quality printed on official parchment quality paper. You can show your employer and they will never doubt that you indeed attended college. You will not find better quality anywhere!!!"

Some of these sites "officially" caution that the diplomas and transcripts are intended for "Novelty and Entertainment Use Only." However, the fake documents you receive do not have a disclaimer written any place on them.

These fakes have not entirely escaped official attention. In Illinois, the legislature passed a law in 2004 aimed at addressing educational fraud. It is now a Class A Misdemeanor to knowingly manufacture or produce for profit or for sale a false academic degree, unless the degree explicitly states "for novelty purposes only."

Safe Hiring Tip ➤ One suggestion to help employers is to include the following language on the employment application:

Please list all degrees or educational accomplishments that you wish to be considered by the employer in the employment decision.

This statement has the advantage of putting the burden on the applicant to determine if they want to report a degree or educational accomplishment. The applicants are on notice that any degree they report can be used by the employer for the employment decision. If the applicants choose to report a worthless degree, or a degree not earned, they can hardly complain if an employer uses that to deny employment, even if the degree was not a requirement of the job

---

How to Recognize Diploma Mills

Webster's Dictionary describes a diploma mill as:

"An institution of higher education operating without supervision of a state or professional agency and granting diplomas which are either fraudulent or because of the lack of proper standards worthless."

A diploma mill issues a paper "diploma" that the student has paid for, and the student performs little or no actual study. Some diploma mills go so far as to provide a phone number or email address for verification-seeking screeners to use fro verification. The phone or an email address is directed to a fake registrar's office, including a very convincing, live fake registrar who will confirm the schools existence and even gets uppity if you suggest there is a fraud.

One problem is that the diploma mills are moving targets. They can change their names overnight and new ones can sprout up as easily as a scam artist can put up a new internet site. There are literally hundreds of websites that offer fake degrees, diplomas, or certificates.

Identifying Diploma Mills

CHEA has an instruction web page on identifying degree mills at www.chea.org/degreemills/default.htm.

A good overall diploma mill identifier is the College and University section in BRB Publication's PRRS-Web or on the CD product.

Two great places to view lists of known diploma mills and unaccredited colleges are at Oregon's list of diploma mills site at www.osac.state.or.us/oda/unaccredited.aspx and at Michigan's "Not Accredited by CHEA" list at www.michigan.gov/documents/Non-ccreditedSchools_78090_7.pdf.

The Bears' Guide to Earning Degrees Nontraditionally and *Bears' Guide to Earning Degrees by Distance Learning* provide good background on off-beat learning and distance education issues and answers.

Safe Hiring Tip ➤ Diploma mills should not be confused with legitimate schools that offer valuable distance-learning programs over the Internet. If an employer is not familiar with a school, the employer should review the school's website to check out its accreditation, curriculum, faculty, and graduation requirements.

Verify High Schools, Trade Schools, and Distance Learning Programs

Verifying High School Degrees

This is easily done if the employer is hiring from a local familiar area, provided the employer understands that during summer vacation and school breaks there may not be anyone at school offices to answer the phone. When employers hire from outside their locale, there are practical problems. First, it is not always easy to locate a particular high school. For the most part, each state will have a website or an office that provides school lists. If a student received his high school degree by testing, such as GED, then there can be delays in obtaining those through the appropriate state or district office.

Verifying Vocational Schools, Trade School Awards or Distance Learning Programs

Not all vocational or trade schools are accredited by recognized accrediting organizations. Each state has an agency in charge of certifying state-approved educational programs. If there are questions about the legitimacy of a vocational or trade school, then an employer should contact the appropriate authority in his state. There are numerous, distance learning programs available on the Internet as well. The same verification rules apply. An employer should determine what accreditation or recognition the programs have, and then evaluate the value of the degree. It is the employer's job to evaluate how a degree or coursework from a vocational or trade school or distance learning program translates into a person's ability to perform a given job. An employer needs to view the school's literature or website to find out about the quality of the facilities and faculty, the course of study required, and other factors that go into determining the value of the education to the job position.

For more information about post-secondary vocational and trade schools, see—

- www.ftc.gov/bcp/conline/pubs/services/votech.htm
- www.ed.gov/students/prep/college/consumerinfo/pubsresources.html
- www.ed.gov/students/prep/college/consumerinfo/index.html

Credentials Verifications

Professional occupational licensing, certifications, and registrations are generally a matter of public record, intended to protect the public from fraud and the unqualified. The Council on Licensure, Enforcement, and Regulation (CLEAR) is an organizational resource for entities or individuals involved in the licensing, non-voluntary certification or registration of hundreds of regulated occupations and professions. CLEAR provides definitions for occupational regulation that that distinguish three levels – Registration, Certification, and Licensure. See www.clearhq.org/.

Types of Agencies Involved

With the above definition in mind, there are several, general types of agencies involved with the registration, licensing, or certification of credentials.

Private Entities

For many professions, the certification body is a private association that has set the licensing or certification standards. An example is the American Institute of Certified Public Accountants, which sets the standards for becoming a Certified Public Accountant (CPA).

State Entities

A state agency can administer the registration, certification, and occupational licensing of an individual intending to offer specified products or services in the designated area. If registration alone is required, there may not be a certification status showing that the person has met minimum requirements. Using the CPA example above, the New York State Education Department, Office of the Professions, oversees the preparation, licensure, and practice of its CPAs.

Local Entities

Local government agencies at both the county and municipal levels require a myriad of business registrations and permits in order to do business (construction, signage, sell hot dogs on a street corner, etc.) within their borders. If you decide to check on local registrations and permits, call the offices at both the county – try the county recording office – and municipal level – try city hall – to find out what type of registrations may be required for the person or business you are checking out.

In order to verify a license an employer needs to require that the applicant provide key information—

- The name or type of license
- The issuing agency
- The state AND date of issuance
- Current status and date of expiration

Nearly every governmental licensing organization can be contacted by telephone. During the verification process, an employer will also want to know if the agency reports any actions against the license or derogatory information about the applicant. That helps to determine if the applicant's license is in good standing.

An agency may be willing to release part or all of the following—

- Field of Certification
- Status of License/Certificate
- Date License/Certificate Issued
- Date License/Certificate Expires
- Current or Most Recent Employer
- Social Security Number
- Address of Subject
- Complaints, Violations or Disciplinary Actions

Many agencies have Internet sites where verifications can be done immediately. An extensive listing of agency websites that offer some type of free search of a licensee list is available for free at www.brbpub.com under the *Free Resources* link or at for a monthly fee at www.searchsystems.net/freepub.php.

Conclusion— Educational Credentials Checking

When it comes to education credentials – employers beware! If an employer is not familiar with the school, check it out. Do not be fooled by a slick-looking website with pretty pictures of a campus and academic scenes and glowing testimonials. The existence of a very academic-looking diploma does not mean anything; fake schools are capable of producing some very convincing worthless diplomas. A common sense approach is a valuable tool in evaluating the worth of a degree. Look first to see if it is accredited by a recognized accreditation agency, then take reasonable steps as necessary to confirm the value of the degree, such as examining the curriculum, the qualifications and reputation of the faculty members, the facilities, the qualifications of the institution's president, or graduation requirements.

Chapter Summary

This Chapter provides information for **Audit Questions 15-16**.

Audit Question #15: Does the firm check past employment?

Best Practices #15:

- It is critical to verify employment to determine where a person has worked even if you only get dates and job title.

- Look for unexplained gaps, target locations to search for criminal records.

- Document all attempts to verify; this demonstrates due diligence.

Audit Question #16: Does the firm check education credentials and achievements?

Best Practices #16:

- Verify the applicant attended and/or obtained a degree or credentials as claimed.

- Verify the school is accredited to issue the diploma or credentials claimed. Insure the school is not a diploma mill.

Chapter 7

Criminal Records Issues Important to Employers

It is paramount that proper policies, practices, and procedures regarding the searching and use of criminal records be incorporated into an SHP. This chapter examines the necessary facts about criminal records that every employer needs to know about properly utilizing criminal records.

Audit Question # 17:

Is the firm conducting an appropriate search for criminal records?

Audit Question # 18:

Does the firm understand the appropriate uses and the limitations on criminal record databases?

Criminal Record Searches are a Critical Part of Due Diligence

Newspapers and law books are full of cases of employers sued for negligent hiring because a criminal record check was not performed or performed incorrectly. The employer's responsibility continues after a person is hired even if there was not a criminal record. An employer also should have policies and procedures to govern post-hire workplace situations.

Timely and attentive management of potential problem situations along with appropriate follow-through and documentation are the keys to avoiding legal claims of negligent retention and negligent supervision. According to all of the available statistics, there is a statistical certainty that unless due diligence is exercised a firm will hire a person who is unfit for the job, or even dangerous. Failure to do rudimentary background checks has lead to innocent people being the victims of crimes in their home or workplace, including murder, robbery, theft, child molestation, sexual assaults, etc. This chapter examines—

- why criminal records are not created equal
- when criminal records may be incomplete or "full of holes"
- the pros and cons of searching different repositories including the so-called national databases
- what employers should know about searching techniques

Misconceptions About Searching Criminal Records

U.S. employers have **misconceptions** about searching criminal records and it is traced to a lack of understanding about these key factors–

- **Criminal records are not created equal.** There are arrest records, records with dispositions, criminal-related records. What may be a felony in one locale may be a misdemeanor in another. There is another caveat – criminal records are not always open to the public. Often, t**he** *best* government databases are often unavailable to employers.

- **State laws on how criminal records can be used by employers vary dramatically from state to state.** What may be permissible to use when making an employment decision in your state may be severely restricted in a neighboring state. In fact, more than 40 states have laws that can place an unsuspecting employer in court if records are improperly used (examined in detail in the next chapter).

- **There is no truly national database of criminal records.** The $15 so-called national search as found on numerous web pages is at best supplemental. These searches as standalone due diligence offer little to no protection to employers in the event of a negligent-hiring lawsuit.

Background screening companies are very knowledgeable about the above issues. A screening firm should be used as a point of reference whenever an employer has questions involving the legal access and use of criminal records.

Why Criminal Records Are Not All Created Equal

Criminal records have three distinct classes – **felonies**, **misdemeanors**, and **infractions**. Felonies are the most serious offenses, usually punishable by a jail or prison sentence of one year or more and/or probation. Misdemeanors are less serious offenses; if a jail term is imposed, it is usually one year or less. However, state laws may vary on the classification. Some offenses may be classified as a felony in one state and a misdemeanor in another state. Whether an offense is tried as a felony or misdemeanor could depend on how the prosecuting attorney chooses to file charges, or how a judge views the offense or the offender. Offenses that can be tried as either a felony or a misdemeanor are commonly referred to as "wobblers."

Infractions are minor offenses not punishable by a jail term such as traffic tickets, municipal code violations, or minor crimes such public drunkenness or disturbing the peace.

The information trail of a criminal record begins with a criminal case tried at one the 10,000+ county, town, and municipal courts, state trial courts, or federal courts. **The court is the most accurate and most up-to-date location to obtain a criminal record.** Courts usually forward records to a central repository. In at least 24 states, the agency responsible for state courts operates a centralized court record repository for the state trial court records. Depending on the state, sometimes county, municipal, or town-level courts participate. There is no continuity from state to state.

The state trial courts, and sometimes the local courts, forward their criminal record information to a centralized state repository controlled by a state law enforcement agency. However, this is where many breakdowns occur, usually regarding case dispositions (see below). Often this database is not public record. The centralized state repositories and the federal courts forward records to the FBI. This information is not available to employers.

Criminal records also exist in other repositories. A number of states have unified court systems that collect case record data, usually statewide. Other *criminal-related* record sources are prison systems, sexual predator lists, federal government sanction and watch lists, and vendor databases.

The Importance of Dispositions

The term **disposition** is frequently used when discussing or searching criminal records. A disposition is the final outcome of a criminal court case; i.e. guilty, innocent, dismissed, etc. A disposition is an important piece of information on a criminal record or record index, along with the defendant's name, some type of personal identifier, the charge, and the case number.

Lynn Peterson, a very highly regarded professional public record searcher, has been gracious to provide her **Criminal Case Flowchart**. Shown on the following page, the flowchart maps the events during a "criminal proceeding" at a court.

While the flowchart may be simplified, it does point out the four key situations when a **criminal record** is **created** or **modified**.

1. **Booking (arrest record)**. Notice that the record is reported to the state central repository of records and then in turn to the FBI. Remember: the defendant is not booked for misdemeanor citations which may not be reported to the state repository. If the case is from a federal court, then the information is not reported to a state agency.

2. **Filing of Charges with Court**. The court docket index begins. Misdemeanor citation records may get picked up here.

3. **Disposition and Sentencing**. Notice that at the sentencing the case is again reported to the state and forwarded to the FBI. Also notice on the chart the dotted line from the "Dismissed box" to "May go to State and FBI" box. **A dismissal is not always automatically reported to the state or FBI.** Courts sometimes neglect to forward information regarding convictions to the state repository.

4. **Incarceration and Jail/Prison**. The jail and prison records are post-court and are considered secondary criminal records. State prison records are readily available online. While some sheriff departments provide online inmate locators, most do not.

CRIMINAL CASE FLOWCHART

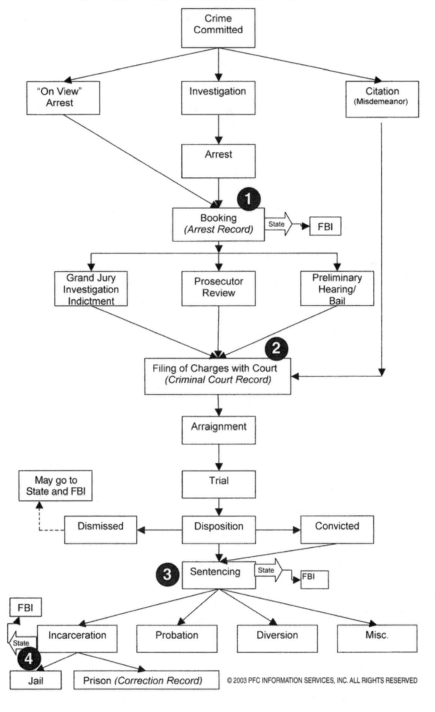

© 2003 PFC INFORMATION SERVICES, INC. ALL RIGHTS RESERVED

The Flowchart's Record Creation Points

Each one of the four record-creation points of Peterson's Flowchart is very significant to employers and other end-users of criminal records. We will reference the significance of these record-creation points throughout this chapter.

The flowchart distinctly illustrates the three different kinds of records that are often generically referred to as "criminal records" – **arrest records**, **criminal court records**, and **correction records**. To an employer, these criminal records vary widely in substance, accuracy, purpose, and legality of use.

Fingerprints, usually taken at the time of a subject's booking, also can become part of a criminal record. The flowchart indicates when major misdemeanors, felony arrest records, and convictions are submitted to the central state repository. In turn, these state repositories submit criminal record activity to the FBI's National Crime Information Center. When these transfers take place, the fingerprints are normally submitted as well.

The Differences Between Federal and State Court Systems

There are two entirely separate court systems in the U.S. – **federal courts** and **state courts**. A search of one system does not include a search of the other system. Each system operates under its own sets of rules, has its own courthouses, clerk's offices, indexes, and judges.

Only about 5% of U.S. criminal records are from federal courts. As of January 2007, 2,258,983 prisoners were held in federal or state prisons or in local jails.[41] Although these next statistics are somewhat older, as of September 30, 2003, 152,459 sentenced offenders were under the jurisdiction of the Federal Bureau of Prisons. Approximately 55% of sentenced federal prisoners were incarcerated on drug charges. During 2004, 109,712 offenders convicted of a federal offense were on community supervision.[42]

Based on the fact that the overwhelming numbers of prosecutions are in state courts, many feel that federal searches have a relatively low rate of return. However, when considering whether or not to include a federal search, especially when hiring for a lower paid position, you should take into account these other factors—

1. **The Nature of Federal Prosecutions.** The old saying, "Don't make a federal case out of it" has some relevance to the type of cases employers might find in federal court. By definition, federal courts are the place where violations of

---

[41] for prisoner number data, see www.ojp.usdoj.gov/bjs/prisons.htm

[42] for data breaking down federal crimes, see www.ojp.usdoj.gov/bjs/fed.htm

federal law are prosecuted. Although in recent years there has been a trend in Congress toward "federalizing" more offenses that have traditionally been associated with state courts, federal crimes still tend to be slanted toward more serious cases, such as large drug cases, financial fraud, bank robbery, kidnappings, and interstate crimes. The majority of criminal cases in federal court are for drug violations. In 2001, of the 82,614 cases commended in federal court by the U.S. Attorneys office, 86% were for felonies. Of those, 43% were drug related. Another 14% involved major immigration offenses.

2. **Federal Sentencing Terms.** The average prison sentence imposed during 2004 was 60 months. Per the studies mentioned above approximately 1/3 of the sentences involved drug cases. In many instances, the tip-off to a federal violation is not a court record search, but a large unexplained gap in the employment history. This underscores a key point made previously –a past employment check can be just as critical as a criminal record check.

The Good, the Bad, and the Ugly about Federal Criminal Record Checks

The "Good"

The federal courts use a centralized online system called PACER that provides search access for the public to almost all U.S. courts.

PACER stands for Public Access to Court Electronic Records. Through PACER, a user can first access the "U.S. Party/Case Index." This index contains certain information from the court files — case numbers and the names of those involved in the case. For an employer trying to determine if an applicant has a federal criminal record, the Party/Case Index is beneficial since it allows one to search by name. The PACER website is http://pacer.psc.uscourts.gov.

The "Bad"

There are two "bads" about PACER. The first is that not every district court in online with PACER, but the website lists the exceptions. However, courts not available through PACER need to be searched through their own electronic access. As a practical matter, that means as long as there are exceptions, it is not possible to perform a true nationwide federal search without identifying the courts not on PACER, and then searching those courts one by one.

The second "bad" is that PACER typically does not provide nearly enough personal identifiers to do a proper name match. If the applicant has a common name and the record shows no date of birth or even a partial Social Security Number, then correct identification can be very difficult. To match the subject, additional documents are needed. Depending upon the court, documents may have to be pulled directly from the courthouse.

The "Ugly"

Even if a federal court document is pulled from PACER, personal identifiers are typically hard to find, unlike the county level courts where there is often a date of birth. If there is a name match only, then other means must be used to determine if that case relates to a particular applicant. For example, if a person was found guilty of a serious offense and the court files indicate a substantial prison sentence, but the applicant in question was employed during that time period, then the case was probably not the same person. If a conclusion cannot be reached by comparing information in the court file to information that has been confirmed by the employer, then it may be necessary to roll up your sleeves and do some sleuthing, perhaps with a phone call to the AUSA (an Assistant United States Attorney who acts as the prosecutor in that district's federal court cases), or call the criminal defense attorney. Case materials will typically reveal the attorneys for both sides.

There is No National Criminal File Available to Private Employers

Contrary to popular belief, obtaining a criminal record is not as easy as going on a computer and getting a thumbs up or a thumbs down. The 10,000+ state and federal courthouses in the United States, spread out over some 3,300 jurisdictions, each has its own records file. Some states have a statewide database, but there is simply no national computer database of all criminal records available to private employers or the public. Period. End of story.

Yes, the FBI and state law enforcement have access to a national computer database called the National Crime Information Center (NCIC). The NCIC is a computerized index of criminal justice information such as criminal record history information, fugitives, stolen properties, and missing persons maintained by the FBI's Criminal Justice Information Services Division in Clarksburg, West Virginia. Some state police agencies have a legislative-mandated program for checking volunteers, health care workers, or other special categories based on using fingerprints.[43] For example, state laws permit or mandate that hiring bodies for teachers or child care workers access the state or federal fingerprint systems that are restricted from the public. However, it is absolutely illegal for most private companies to obtain criminal information from law enforcement computer databases without specific legal authorization. And unless your industry has specific access to fingerprint checks, you cannot access the FBI database.[44]

Take Caution When Using "National Databases"

A new tool being touted to employers is a "national database search" of criminal records. A number of vendors advertise they have, or have access to, a "national database of criminal record information." These services typically talk about having 160+ million records from 38 or more states. When sexual offender data are added, these services claim even more states and records are covered. Unfortunately, this form of advertising can create an impression in an employers' minds that they are getting the real thing — access to the nation's complete criminal records. Nothing could be further from the truth.

These databases are compiled from various state repositories, correctional lists, and county sources. There are a number of reasons why this database information may not be accurate or complete. It is critical to understand that these multistate database searches represent a research tool only, and under no circumstance are they a substitute for a hands-on search at the county level.

---

[43] A state fingerprint program should not be confused with certain "statewide" searches based upon name matches that are available in most states. Those will be reviewed under the section on where to search for criminal records.

[44] There are three situations where information from the FBI records is provided to private employers. First, a state may pass legislation authorizing such a check. Examples are school teachers, childcare workers and water-treatment plant workers. Second, the federal government may require an FBI criminal check. Examples are nuclear plant workers, aviation or certain other positions in transportation. Third, some types of employers have been given direct access to the FBI, such as banking institutions through the American Banking Association (ABA). One difficulty for employers – if there is "hit" on the FBI rapsheet – is that the report can be very confusing and it can be difficult to determine the nature and current status of the record without going to the courthouse and examining underlying court documents. The U.S. Congress requested in 2004 that the Justice Department conduct a study on the feasibility of opening up the FBI database to private employers directly. A report was issued by the Justice Department that examined a host of issues involved with opening up direct employer access to all private employers to the FBI criminal records. As of the printing of this book, there is still no direct employer access to the FBI criminal records to all private employers. The report, *The Attorney General's Report on Criminal History Background Checks* can be found at: www.usdoj.gov/olp/ag_bgchecks_report.pdf

Also, just because a person's name appears in one of these databases does not mean the subject is a criminal. On the other hand, if a person's name does not appear, this likewise should not be taken as conclusive the person is not a criminal. In other words, these databases can result in *false negatives* or *false positives*. An over-reliance can cause one to develop a false sense of security.

Our discussion of vendor databases will focus on two areas – *value* and *limitations*.

Database Value

Database searches are of value because they cover a much larger geographical area than traditional county-level searches. By casting a much wider net, a researcher may pick up information that might be missed. Thus, a subject name cleared by a traditional county-of-residence search could have criminal records found in other counties in vendor databases. In fact, it could be argued that failure to utilize such a database demonstrates a failure to exercise due diligence given the widespread coverage and low price.

Overall, the best use of these databases is as a secondary or supplemental research tool, or "lead generator" that shows a researcher where else to look.

Database Limitations

A vendor's compiled data typically comes from a mix of state repositories, correctional institutions, courts and any number of other counties agencies. That is the way the databases can be more accurately described as multijurisdictional databases. The limitations of searching a private database are the inherent issues about completeness, name variations, timeliness, and legal compliance.

Completeness Issues

The various databases that vendors collect may not be the equivalent of a true all-encompassing multistate database. First, the databases may not contain complete records from all jurisdictions — not all state court record systems contain updated records from all counties. Second, for reporting purposes, the records that are actually reported may be incomplete or lack sufficient detail about the offense or the subject. Third, some databases contain only felonies or contain only offenses where a state corrections unit is involved. Fourth, the database may not carry subsequent information or other matter that could render the results not reportable, or result in a state law violation concerning criminal records use.

The result is a crazy quilt patchwork of data from various sources, and lack of reliability.

Name and Date of Birth Issues

An electronic search of a vendor's database may not be able to recognize variations in a subject name, which a person may potentially notice if manually looking at the official index. The applicant may have been arrested under a different first name or some variation of first and middle name. A female applicant may have a record under a previous name. Some database vendors have attempted to resolve this problem with a wildcard first name search (e.g. instead of Robert, use Rob* so that any variations of ROB will come up). However, there are still too many different first and middle name variations. There is also the chance of name confusion for names where a combination of mother and father's name is used. In addition, some vendors require the use of date of birth in order to prevent too many records from being returned. Also, if an applicant uses a different date of birth it can cause errors.

In some states a date of birth is not in the court records. If databases match records by date of birth, searching when no DOB exists is of little value since no hits will be reported. In those situations, it is necessary to run a search in just the state in question and then individually review each name match. This can be tedious, especially if a common name is being searched.

Timeliness Issues

Records in a vendor's database may be stale. Records are normally updated monthly, at best. Even after a vendor receives new data, there can be lag time before the new data is downloaded into the vendor database. Generally, the most current offenses are the ones less likely to come up in a database search. Also, consider that the vendor data may not go back far enough.

Legal Compliance Issues

When there is a "hit," an employer must be concerned about legal compliance. If an employer uses a commercial database via the Internet, the employer must have an understanding of the proper use of criminal records in that state. If the employer acts on the face value of database search results without any additional due diligence research, potentially the applicant could sue the employer if the record was not about him.

If a screening firm locates a criminal hit, then the firm has an obligation under the FCRA Section 613 (a)(2) to send researchers to the court to pull the actual court records. This section requires that a background-screening firm must...

"...maintain strict procedures designed to insure that whenever public record information, which is likely to have an adverse effect on a consumer's ability to obtain employment, is reported, it is complete and up-to-date. For purposes of this paragraph, items of public record relating to arrests, indictments, convictions, suits, tax liens, and outstanding judgments shall be considered up-to-date if the current public record status of the item at the time of the report is reported."

As discussed in Chapter 3, FCRA section 613(a)(1) provides an alternative procedure. Instead of going to the courthouse, a CRA can notify the consumer that public record information is being reported by the consumer reporting, and give name and address of the requester. However, some states arguably do not permit this alternative procedure. This is a potential compliance issue for employers who operate in states that do not allow the "notification" procedure to be used instead of the "strict procedure" method of double-checking at the courthouse.

The best approach for an employer is to insist that a CRA always confirms the details of a database search by going to the courthouse to review the actual records.[45] Additional information about the FCRA and databases is covered in the next chapter.

Conclusion About Using Private Databases—

Criminal record vendors and background firms should make clear, and employers need to understand, the exact nature and limitations of any database they access. These private database searches are ancillary and can be very useful, but proceed with caution. In other words, it cannot be assumed that a search of a proprietary criminal database by itself will show if a person is or is not a criminal, but these databases are outstanding secondary or supplemental tools with which to do a much wider search.

Take Caution When Using Government Databases

A public online database is maintained by an official government body where records are available online to the public for name look-ups. Some public databases are free to search, while others are commercial systems with fees and access restrictions involved.

---

[45] For a detailed discussion about the legal uses of a database, see an article co-written by Les Rosen and national FCRA expert Carl Ernst called *"National" Criminal History Databases* at www.brbpub.com/CriminalHistoryDB.pdf.

There are four primary sources of government online databases—

1. PACER System at the federal courts
2. Single court or regional systems
3. State court administrators' statewide systems
4. State criminal record agencies (i.e. state police, DPS, etc.)

It has been estimated that upwards of 35% of the courts in the U.S. have some sort of online access capability and the number is growing, With online access, employers can go to the website and do name searches to see if their candidate is listed on an index of criminal cases.

However, just as with PACER, there are inherent problems when using some of these systems.

- Typically, court website searches are only of a record index. If there is an index "hit," the site does not give the searcher the full case file information. This means that arrangements must be made to retrieve actual court records.

- Online searches also have limitations on names and identifiers. For example, the Los Angeles County online access system only searches on the basis of the exact information input. So, if you have a Robert Smith who was charged under the name "Rob Smith" or "Bob Smith," you can get a "false negative." A related problem is the online index may contain only names with no identifiers. If the name does not appear (assuming you ran the right first name), then the person is clear. If you run a common name and get matches, someone is then required to go to the courthouse and pull files to determine the proper identity.

- For various reasons, many state databases can have "gaps." For example, Florida has the Florida Department of Law Enforcement (FDLE) database online and it is dependent upon courts submitting case information to it, which takes place per the courts' schedule. States that take records directly from the courts have the more accurate databases. North Carolina draws its data online directly from every court on a real-time basis. That is the safest type of database to use, assuming the researcher knows the ins and outs of the database.

Remember those TV shows where a professional stunt person would perform, and the announcer would say, "Remember, we are professionals. Do not try this at home." To avoid getting false results, there is an element of training and experience needed when using some databases. For example, there are at least two states with two sets of statewide databases that both must be searched.

Unless a researcher knows this, searches will be incomplete. An employer or researcher without expertise in using databases can easily error and miss a record.

Let's review the pros and cons of using these web-based systems at the state level.

Using State Criminal Record Agencies

All states have a central criminal justice agency such as the Department of Public Safety or Department of Justice where an employer can obtain a state criminal record. Many employers and state licensing boards depend on these state criminal record repositories as their primary resource when performing a criminal record background check. But in some states this can be a questionable practice if this is the only resource used, even if fingerprints are submitted.

There are four reasons why the completeness, consistency, and accuracy of state criminal record repositories are open to concern—

- Level of Automation
- Level of Quality Control
- Timeliness of Receiving Arrest and Disposition Data
- Timeliness of Entering Arrest and Disposition Data into the Repository

The Disposition Reporting Factor

Remember the Criminal Case Flowchart? One of the key record creation points is when a case receives a disposition. A problem is this: in many states there is no automated system that insures the disposition is reported by the courts to the state. This includes a guilty or a not-guilty verdict. Thus a record search may indicate an open case when in fact the case was dismissed, or the subject may have already been acquitted, or served time or probation.

The lack of dispositions can complicate things. State and federal laws are very strict about what records employers can and cannot use when making hiring decisions. There can be strict compliance rules in place. Many states have enacted laws that prohibit disclosure of criminal information if a disposition is missing.

The Ease of Access Factor

Consider the following statistics from BRB Publications[46] about restrictions on criminal record requests made to the state repositories by the public —

---

[46] Taken from the *Public Record Research System*, BRB Publications, Inc. www.brbpub.com

- 23 states release criminal records (name search) to the general public without consent of the subject.
- 18 states require a signed release from the subject.
- 9 state require submission of fingerprints
- 6 states have closed their records.

Several states, Minnesota for example, offer access to two types of records – limited or full – depending if the requester presents a signed release by the applicant.

Employers who use the services of pre-employment screening firms will find these screening experts have plenty of good suggestions on which state's database resources to search for criminal records.

Using Statewide Court Databases and Websites

For the same reasons discussed, these sources must be approached with caution and in most cases are not the primary sources of criminal record information for employers. First, consider this: many statewide systems are only clearinghouses for those counties that choose to deposit records. There are no guarantees that all counties are up-to-date or even participating. In the event of a hit during a database search or online search, the physical files still may need to be pulled for inspection.

Again, employers can rely on pre-employment screening firms to have plenty of good suggestions on which state's database resources to search for criminal records.

Record Searching at Courthouses

When searching criminal records for employment purposes, the access method most often used is to physically visit each relevant county courthouse and look up the record. That is done for two good reasons. First, it is reliable and usually the fastest method. Indexes and records can be viewed immediately. Second, if there is a potential match, the on-site researcher can make arrangements to view the file, looking at case details and finding identifiers to be certain it is indeed the person.

State court searches are performed in the clerk's records office, by human beings. Access methods can vary from court to court. For various reasons, a court may have rules on who performs the actual search. Some courts require that the names to be searched are to be handed over to the court clerk who performs the actual search. Some courts have computer terminals that a researcher can view in person. Some courts index names in other searchable formats such as ledgers, microfiche, or microfilm. Methods of file storage can vary from court to court.

To obtain the most accurate records an employer or screening firm must typically go to the local courthouse, talk to the court clerk, learn the system, and search the records.

Safe Hiring Tip ➤ In some counties, there are official databases available online that are the functional equivalent of viewing the public access terminal at the courthouse. However, for all of the reasons discussed, if there is a "hit," there still may be a need to go to the courthouse to look at the actual court files to obtain identifiers and discover details about the case, since online resources are often just summaries or indexes without sufficient details, like dispositions.

Record Searching Tips

Listed below are key factors applicable for criminal record searching.[47]

Start by Doing a Name Search

- The first step involves the researcher looking on an index for the applicant's name, or the absence of it. If the name is not shown, then the search is marked "clear."

- The critical point in doing a name search depends upon a human being either entering data in a computer or visually reviewing a list of names. As with any human endeavor, errors are possible. Any human error in data input, or when looking at a list of names, can result in a "false negative," meaning a person who in fact has a criminal record is reported as "clear" when in fact he is not.

- Names can also be missed if there is a variation of the name. For example, if looking for "Robert Smith" a researcher must also look for a "Rob Smith" or a "Bob Smith." If a researcher was looking for a "James Evans" and the person was arrested under "Jim Evans," then the name could be missed. If the applicant is a "Junior," a court index may list that at the very end instead of in alphabetical order. If an applicant was arrested under the name "Joe Smith, Jr," a search under the "S" category may miss it.

- A researcher also faces cultural complications when it comes to naming conventions. In some cultures, a person uses both the maiden name and the family surname. For

---

[47] For those readers who wish to know more about how to perform court record searches, a useful resource is the *Public Record Research Tips Book* by Michael Sankey (2008, Facts on Demand Press).

example, Spanish names are often based upon a first name, the mother's maiden name, and then the father's family name. However, if an applicant only goes by the mother's name, a completely different search strategy is needed. If a search is conducted for the name Juan Garcia Hernandez, and a person was arrested under the name Juan Garcia, then there is a strong likelihood the record will be missed.

- A similar problem exists with former names and aliases. A common former name issue is with a female applicant who has changed her last name as a result of marriage. An employment application or screening form should ask for previous names. It should also ask for the date of the name change.

Safe Hiring Tip ➤ A second name search should not be referred to as a "maiden name" search since that clearly indicates that an employer is obtaining information on martial status, which is a prohibited basis upon which to make an employment decision. The second name search should be referred to as a "previous name search."

If There Is a "Hit," a Researcher Must Pull the Court File to Confirm Identity

- If a researcher finds a criminal record in the name of the applicant, does that mean the applicant cannot be employed? The answer is an emphatic NO. The location of a criminal record by a name match is just the start of the process. If there is a name match, then the researcher needs to determine if the person located is truly the applicant.

- A researcher needs to locate an identifier in order to match the court record to the applicant. Commonly used identifiers are—

  o Date of birth
  o Driver's license number
  o Social Security Number

Safe Hiring Tip ➡ If there is a name match on an index without identifiers, then the researcher must review each possible court file that bears the same name of the applicant, in order to determine if a file includes a matching identifier.

Looking at Court Dockets and Files

- The court docket and/or clerk minutes contain the events that occurred at each court appearance – essentially the history of the case. The docket will include the exact law section that the defendant is charged with, the plea entered by the defendant, and in the event the defendant either pleads guilty or is found guilty, it will contain the sentence imposed as well as the exact charges for which the defendant was convicted. This file also may contain identifiers.

- In order to review the case file to look for identifiers, a court researcher must typically ask court personnel to find – pull – files. In some courts, there are limits to how many files a court clerk can pull. Further delays are possible if the file was placed in storage. Although citizens generally have a right to access public files, the speed at which a court clerk chooses to obtain the files is up to that court clerk. Even when an employer performs background checks in person, there can be delays.

- Assuming the criminal file is examined and identifiers are located, that still does not mean the criminal matter can be used in the consideration of the applicant's employment. There are a number of reasons a criminal record may not be legal to use (see the next chapter). In order to determine if the record may be used, a researcher must obtain details about the case — the nature of the offense, the offense date, future court dates, sentencing, probation terms, and whether the case is a felony or a misdemeanor.

- Information can be gleaned just from the public documents, typically a complaint, indictment, or some sort of charging document that would normally state the basis of the charges and may reveal the victim or additional case details. The court may state certain terms and conditions in the sentencing that may shed light on the case. If the defendant was convicted of assault, and the court orders the defendant to attend a drug program, that may indicate drugs were involved. But get the details before making a hiring decision.

Set Courthouse Searching Guidelines

Since you cannot search every county courthouse, the key is to choose which counties are relevant. Consider these guidelines when establishing criminal record searching procedures for an SHP—

- **County of Residence:** At a minimum, employers should search the county of residence or the last place where the applicant spent the most time. Although there are no conclusive studies to prove the point, many criminal justice professionals have observed that the county of residence is the most likely location for a criminal to commit a crime. Many background screening firms have found that employers get the biggest bang for the buck by searching the county of residence – assuming a person has not moved there recently.

- **Last Three Counties:** Some employers have a policy to search the last three counties lived in. *Three* is not based upon any court case or official government recommendation; rather, it is based upon the experience of screening firms showing that most applicants have lived in an average of two to three counties in a seven-year period.

- **Seven-Year Search:** A much higher degree of protection is a seven-year county search of all places where the applicant lived, worked, or studied, based on his application. The county names can be determined as a result of verification of past employment and all past addresses provided as part of a Social Security Trace. The Social Security Trace is discussed in detail in Chapter 9.

- **Adjacent County or Metro Searches:** An employer can go to an even higher level by also searching metro areas of adjacent counties. This search recognizes the fact that there is nothing to prevent a person with a criminal record from crossing county lines. For example, if an employer wanted to search for criminal records for a person who lived in Boston, the employer would likely check Suffolk County. However, a metro search would include Norfolk, Middlesex, and Essex Counties.

  Here are other examples. The first county named is where the city is located. [48]

  - San Francisco - San Francisco, Alameda, Contra Costa, Marin, San Mateo
  - San Jose - Santa Clara, Alameda, San Benito, San Mateo, Santa Cruz, Stanislaus
  - Atlanta - Fulton, Clayton, Cobb, Dekalb, Douglas
  - Chicago - Cook, Dupage, Kane, Lake, Will

---

[48] A database of all adjoining counties in the U.S. is available through BRB Publications. The adjoining county data is available as a CD-Rom product and as part of an online subscription service. See www.brbpub.com

- o Baltimore - City of Baltimore, Anne Arundel, Baltimore, Howard
- o Detroit - Wayne, Macomb, Monroe, Oakland, Washtenaw
- o Dallas - Dallas, Collin, Ellis, Kaufman, Tarrant

- **Looking for Criminal Offenses in Counties with Multiple Courts:** While most counties have a central court where all felony records can be reviewed, some jurisdictions have multiple lower level courts such as municipal courts or justice of the peace courts. Local courts may not report all convictions to a central court. The good news, however, is that these outlying lower courts usually handle minor cases. If these cases were more serious, then they would typically be sent to the central court. Therefore, it is not likely an employer is missing much if he fails to check the small courts. In addition, these local courts can be difficult to search, have irregular hours of operation, or may be located in remote areas. One plus is that if the offense is driving related, such as a driving-under-the-influence case, it should be reported to the state motor vehicle department and should show up in a driving record.

  For example, in Darlington County, South Carolina, there is a central circuit court where felonies and most misdemeanors are available. There are also four magistrate courts with minor case offenses. It is not practical for employers to go driving all over the county in case there is a minor record in a remote lower court not reported to that central circuit court.

One of the inherent advantages of working with a reputable employment screening firm is that these firms are well aware of the above factors.

Watch for Non-Criminal Offense Records

Employers need to proceed with caution before utilizing "non-criminal" offense records. Some states, such as New York and New Jersey, have created categories of minor offenses that are specifically deemed to be "non-criminal." Examples of such offenses can be traffic violations or violations related to "disturbing of the peace." New Jersey has a system for "offenses," which are typically brought in lower courts in order to expedite less serious matters. An expert in New Jersey criminal searches states that a "non-criminal" offense can be brought in more than 500 municipal courts for offenses that do not exceed six months in custody.

For the unsuspecting employer, this "non-criminal" case can cause complications. For example, assume a job candidate stated in his application that he had not been convicted of a crime. A background screening report revealed that he did have a court record for disorderly conduct, but in a state that had labeled such a record as being "non-criminal." In that case, an employer cannot assume that the applicant had been untruthful, since technically the applicant was not convicted of a crime.

On the other hand, there is nothing that prevents an employer from utilizing information properly obtained that is a valid predictor of job performance, and non-discriminatory where state law has not prohibited the employer from considering it. The "non-criminal" disposition could have resulted from a more serious matter that may demonstrate behavior that is inconsistent with the job, such as violence. However, it is the underlying behavior that is being considered, and it can be difficult to discover the underlying factual basis of the "non-criminal" matter.

Most employers have questions in their application forms about past criminal convictions. Employers in states that have such non-criminal offenses may want to change the language on their application forms to include asking about "non-criminal offenses or violations," provided there is no prohibition in their state about asking. Employers should contact their legal department or outside attorney to review the application form. Employers also should keep in mind that their applications should contain language advising applicants that a criminal conviction will not be used to automatically deny employment.

Using Misdemeanors Records

One of the biggest mistakes an employer can make is to only ask about or search for felonies, or the job application only asks about felonies. This practice is partly because in many states there are limitations on asking about misdemeanors (it is important to first be aware of the rules in your state). In some other states a misdemeanor may be a very serious offense. An employer certainly wants to know if an applicant has been convicted of—

- Resisting arrest
- Battery on a police officer
- Possession of drug paraphernalia
- Illegal gun possession
- Commercial burglary
- Assaulting a child or spouse

In many states, these violations are misdemeanors, not felonies.

In some instances, a misdemeanor case can be extremely relevant to a job, and even more relevant than a felony. For example, petty theft may be a misdemeanor, but if an applicant was being considered for a bookkeeping position, that misdemeanor record would be good information to have. Another example: a driving under-the-influence citation can be a misdemeanor, but a very relevant one to any position involving driving.

It is not unusual for felony charges to be reduced to a misdemeanor through a plea bargain. When some element of the case may be hard to prove, the felony charge can be reduced to a misdemeanor by plea bargaining. There may have been mitigating circumstances in either the crime itself or in the life of the perpetrator, so that a prosecutor feels a misdemeanor is appropriate under the circumstances. Sometimes one "bad actor" commits a crime against another "bad actor," leading to one person with a criminal record testifying against another with a criminal record after having bargained for a lesser penalty in exchange for cooperating with authorities. In large jurisdictions with more crimes to prosecute than there are resources, there may be more pressure to plea bargain cases out of the system.

The bottom line— because a misdemeanor can be the result of behavior that may otherwise have been serious enough to be considered a felony, and is only a misdemeanor due to a plea bargain, employers cannot ignore misdemeanors.

Sources of Criminal-Related Records

In addition to the sources already mentioned, there are other searchable resources available to employers. These include driving records, the local prison system, the Federal Bureau of Prisons (BOP), and sexual offender databases.

What each of these searches has in common is that, in theory, the records should have already been found elsewhere. A search of state and federal prisons should indicate the same record found during a court search. The driving records and sexual offender databases are compilations of a particular category of conviction that also would have generated a criminal record.

Given the limitations inherent in criminal records, checking these "secondary sources" provides an extra layer of due diligence protection. However, each of the searches has a drawback.

State Motor Vehicle Records – MVRs

For purposes of criminal records, note that the matters reported on driving records are driving related only, obviously not nearly a complete resource of criminal records. On the plus side, an MVR search is a true statewide search. MVR records are discussed in more detail in Chapter 9.

State Sexual Offender Registers

State sexual registration requirements became mandatory on May 17, 1996 when a law, popularly now known as Megan's Law, was signed by President Clinton. This law had two primary goals: (1) to require each state and the federal government to register sexual predators; (2) to provide for community notifications.

A more detailed discussion of the uses and limitations of these sex offender registries is provided in Chapter 9.

Federal Prison Locator

The Federal Bureau of Prisons (BOP) has an inmate locater at www.bop.gov. The site contains information about inmates going back to 1982. However, as a research tool, the database has the same drawbacks as most other large databases of names. If an employer already has the inmate's prison number — or another government number, such as the FBI or INS number — then the look-up is easy. However, for a pre-employment inquiry, an employer presumably would not have that number. There may be additional look-up options that allow lookup by other factors such as race, sex, and age usually. Due to rules concerning the use of race as a factor in employment, it is unlikely that any employer will use that search option. In addition, many employers have the same sensitivity about age. This leaves only a name search. Any database that depends upon a name look-up inherently has problems; plus, when information is entered into a database from numerous sources, there is increased likelihood of discrepancies. As a result, this is another database that requires a researcher to run all sorts of first name variations, including just the first letter of the target's first name.

State Prison Records

A number of states have state prisoner locator services on the Internet. Each state with a locator operates differently. Some sites contain only current prisoners, some contain those on parole, and others contain historical information. Again, as with any database, a researcher needs to fully understand the look-up logic and be prepared to run a number of name variations.

There are two excellent resources to find these websites.

- www.corrections.com/links/index.asp (Inmate Locator link)
- www.brbpub.com/pubrecsites.asp

Many of the state correctional databases are included in proprietary databases compiled by vendors, as described earlier.

Chapter Summary

This Chapter provides information for **Audit Questions 17-18**.

Audit Question #17:   Is the firm conducting an appropriate search for criminal records?

Best Practices #17:

- The criminal information was verified and the information is current.
- The company's specific **practices** are documented.
- The company uses **written forms** and **procedures.**
- The company is knowledgeable about criminal record searching matters and understands how county searches are performed.

Audit Question #18: Does the firm understand the appropriate uses and the limitations on criminal record databases?

Best Practices #18:

- The company knows that statewide searches and multi-jurisdictional vendor searchers represent a research tool only, and under no circumstances are they a substitute for a hands-on search at the county level.

Chapter 8

Limitations and Legal Use of Criminal Records

It is important that an employer assess and apply a complete understanding how criminal records with negative information are used during the hiring process and post-hiring phase. This is an essential part of an SHP.

Audit Question # 19:

Is the firm's policy and procedures for the use of negative criminal information legal and compliant with federal and state laws?

How to Deal with the Discovery of a Criminal Record

There are three instances when a criminal record may be "discovered" by an employer—

1. When the applicant reports the record on an application or during an interview.
2. When an undisclosed record is uncovered during the background check.
3. When an arrest and conviction occurs after employment.

Each of these situations is a potential minefield unless the employer has an SHP with specific written policies in place to deal with such matters.

When the Applicant Reports the Record

This is a critical rule—

You cannot automatically reject or deny employment due to a criminal record.

When an applicant accurately tells an employer about a criminal record, and there is no element of surprise or dishonesty, then the issue arises as to what an employer can legally do and should do.

Discrimination and the No Automatic Disqualification Rule

If the decision not to hire is based upon a criminal past, then an employer needs to have a business justification The U.S. Supreme Court ruled in *Griggs v. Duke Power*, 401 U.S. 424 (1971) that a plaintiff can allege employment discrimination without proving a discriminatory intent.

As a result of *Griggs* and ensuing cases, the EEOC has made it clear the automatic use of a criminal record without showing a business necessity can have a discriminatory impact by disqualifying a disproportionate number of members of minority groups. The key term is, of course, *business necessity.*[49]

Here is the EEOC's position regarding the use of criminal records—

"(a)n employer's policy or practice of excluding from employment on the basis of their conviction records has an adverse impact on Blacks and Hispanics in light of statistics showing that they are convicted at a rate disproportionately greater than their representation in the population.

---

[49] Important court cases on the subject were summarized recently in El v. Southeastern Pennsylvania Transportation Authority, 479 F.3d 232 (3d. Cir. 2007).

Consequently, the Commission has held and continues to hold that such a policy or practice is unlawful under Title VII (the Equal Employment Opportunity law) in the absence of a justifying business necessity."[50]

The EEOC defines business necessity in its 2/4/87 Notice–

- "The (employer) must show that it considered these three factors to determine whether its decision was justified by business necessity:

- The nature and gravity of the offense or offenses,

- The time that has passed since the conviction and/or completion of the sentence, and,

- The nature of the job held or sought."[51]

This means an employer cannot simply say, "No one with a criminal record need apply." That, statistically, could end up having an unfair impact on certain groups. Instead, if an applicant has a criminal record, the employer must determine if there is a rational, job-related reason why that person is unfit for that job. In other words, an employer must show that the consideration of the applicant's criminal record is job-related and consistent with business necessity.

How do you apply this test? Each element of the test has a different meaning.

1. **The nature and gravity of the offense or offenses**.

  a. **Nature of the offense** generally means the characteristics that underlie that type of offense. For example, a theft offense has character traits of dishonesty. Robbery, which involves theft as well as an element of threatened violence or actual violence, has the character traits of both theft and violence. These are both offenses of moral turpitude, which are acts or behavior that gravely violate the accepted standard of the community.

---

[50] see EEOC Notice N-915 (2/4/87)

[51] Long-time employers, HR, and security professionals involved in employment decisions may recall a different set of rules. The EEOC changed the earlier rule in the 2/4/87 Notice. Prior to that, business necessity was established by a two-step process. The first step involved showing the conviction was job-related. If it was job-related, then the employer had to demonstrate that the applicant could not safely and efficiently perform the job based upon: (1) number of offenses and the circumstances of each offense; (2) length of time between the offense and the employment decision; (3) applicant's employment history; and (4) efforts at rehabilitation. The revised 2/4/87 standard eliminated the need to consider an individual's employment history or efforts at rehabilitation; however, as a practical matter, an employer may wish to consider these points if he intends to hire a person with a criminal record.

b. **Gravity of the offense** generally refers to the seriousness of a crime, or the degree of harm it causes. For example, a crime that involved great bodily injury or risk of death is likely very grave, as are most sexual offenses. On the other hand, a one-time driving-under-the-influence charge, where the applicant has no prior offenses, and, in fact did not hurt anyone, may not be as grave.

2. **The time passed since the conviction and/or completion of the sentence.**

Age of the offense is another way of saying *as an event recedes in time, it becomes less important.* In addition, an employer may wish to consider what a person has done since the criminal conviction.

3. **The nature of the job held or sought.**

This refers to the characteristics needed to safely and efficiently perform that job, such as a person working with children or the aged, or going into the homes of a vulnerable population, which certainly requires someone who is honest and law-abiding. The same considerations apply for positions that involve handling money. On the other hand, for a worker on an assembly line who is supervised, a past theft conviction may certainly not be as relevant.

Let us take these criteria and apply them to different facts in order to illustrate how an employer may analyze a disclosed criminal record. This following example is meant to show how the criteria may apply—

Assume a person had a robbery conviction four years ago. He is applying to work in the warehouse of a furniture store where the duties include furniture delivery to customers. Under these facts, an employer could find a business necessity not to hire. The nature of a robbery is that it is a violent crime showing theft, dishonesty, and violence. In addition, any offense involving use of a weapon can be considered very grave. When analyzing an event that occurred just four years ago, an employer might be concerned that the behavior was too recent, and there have not been any intervening events to show the applicant does not still possess the character traits showing a propensity to re-offend. In addition, any position that involves sending someone into a home requires extra sensitivity.

However, assume the crime occurred ten years ago, and in the intervening years the person has successfully held jobs and has good recommendations. Also, assume the job involves working on a supervised roofing crew. Using these, an employer is apt to come to a different decision.

Because there are so many different possible crimes covered by the criminal codes of the 50 states as well as federal law, it is difficult to create an exact table that outlines for employers what particular crime is disqualifying and what crime is not. There also would be EEOC and state discrimination law considerations, even if such a table were possible. See the section "Suggested Language for Employer Policies" later in this chapter.

In fact, even if there were an overall table of crimes, it still would not tell employers in all instances what crimes are disqualifying because each particular event and person is unique. For example, a one-time battery during the course of an argument with a neighbor by someone with no criminal record and an excellent work history may well be treated differently than a battery by a person with a history of violent criminal acts and a very poor work history. The very point is to give an applicant individualized consideration

Instead, have a policy that says, as an employer, you maintain a safe workplace and will conduct a strict review of any applicant with a criminal record, without automatic disqualification. If you decide to hire someone with a criminal record, then document the reasons for your decision. This documentation will be important in case a third party later sues you for injury caused by this applicant, or in case a future applicant with a similar record is not hired and sues.

Be Aware of State Discrimination Laws

The states listed below have discrimination restrictions on the use of criminal records, including convictions and arrests law similar to the EEOC rules. Some states impose rules that are more stringent than the EEOC. Even in states without a separate set of rules in this area, the federal rules would apply. Employers in the states listed below[52] should check with their employment lawyer or screening company. Employers in states NOT listed should probably check as well in order to ensure there are no restrictions.

Alaska, Arizona, California, Colorado, Connecticut, Delaware, District of Columbia, Florida, Georgia, Hawaii, Idaho, Illinois, Iowa, Kansas, Louisiana, Maine, Maryland, Massachusetts, Michigan, Minnesota, Missouri, Nebraska, Nevada, New Hampshire, New Jersey, New York, North Dakota, Ohio,

---

[52] The list of states is provided for educational purposes only, and no representation is made that this list is accurate or current.

Oklahoma, Oregon, Pennsylvania, Rhode Island, South Dakota, Texas, Utah, Vermont, Virginia, Washington, West Virginia, and Wisconsin.

An example of how complex discrimination issues can be is illustrated by a press release issued by the University of Chicago, Nov 21, 2006. The press release related information about an article[53] that found employers who performed background checks ended up hiring more black workers, especially black men. The reason, according to the study, was that in the absence of a criminal background check, some employers may use race to infer past criminal activity. The article indicated in a survey of 3,000 establishments in some major American cities found that employers who are averse to hiring ex-offenders were the most likely to statistically discriminate. This study is an example of how criminal background checks can actually help prevent discrimination by proving applicants do not have criminal records, and thereby overcoming assumptions employers may make. Making criminal records harder to obtain can have the unintended consequence of harming law-abiding citizens. According to the authors of the study, "curtaining access to criminal history records may actually harm more people than it helps and aggravates racial difference in labor market outcomes."

When the Applicant Lied and Did Not Reveal a Criminal Record

If a background check locates criminal matters that an applicant misrepresented or lied about, then the dishonesty can be the grounds to deny employment. This can come about in two different ways. An applicant may indicate on an application form that he or she has no criminal record, or fails to check the box either way. Or, the applicant may self-report an offense. As discussed in the chapter on applications, it is important to carefully review an application during the hiring process. Employment applications should ask about criminal records in broad, clear language, and inform applicants that *dishonesty is a basis to deny employment*.

Here is a common scenario to watch out for. An employer uses an application form that only asks about *felonies*. The applicant's background report comes back and reveals convictions on serious

---

[53] The article is Perceived Criminality, Criminal Background Checks and the Racial Hiring Practices of Employers. Journal of Law and Economics: 49:2. Authors: Harry J. Hold, Steven Raphael and Michael A Stoll.

misdemeanors. The employer's first reaction is to deny employment because the person lied. The applicant did not lie — the question was answered truthfully. As a result the employer must make a decision based upon the three-part EEOC test discussed earlier — are the crimes job-related?

If the question on the application was worded properly and the employer caught the applicant in a lie, then it is the LIE that forms the basis for the termination of the hiring process.

When Arrests and Convictions Occur After Employment

An employer should review his employee manual on the subject of arrests. In Chapter 2, suggested language for the employee manual was offered on employment screening and safe hiring. The language below covers employees who are on the job and are arrested for a criminal act *after* being hired.

Sample Statement

ABC Company Policy on Employees Arrested for a Criminal Act

In addition, in order to ensure a safe and profitable workplace, all employees are required to report to their supervisor if they are arrested, charged or convicted for any criminal offense including a DUI or DWI, with the exception of minor traffic offenses unless the employee is in driving position.[54]

If an employee is arrested, charged, or convicted for any offense, then the employee must report the matter to his direct supervisor and submit a police report or other documentation concerning the arrest and/or charges. The report must occur within two business days of the arrest.

The employer will review the underlying facts of the matter. The employer will not take any adverse action based only upon the fact of an arrest. Any action will be based upon the underlying facts of the arrest. Any action will be considered on a case-by-case basis taking into account the underlying facts and the totality of all the circumstances. At the employer's discretion, actions may range from *no action*, to *leave with or without pay*, to *termination*.

Noncompliance with the above stated requirement constitutes grounds for termination. Furthermore, misrepresentation of the circumstances of the events can serve as grounds for termination.

---

[54] Driving position is any position where the employee drives on company time or for the benefit of the company.

> Employees who are unavailable to report for work due to incarceration are subject to suspension or termination in accordance with the terms of the employee manual.

Before implementing this policy, employers should contact their legal counsel concerning the laws in their state. It is important to note that the employer should not take action due to the mere fact of the arrest. That could violate the EEOC policy. The employer needs to base any decision on the underlying facts of the arrest or on the conviction. If, as a result of an arrest, a person is incarcerated, the inability to come to work may give grounds for an employer to terminate employment.

The topic of "continual screening" after an employee hired is discussed in detail in Chapter 10.

Arrest Only Records are Subject to Special Rules

An SHP often must deal with a critical point: the **difference between an arrest and a conviction**. An arrest is the process by which a criminal case is initiated by means of a police officer taking some action to initiate criminal charges. It can be a physical arrest, where the person is taken into custody, or some alternative form of custody such as a citation or order to appear in court. However, if NO CONVICTION occurs as a result of the arrest, then in terms of pre-employment screening, this action or record is considered an "arrest only."

If there are usage limitations for convictions, then it stands to reason there would be even more stringent limitations for an arrest. Why? Because an arrest itself is only a police officer's opinion. An arrest only does not prove underlying conduct, and only underlying conduct may be considered.

More about Arrest Charges

Before we examine when and why arrest records are so important, let us discuss why an arrest may not turn into a conviction. There can be a number of reasons, including—

1. A prosecuting attorney may determine there is insufficient evidence to file the charges, and a criminal charge is never filed in the courthouse.

2. In some jurisdictions, arrestees for certain offenses are taken before a magistrate for a probable cause determination or a grand jury. At that point in the system, charges may not be filed or are dropped.

3. In some instances, even after the charges are filed, a district attorney may end up dropping the charges for any number of reasons, such as insufficiency of the evidence or inability to obtain witnesses.

4. In some cases, the criminal charges may be dismissed by a court based upon motions brought by the defendant, alleging such things as illegal search and seizure, or some other deficiency.

5. Finally, a person could be found not guilty as a result of a court trial or jury trial, meaning the underlying facts of the arrest were insufficient for a determination of guilt.

In each of the first four instances, the end result was never a judicial determination on the guilt or innocence to the person arrested. Therefore, the arrest itself is only an opinion of the police officer and not facts of conduct or behavior. As the U.S. Supreme Court has ruled, "the mere fact that a (person) has been arrested has very little, if any, probative value in showing that he has engaged in misconduct." *Schware vs. Board of Bar Examiners*, 353 US 232, 241 (1957)

What about a **Pending Case?** A criminal case also can be in the gray area between an arrest and a conviction. This occurs in a case where an arrest has been made, a court case has been filed and a public record has been created, but the case is still in court pending a resolution. There has been no factual determination of the truth of the charges, nor have they been dismissed. Since a case has been filed, a search of courthouse records *may* uncover the pending case. In California, an employer is specifically not prohibited from asking an applicant about an arrest for which the employee or applicant is out on bail, or on his own recognizance pending trial.[55] In addition, since showing up for work is normally an essential function of any job, a pending court case may have relevance since an applicant may miss work to go to court and if convicted, may not be able to come to work. There are other criminal dispositions as well that can fall into a gray area such as a deferred adjudications or diversion programs. It is up to the rule of each state as to whether such matters can be considered.

Arrest Records and EEOC Rules

Under the EEOC rules, when making employment decisions, there are strict limitations on using the fact an applicant has been arrested. In addition, many states have similar limitations. The EEOC requires a business justification before using a *conviction* as

---

[55] see California Labor code section 432.7

the basis of an employment decision. The EEOC published a detailed notice about the use of arrest records at EEOC Notice N-915-061 (9/1990). The EEOC obligates employers to determine the facts of arrests as follows—

- An employer must look beyond the arrest and determine the underlying acts in order to understand what actually happened.
- Then the employer must determine whether the conduct is relevant to an employment decision.

If an employer locates an arrest, then it can be very difficult to determine the underlying conduct. It may well require phone calls to the local police or prosecutor, and they may not be willing to cooperate. Under the EEOC rules, the inquiry does not require an "informal 'trial' or extensive investigation," but more must be done than to simply ask the applicant to give his side and then ignore it without some reasonable effort to determine if a credible explanation exists. Many employers find that it is just not practical to try to consider the underlying facts. What if the applicant went to trial and was found not guilty?

Because of the difficulties, the EEOC concludes—

"Since using arrests as a disqualifying criteria can only be justified where it appears that the applicant actually engaged in the conduct for which he/she was arrested and that conduct is job-related, the commission further concludes that an employer will seldom be able to justify making broad general inquiries about an employee's or applicant's arrests."

Even if the employer is able to establish the underlying conduct, the employer must then go through an analysis to determine if there is a business justification to deny the employment similar to the analysis used for a conviction. However, the EEOC notes that where the position involves security, or "...which gives the employee easy access to the possessions of others, close scrutiny of an applicant's character and prior conduct is appropriate where an employer is responsible for the safety and/or well being of other persons."

As a practical matter, employers need to think long and hard before using information from an arrest in the view of clear EEOC rules.

Arrest Records and FCRA Considerations

If a third party is used, employers need to make sure that the criminal information is used in accordance with the FCRA. What if employers obtain the information themselves without the use of outside third parties? This procedure can trigger the FCRA even if an employer does not intend to.[56]

Time Limits on Use of Criminal Records and Arrest Records

The age of the conviction or an arrest is a critical issue. Under the FCRA, as amended effective November 1998, there is no limit on how far back a background screening firm can go in obtaining criminal records. Prior to that amendment, there was a seven-year limitation unless a new hire was expected to have an income of more than $75,000 a year. Several states have a seven-year limitation rule and the FCRA has a seven-year limitation on arrest-only records.

Even the EEOC has some bearing on time limits. If employers go back further than seven years, recall the EEOC position that the older the conviction or arrest, the less relevant it may be.

Special State Rules For Using Criminal Records

Many states have their own procedural rules on the proper use of criminal records that employers and screeners must follow when obtaining background reports. These rules are aimed generally at not shutting out ex-offenders from job opportunities. Many states have limits on what information an employer can use or whether employers can utilize arrests not resulting in convictions.

Brief summaries of some of the state rules are listed below. The listings are for general information only. These materials contain generalizations and do not constitute legal advice. Specific factual situations should be discussed with your legal counsel. Laws also can change. In addition, there is another set of separate state rules for using a third party background-checking firm.

States with some sort of prohibition against employers using arrest-only records—

California, Hawaii, Illinois, Massachusetts, Michigan, Nevada, New York, Pennsylvania, Rhode Island, Utah, Virginia, Washington, Wisconsin (unless position is bondable).[57]

States that prohibit or restrict consideration of misdemeanors in some way—

California, Hawaii, Massachusetts.

---

[56] The FCRA considerations, as well as state laws similar to the FCRA, are discussed in detail in Chapter 3.

[57] Even in states without prohibitions, arrest only records are subject to EEOC limitations

States that prohibit or limit the use of Expunged or Sealed Records—

California, Colorado, Hawaii, Illinois, Ohio, Oklahoma, Oregon, Rhode Island, Texas, Virginia, Louisiana, Maryland, New Jersey, South Dakota, Utah, Virginia.

States that limit the use of First Offense Records—

Georgia, Massachusetts.

States that prohibit employers from using certain records based on age of record—

Hawaii, Massachusetts.

Note that a court record by itself may be insufficient to determine the true nature of the offense since the final outcome may be influenced by a plea bargain or other resolution not reflecting the true offense. A firm may need to attempt to verify the true nature of the offense by contacting, or at least attempting to contact, a person in authority such as a parole or probation officer, a police officer, or a prosecuting attorney. Again, documentation is a must.

Special Rules About Mandatory Criminal Record Checks

In some regulated industries, state or federal law mandates criminal record checks be performed. It is not a matter of criminal propensities or statistics – it is the law.

All states have regulations requiring criminal background checks for jobs that involve contact with populations who are vulnerable or at risk. This may include teachers, childcare workers, health-care professionals, workers who care for the elderly or those at risk. Another example is a professional licensing board. Per state law, these boards are state agencies that oversee the certification of workers in certain professions. Employees subject to such regulations are normally aware of the licensing procedures or industry contacts. A list of professions that require a criminal record background check includes private investigators, security guards, security brokers, insurance agents, bail bondsmen, jockeys, casino workers, and so forth.

Mandatory criminal record checks are typically done with a fingerprint check of state and federal criminal records. Usually the checks are arranged for the employer directly through the specific state licensing agency rather than using the services of a professional background screening company.

There are also federal rules for certain industries. The Federal Aviation Administration (FAA) has rules for mandatory background checks for workers employed by airport operators as well as employees having unescorted access to restricted areas. Similarly, the banking industry has certain mandatory background checks.

The clear trend is toward the government getting into the background checking business by making criminal record checks mandatory.

Three Common Employer Policy Mistakes When Using Criminal Records

Given all the EEOC, FCRA, and state restrictions, what **policy** should an employer have regarding the use of criminal records? First, let us review what employers should *not* do—

1. **Having a policy that flatly prohibits employment of an applicant with a criminal record or employment for persons with certain crimes.**

   According to the EEOC, a flat policy against anyone with a criminal conviction is likely to have an adverse impact on members of a protected class, and therefore could be contrary to the rules of the EEOC. The EEOC covers this topic in Notice N-915 (7/29/87), (see the Appendix.) If challenged, the employer has a duty to present statistical data concerning applicant data flow to demonstrate that a flat policy against hiring anyone with a conviction would not have an adverse impact. However, the EEOC also cautions that such data could also be challenged if the applicant pool artificially limits members of the protected groups from applying in the first place. According to the EEOC notice, "if many Blacks with conviction records did not apply for a particular job because they knew of the employer's policy and they therefore expected to be rejected, then applicant flow data would not be an accurate reflection of the convictions' policy actual effect." Notice N-915 (7/29/87).

   Unless an employer plans to hire a professional statistician and a team of labor lawyers and demographics experts, the best policy is to not have a flat and automatic prohibition on applicants with criminal records.

2. **Having a scoring policy, where a conviction of certain crimes automatically eliminates an applicant.**

   Another potential mistake employers make is to have a flat prohibition on certain crimes. For example, an employer may have a flat and automatic prohibition against hiring someone with certain convictions such as theft, robbery, violence, or drugs.

Some employers go even further and have a "scoring" system whereby an employer uses the services of a screening firm to automatically eliminate an applicant. Some employers use a "traffic light system." If the applicant has no criminal records, then he is given a "green light." If the applicant has a disqualifying criminal record, such as a violent crime, the screening company gives the applicant a "red light." If there is a crime that is not on the employer's automatic elimination list, that person receives a "yellow" or "caution light" so that the crime can be reviewed with the employer.

The same EEOC Notice mentioned above also addresses this issue. According to the Commission, past decisions were based upon national or regional statistics for crime as a whole. However, if the employer can present more narrow regional or local data on conviction rates for all crime or the specific crime showing that protected groups are not convicted at disproportionably higher rates, then the employer may be able to justify such a policy. In addition, the employer can show that the policies in fact did not result in disproportionately higher rates of exclusion. This is a tough sell for an employer.

In view of the legal exposure for discrimination and the potential high cost of defending the process, employers may consider changing the red flag from automatic disqualification to a policy of "strict scrutiny of the offense," pursuant to the EEOC three-part test. Now the red-flagged person will go through a special process whereby the employer reviews the details of the past offense, the applicant, the job, and then reaches an individualized, documented decision.

3. **Having no policy.**

As a general rule, it is a best practice for employers to have written policies on important issues. Without a policy, an employer's actions in denying employment may become harder to defend. Having no policy also subjects an employer to claims of a discriminatory practice.

Flat Polices Are Inherently Unfair

Some security and HR professionals have suggested that a flat policy against criminal offenders is inherently fairer because an employer is not required to make a distinction between candidates. A flat policy is fair, they suggest, because it is applied regardless of the person. In fact, the opposite is true. A flat policy that judges a person by his or her status or membership in a category (e.g. criminal offender) is inherently prejudicial because it denies individualized consideration. In other words, a person is being pre-judged not based upon who he is, but upon the label attached to him. The root of the word prejudice is to "pre-judge."

Of course, this means that an employer could be placed in a situation where he has two applicants with identical criminal records, but one gets a job offer and the other does not. That can happen because one applicant has engaged in substantial rehabilitation and has great references. In this decision, an employer needs to document why the two individuals are being treated differently. The answer is simple— although they committed the same crime, they are different people with different qualifications.

Suggested Language for Employer Policies

An important step in the creation and implementation of an SHP is documenting company policies. Let's look at two areas that should be covered.

Policy on Use of Criminal Records

Here is sample policy language for an employer's policy on criminal records. The sample is offered for the purpose of illustration only your own policy should be reviewed by legal counsel before utilizing any language.[58]

Sample Policy Statement

ABC Company Policy on Use of Criminal Records

To ensure that individuals who join this firm are well qualified and have a strong potential to be productive and successful, and to further ensure that this firm maintains a safe and productive work environment that is free of any form of violence, harassment, or misconduct, it is the policy of this company to perform pre-employment screening and credentials verification on applicants who are offered and accept employment. A pre-employment background check is a sound business practice that benefits everyone. It is not a reflection on a particular job applicant.

---

[58] Sample written policies regarding aspects of safe hiring and pre-employment screening are provided in Chapter 2.

The background check also may include a criminal record check. If a conviction is discovered, then the criminal offense will be closely scrutinized to determine if the conviction is related to the position for which the individual is applying or would present safety or security risks before an employment decision is made. The employer will take into account the nature and gravity of the offense, the nature of the position applied for, and the age of the criminal conduct. A criminal conviction does not necessarily automatically bar an applicant from employment.

Using a Conditional Offer of Employment

A criminal background check can take a little time — several days or weeks — depending on the government agencies involved and who is doing the check. Meanwhile, an employer may have a difficult position to fill, or have concerns about losing a good candidate who has cleared the earlier safe hiring steps and seems to be a good fit for the job. The employer may choose to make a contingent offer of employment based upon the receipt of an acceptable background report.

If a contingent offer is made, then the following language is recommended for the offer letter—

Sample Policy Statement

ABC Company Policy on Conditional Employment

This offer of employment is conditional upon the employer's receipt of a pre-employment background screening investigation that is acceptable to the employer at the employer's sole discretion.

This suggested language specifies the report must meet the **employer's satisfaction**, so there can be no debate over what constitutes a satisfactory report. If candidates have not been forthcoming up to this point, then many will self-elect to decline an offer letter that is tentative, pending results.

With All of These Rules, Are Criminal Records Still Worth Accessing?

An employer may well be scratching his head wondering if it is worth the trouble to do a criminal records check given all the rules and procedures involved. If the employer makes a mistake, then he risks a lawsuit from a disgruntled applicant accusing the employer of violating the applicant's rights. Or, an employer may be concerned about the EEOC or a state authority becoming involved if an applicant were to complain of discriminatory practices.

Even with these complications, experts agree that it is incumbent upon employers to check for criminal records. Here is why: the chance of being sued, much less being sued successfully, by a person with a serious criminal record is remote. As long as the employer does not engage in the automatic disqualification of applicants with criminal records and treats every applicant fairly, the chance of a lawsuit is remote.

On the other hand, according to all of the available statistics, there is a statistical certainty that unless a firm exercised due diligence, it will hire a person who is dangerous or unfit for the job. As discussed in the Introduction, the legal and financial fallout can be a never-ending nightmare.

To put it another way, *the number of lawsuits from disgruntled applicants with criminal records is minimal. The potential lawsuits or harm from not doing a criminal check is enormous.*

Can They Sue?

Attorneys are often asked by employers, "Can they sue me?" The answer is always "YES." Anyone in the U.S., for a modest filing fee, can sue anyone else for nearly anything he wants.[59] The key term is a *successful lawsuit*. There is never a guarantee that a lawsuit will not be filed, but an employer should be concerned of the risk associated with a successful lawsuit.

Whether or not to use criminal records ultimately comes down to a risk management decision where an employer has to weigh the cost versus the benefit.

- **Costs:** Overall costs include the time, money, and effort spent in obtaining the criminal report, as well as the potential, though not very realistic, risks of a lawsuit from a disgruntled applicant.

- **Benefits:** The benefits can range from merely avoiding an unpleasant situation to avoiding the loss of life and the loss of the business.

On a cost-benefit basis, employers are clearly ahead by doing criminal checks.

Persons With Criminal Records Should Still Be Able to Find Jobs

As always, there are two sides to any story. On one hand, employers have an incentive to conduct background checks

---

[59] The exception is certain people who have abused the system by filing multiple lawsuits of doubtful validity can be declared a "vexatious litigant" and not be allowed to sue without court approval.

because of the overwhelming evidence of the importance of criminal records in anticipating future behavior.

However, as we review criminal records, it is important to keep in mind that no one is suggesting that just because a person has a criminal past, he can never be hired. Unless our society wishes to create a permanent criminal class, it is critical for ex-offenders who have paid the price to society to be able to get a J-O-B. Without a job, ex-offenders can never become tax-paying, law-abiding, productive citizens. Logic and statistics suggest that ex-offenders who are not able to find and keep gainful employment are likely to re-offend. Unless our society wants to spend an inordinate amount of tax money on building prisons, ex-offenders need a chance at a decent career. In fact, the law provides that a criminal record cannot be used to automatically deny a job. For information on job hunting from the point of view of a person with a criminal record, see: www.privacyrights.org/ar/rosencrim.htm.

A person with a criminal record does not have a big scarlet C for criminal emblazoned on his forehead so that he can never rejoin society. There are certain jobs that are just inappropriate for individuals with certain backgrounds. For example, a person with an embezzlement record may not be a good candidate to be a bookkeeper. However, such a person may do perfectly well in other jobs. There is a job for everyone, but not everyone is suitable for every job.

There is also research to suggest that the longer an offender is able to stay out of jail, the less likely he is to re-offend, and after three years, the risk may fall off rapidly. Issues concerning the use of criminal records as a valid predictor of future criminal behavior as well as concerns over giving ex-offenders an opportunity to re-enter society are reviewed in a report to the American Bar Association in 2007. See:

http://meetings.abanet.org/webupload/commupload/CR209800/newsletterpubs/SealRescleanRC6507alfsasFINAL.pdf

Chapter Summary

This Chapter provides information for **Audit Question 19**.

Audit Question #19: Is the firm's policy and procedures for the use of negative criminal information legal and compliant with federal and state laws?

Best Practices #19:

- There are written guidelines to follow and procedures and decisions documented in a file.

- There is there a review process, with a particular person in the organization in charge of the process.

- Similarly situated applicants are treated the same.

- There is a mechanism to ensure that information remains private and secured, and only appropriate decision makers view the information? (e.g. reports with negative information are not sent through office mail to a hiring manager's desk).

- **Legal compliance FCRA—** If a third party obtains information under the FCRA, then there is a procedure to ensure that pre-adverse action and post-adverse letters are handled as required by law.

- **Legal Compliance EEOC—** If the negative information is a criminal record, then the firm understands and follows the EEOC rules concerning the use of criminal records. Under EEOC rules, an employer may not deny employment to an ex-offender unless it is a business necessity, determined by reviewing the following three factors—

    1. The nature and gravity of the offense;

    2. The nature of the job being sought or held; and

    3. The amount of time that has passed since the conviction or completion of sentence.

Chapter 9

Other Important Screening Tools for Employers

To this point we have analyzed many of the core screening tools and how they can be integrated into an SHP.

Chapter 9 examines other resources of information that can prove to be valuable screening tools. These resources should be considered for some screening programs. Whether or not to use some of these sources may depend on the position being filled by the applicant. However, use of the Form I-9 tool is mandatory.

Audit Question # 20:

Does the firm use other screening tools and, if so, is the information used in accordance with safe hiring guidelines?

Screening Tools to Consider

The following useful screening tools are examined in this chapter—

- ➤ Form I-9 and E-Verify
- ➤ Social Security Trace and Verification
- ➤ Credit Reports
- ➤ Driving Records
- ➤ Drug Testing
- ➤ Internet and Social Networking Sites
- ➤ Civil Lawsuits
- ➤ Judgments, Liens, and Bankruptcies
- ➤ Military Records
- ➤ Security Clearances
- ➤ Sexual Offender Registries
- ➤ Workers' Compensation Records
- ➤ International Screening

Form I-9 and E-Verify

Form I-9 Form

Most HR personnel and hiring managers are no doubt aware of Form I-9. To summarize, the Immigration Reform and Control Act of 1986 (IRCA) mandates that U.S. employers verify the employment eligibility status of newly hired employees, making it unlawful to knowingly hire or continue to employ unauthorized workers. The Immigration and Naturalization Service (INS), now part of the Department of Homeland Security (DHS), created Form I-9. Use of this form is mandated to all U.S. employers.

The I-9 Form consists of three parts. Section 2 must be completed by the employer within three business days of a new hire. This section certifies that the new employee's identity documents are or appear to be genuine.

As of December 26, 2007, any employer who fails to use the amended Form I-9 may be subject to civil penalties as enforced by the DHS. Use of the Form I-9 should be written into a company's SHP documentation.

E-Verify

In 1996, Congress enacted the Illegal Immigration Reform and Immigrant Responsibility Act to further help deter illegal immigration into the U.S. This act also created the **Basic Pilot Program**, a voluntary program eventually allowing employers in all states to verify employment eligibility of prospective employees through both the Social Security Administration (SSA) and INS.

In 2007, the Basic Pilot Program was renamed **E-Verify,** and the federal government added enhancements to the system. Utilizing databases administered by the DHS and SSA, employers now can utilize the E-Verify system to check the information on Form I-9 to determine that individual's employment eligibility.

To participate in the E-Verify (Basic Pilot) Program, an employer must first register. As part of the registration process, an employer must execute a Memorandum of Understanding (MOU) that sets forth the responsibilities of the SSA, the U.S. Citizenship and Immigration Services Bureau, and the employer. Although the program is voluntary on the federal level, some states such as Arizona have made it mandatory.

Employers who participate in E-Verify complete the Employment Eligibility Verification Form (Form I-9) for each newly hired employee as is required of all employers in the U.S. E-Verify employers may accept any document or combination of documents acceptable on the Form I-9, but if the employee chooses to present a List B and C combination, the List B (identity only) document must have a photograph.

After completing the Form I-9 for a new employee, E-Verify employers submit an electronic query that includes information from Sections 1 and 2 of the Form I-9. After submitting the query, the employer will receive an automated response from the E-Verify system regarding that individual's employment eligibility. In some cases, E-Verify will provide a response indicating a tentative non-confirmation of the employee's eligibility. This does not mean that the employee is necessarily unauthorized to work in the U.S. Rather it means that the system is unable to instantaneously confirm that employee's eligibility to work. In the case of a tentative non-confirmation, the employer and employee must both take steps specified by E-Verify in an effort to resolve the status of the query.

The new I-9 form is located at www.uscis.gov/files/form/I-9.pdf.

The USCIS also issued a 47-page handbook on I-9 compliance. See www.uscis.gov/files/nativedocuments/m-274.pdf.

The Social Security Trace and Verification

A standard tool offered by nearly every pre-employment screening firm is the Social Security Trace. A second tool – called a Social

Security Number Verification – is usually offered as part of a trace or can be a stand-a-lone search.

The Verification

The verification is a check of the Social Security Number (SSN) against an SSA database that indicates the date of issue and the state that issued the number. Often a screening company will do an additional check against an index of SSNs that belong to deceased persons, called the Death Index.

This is how the verification works. The first three digits of the SSN relate to the state of issue. The middle two digits are the "group numbers" that indicate the range of years when the SSN was issued. By understanding the methodology behind these two sets of numbers, an employer can determine the state of issue and the approximate year of issue. The last four numbers are unique to the individual who received the SSN. For example a Social Security Number 548-72-xxxx is a California number. The '548' is associated with California. The '72' is the group number that helps to determine when that SSN was issued. The last four digits belong uniquely to the individual.

Thus, the SSN Verification is a quick way to determine if an SSN may or may not belong to a person, based on age and/or if the number belongs to a deceased person. There are a number of resources and even web-services screening companies and employers may utilize these to perform the verification.

Remember: not all employers want date of issue or date of birth due to discrimination problems associated with knowing an applicant's age.[60]

The Social Security Trace

The Social Security Trace is a much more in-depth searching tool than the SSN Verification. In fact, when an employer orders a Trace from an employment screener, the verification also is often provided.

A Trace is performed submitting an SSN to a vendor in order to obtain the top portion of a credit report. Ergo, this report is often referred to as a **credit header.** The credit header is compiled from identifying information obtained by credit bureaus when individuals apply for credit cards, provide a change of address to a credit card company, or engage in any credit-related transaction. For example, anytime a person applies for a credit card, the data – including the person's SSN, as well as a name and address – goes into large

---

[60] Discrimination and age issues are discussed in Chapters 3 and 5.

computer databanks kept by the major credit bureaus. If two years later a person moves and submits a change of address card, then that new data also goes into the computer memory.

Using a Trace and Importance of Past Addresses

The information found on a Trace may provide information about a person's past addresses and it may help to discover any issues of identity fraud. Some employers use the Trace to look for discrepancies and to cross-reference what an applicant has told them. For example, since a Trace may indicate a year and state of issue or additional names used, that may lead an employer to question what an applicant provided or to look for additional information.

Past addresses are critical because it helps employers determine where to search for criminal records. In addition, there may be an occasion when names or addresses are incorrectly associated with a SSN. This can occur for a variety of reasons. For example, if a data entry clerk for a credit card company accidentally switched two numbers in an SSN while entering a change of address form, the credit bureau records may link the wrong name and addresses to a SSN. Sometimes, members of the same family may have their credit history intertwined. If a father and son have similar names, the databases can end up "merging" their data, odd locations may appears causing results.

What a Social Security Trace Is Not

Many employers mistakenly believe SSN searches are an "official review" of government records. The Trace information is provided by vendors and not accessed directly from government records, and therefore is not an official verification of an SSN. A Trace report may contain data from the SSA's list of deceased individuals, but usually the substance of the report is created from data found in the databases of private firms and in credit headers.

In addition, it is critical to understand that a Trace report is NOT an official registry of current or past addressees. For a number of reasons, current and past addresses will not appear on a Trace report if the applicant never used those addresses in any dealings of interest to the major credit bureaus. On occasion, the report may show no names or addresses associated with an SSN. This can occur when a person has never applied for credit; either he is too young to be in the credit bureau records or he is new to the U.S. and has recently obtained an SSN.

An employer should never make a direct hiring decision based upon the absence of an address in a Trace. Although Trace reports can be helpful for identity purposes and for determining where to search for criminal records, they are not positive proof of identify or the validity of an SSN. However, unusual information in a Trace report can be the basis for further research of an applicant.

Where to Obtain a Social Security Trace

With the applicant's signed release, the Trace can be obtained directly from major credit bureaus or through employment screening firms. Some employment screening firms provide enhanced Trace searches using name and address information gathered from a number of additional sources. Remember: the data is gathered by private organizations and originates from multiple sources, including billions of public and private records.

How to Verify a Social Security Number <u>After</u> an Employee Is Hired

The method for employers to officially verify an SSN after employment is to contact the SSA. The SSA will verify SSNs to ensure the records of employees are correct for the purpose of completing Internal Revenue Service Form W-2 – the employee Wage and Tax Statement. A background screening firm or employer cannot use this service – now known as SSNVS – prior to an offer of employment being made. So employers typically call later as part of the new-hire paperwork and during the I-9 process, which is the process employers undergo to confirm an applicant has a legal right to work in the U.S.

Legal Policy – Don't Discriminate or Misuse SSNVS

The SSA also has posted a Legal-Use Policy on its webpage...

"...SSA will advise you if a name/SSN you submitted does not match our records. This does not imply that you or your employee intentionally provided incorrect information about the employee's name or SSN. It is not a basis, in and of itself, for you to take any adverse action against the employee, such as termination, suspending, firing, or discriminating against an individual who appears on the list. SSNVS should only be used to verify currently or previously employed workers. Company policy concerning the use of EVS should be applied consistently to all workers, e.g. if used for newly hired employees, verify all newly hired employees; if used to verify your database, verify the entire database. Any employer that uses the information SSA provides regarding name/SSN verification to justify taking adverse action against an employee may violate state or federal law and be subject to legal consequences. Moreover, this makes no statement about your employee's immigration status."

The SSA toll-free phone number is 800-772-6270 and is open weekdays from 7:00 a.m. to 7:00 p.m. EST. An employer also will be asked for the company name and EIN.[61] More information is available at www.ssa.gov/employer/ssnv.htm.

Using Credit Reports

For some companies, a credit report has become a screening tool to evaluate a candidate and to exercise due diligence in the hiring process. However, to job applicants a credit report can feel like an invasion of privacy or a violation of their rights. Of all the potential tools available to the employer to make safe hiring decisions, a credit report comes closest to invading a perceived zone of privacy since it directly reflects where and how we spend money in our personal lives. A credit report can indicate where you shop and the amount you spend.

Job applicants do have substantial legal protection concerning the use of credit reports for employment. In fact, an employer cannot obtain a credit report without an applicant's written permission. An employer cannot use it to deny a job until the applicant has had the chance to review the report. Therefore, employers should approach credit reports with caution, making sure they are used only for valid business-related reasons. Employers are only to use information that is fair, recent, and relevant.

A common misperception is that "credit scores" are used for employment purposes. Credit reports for employment purposes will have a credit history that will show, for example, if a person misses payments. But an employment credit report does *not* contain the credit score. The three major credit bureaus use a special reporting format that leaves out actual credit card account numbers, credit risk scoring, and age. Even though there is research suggesting that credit scores can have a discriminatory impact, credit scores simply are *not* used for employment purposes.

Why Employers Use Credit Reports

Employers seek employment credit reports on job applicants for a variety of reasons. Since scoring is not allowed, the use of credit

---

[61] Employer Identification Number

reports tends to be on a judgment-call basis, meaning the credit report is utilized in conjunction with all other available information.

Some employers take the position that a credit report shows whether an applicant is responsible and reliable by looking at the way an applicant handles his personal affairs. The logic is that a person who cannot pay his own bills on time or make responsible personal financial decisions may not be the best fit for a job which requires handling of the company's funds or for making meaningful decisions.

Employers may request credit reports to alert them to applicants whose monthly debt payments are too high for the salary involved. The concern is if a person is under financial stress due to a monthly debt that is beyond his salary, then that can be a "red flag." One of the common denominators in cases of embezzlement is a perpetrator in debt beyond his means, or has excessive financial pressure due to personal debt.

Employers hiring sales positions may require that a salesperson utilize a personal credit card. A credit report may help to indicate a potential candidate's ability to use a credit card wisely. There have been employers who discovered months into the employment relationship that the reason a salesperson was not making his quota was because the person was not able to fly or travel due to an inability to cover advance travel expenses.

The credit header in a credit report also helps verify identity. However, an employer does not order an entire credit report just to obtain the credit header.

On credit reports, an employer also may look for negative public records and determine if they are related to employment. For example, a tax lien may indicate someone has not paid attention to his affairs or is under financial stress. If there is a bankruptcy in the credit report, then the employer should *not* utilize the bankruptcy without talking to the attorney. A form of discrimination could be construed by denying employment based upon bankruptcy proceedings. Federal law expressly prohibits a private employer from discrimination solely on the basis of a person exercising his rights under the bankruptcy laws.[62]

Are any alerts from the credit agencies found? Some bureaus issue fraud alerts based upon a variety of criteria, if there is suspicion of fraud or abuse.

---

[62] See 11 USC 525

Best Practices for Employers Using Credit Reports

Employers should approach the use of credit reports with caution, having polices and procedures in place to ensure the use of credit information is both relevant and fair. Consider the following best practices—

- An employer should first determine if there is a sound business reason to obtain a credit report. Many employers limit credit reports to management and executive positions, or to positions that have access to high levels of cash, assets, company credit cards, or confidential information. Employers are well advised to run credit reports on bookkeepers or others who handle significant amounts of cash.

- Unless the information in a credit report is directly job related, its use can be considered discriminatory. For example, running a credit report for an entry-level person with low levels of responsibility or no access to cash is probably not a good practice. Running mass credit reports on all applicants, regardless of the position, can have the effect of discriminating against certain protected classes. Although an employer may want to run credit reports on perspective cashiers, it is not necessary since most employers do a drawer count at night and if money is missing an employer will know almost immediately.

- Employers should avoid making negative hiring decisions on credit report information that is old, relatively minor, or has no relevance to job performance. For example, poor credit caused by medical bills may have nothing to do with employment.

- An employer needs to ensure that credit information is accurate. In order to protect a consumer's rights and guard against error, an employer must carefully follow the requirements of the FCRA, and any applicable specific state rules.

- Mistakes are always possible. Although credit bureaus make efforts to be accurate, credit reports are based upon millions of pieces of data assembled by human beings and computers. According to screening expert Dennis L. DeMey, author of *Don't Hire a Crook*—

  "Keep in mind that there may be mistakes. Also, different credit bureaus can have different information. One credit bureau may have extensive information on the subject whereas another may have very little. Lenders do not necessarily utilize and/or communicate with every bureau. Consequently, one bureau may be more up-to-date than another in a specific region. In instances where such a search is critical, it is wise to verify by using more than one bureau."

Credit Reports and EEOC Considerations

If the use of credit reports for employment decisions results in the unfair exclusions of applicants with poor credit, then it may have EEOC implications. Even though a credit report may appear neutral on its face, if its use results in a "disparate impact" upon members of protected groups, a claim can be made that the use of credit reports is in fact discriminatory.

The EEOC has launched a new initiative called E-RACE – Eradicating Racism and Colorism From Employment. According to the EEOC, the use of credit, although it appears facially neutral, can have a discriminatory impact. See www.eeoc.gov/initiatives/e-race/why_e-race.html. According to an interview with an EEOC official that appeared in the April, 2007 issue of Society for Human Resource Management's magazine[63], unnecessary credit reports can end up being a subtle form of discrimination and are best utilized when there is a legitimate business need. Statistics by the Texas Department of Insurance seemed to suggest that members of protected groups do have lower credit scores. Even though an employment credit report does not provide a credit score, the credit history is included.

The state of Washington has addressed these concerns through a law passed in 2007 that prohibits employers from obtaining a credit report as part of a background check unless the information is—

"...substantially job related and the employer's reasons for the use of such information are disclosed to the consumer in writing; or required by law." (See: RCW 19.182.020)

A recent study reported by the Society for Industrial and Organizational Psychology questioned whether credit checks have any validity in predicting the job performance of employees. According to the report, two Eastern Kentucky University researchers studied credit reports of nearly 200 current and former employees working in the financial service areas of six companies. The results suggested that a person's credit history is not a good

---

[63] See www.shrm.org/hrnews_published/archives/CMS_020975.asp

predictor of job performance or turnover. The full report is found at www.newswise.com/articles/view/502792/.

Considerations when Negative Information is Found

Before utilizing negative information found in a credit report, the employer should consider—

- Is the negative information a valid predictor of job performance?
- Is the information current and correct?
- Is negative information reported that is outside the applicant's control such as the result of a disputed bill, medical bills, dissolution of marriage, or some other problem?
- Is there any reason not to consider the negative information? For example, an employer generally should not consider a bankruptcy.
- Is the employer consistent in the use of negative information? For example, have other applicants been hired with the same type of negative information and, if so, is there a rational reason why it was overlooked for others? Is there a company hiring policy or some documentation put in the file to demonstrate that the employer is consistent?
- Has any decision or conclusion been documented?
- Is the applicant being afforded all of his legal rights?

Safe Hiring Tip ➤ To prevent the misuse of credit reports, the credit bureaus have significantly increased safeguards. Before a background firm may issue a credit report to an employer, the background firm must essentially conduct a background check on the employer. This includes an on-site inspection to ensure the employer is a legitimate business with a proper and permissible purpose for using an employment credit report.

Understanding Legal Limits and Consumer's Rights

The job applicant must provide written authorization before an employer can request a credit report. Under the FCRA, an applicant has a series of additional rights. If an employer intends not to hire someone based upon information in the credit report, then the applicant must first receive a copy of the report and a statement of rights. The applicant has a right to review the credit report and to dispute any information believed to be inaccurate or incomplete. This right applies even if the employer has additional reasons not to hire the person or even if an applicant has excellent credit, and even if there are other concerns such as a reported high debt level. For example, an employer may be concerned that an applicant's debt level is higher then the job pays even though the applicant has a perfect payment record. If the employer did not give the applicant his right under the FCRA to review the credit report for errors, then the applicant would have been unfairly eliminated. If a final decision is made, then an applicant is entitled to a second confirming letter. In California and certain other states, job applicants also must be given the opportunity to request a free copy of a report originally obtained by an employer.[64]

Because of the potential for errors on credit reports, an applicant has a right to review a report before it is used to adversely affect his employment.

If job applicants are concerned about their credit reports, then they should first contact all three major credit bureaus and request a copy. Typically, there is a fee not exceeding $8, but in some circumstances reports are free. Under federal law that took effect in 2004, applicants have a right to a free credit report once a year.[65] Credit reports, as well as information on costs and procedures to dispute information, can be obtained from the following sources—

- Trans Union: www.transunion.com - 800-888-4213
- Equifax: www.econsumer.equifax.com - 888-532-0179
- Experian: www.experian.com - 800-972-0322

If there is an error or explanation the applicant cannot resolve with the creditor, then the applicant should write a detailed letter to the three credit bureaus, who have 30 days to investigate and resolve the dispute. If the report is corrected, the applicant may request the agencies to notify anyone who has received the report for employment in the past two years. If the dispute is not resolved to the applicant's satisfaction, the applicant has a right to place a brief statement on his credit report. All of these rights are explained in detail on the FTC website at www.ftc.gov/bcp/menu-credit.htm.

If a job applicant wants to clear bad credit, there are excellent credit-counseling services available. The National Foundation for Consumer Credit, a non-profit organization with more than 1,400 affiliates throughout the U.S., provides this service; see www.nfcc.org. Unfortunately, there also are scam artists who make false or misleading claims; the FTC issues warnings about these scams and provides information for consumers on the FTC website.

---

[64] Under the FACT Act passed in 2003, consumers now have the right to request a free copy of their credit report every year, see www.ftc.gov/bcp/conline/edcams/credit/ycr_free_reports.htm for information.

[65] In some states, this right for a consumer to receive a free credit report already existed.

Driving Records

Many employers utilize driving records, also known as MVRs, as a safe hiring tool, often regardless if the position applied for involves driving or not. An MVR is a historical index of a driver's moving violation convictions, accidents, and license sanctions. Depending on the state's record reporting procedure, an MVR can show activity anywhere from three years to a lifetime.

There are four important rules about state motor vehicle records to keep in mind—

1. Each state maintains its own separate database of licensed drivers, vehicle registrations, vehicle ownership, accident reports, and other associated records.

2. There is NO national database of driving records. [66]

3. The federal Driver's Privacy Protection Act (DPPA)[67] sets specific standards for when the personal information can be included on records, but not necessarily on whom can access records.

4. Many state jurisdictions impose restrictions on the access of motor vehicle records per DPPA. But many state agencies permit the public to obtain **sanitized records** – no personal information shown – without the consent of the subject.

Due to the DPPA, sometimes the version of the MVR report provided to employers by a background screening firm will contain the applicant's name and driving record, but with personal data – date of birth, address, physical characteristics, etc. – removed.

The License Status Report

A status report – the top or header portion of a driving record – can sometimes be obtained as a separate record. The license status report generally indicates three important pieces of information:

1. The type or 'class' of license issued which in turn tells what types of vehicles (commercial, non-commercial, motorcycle) can be operated. Different commercial license classes regulate the size or weight of the vehicle licensed to be driven.

2. Any special conditions placed on the license holder. These permissions and limitations are known as endorsements and restrictions. A typical restriction is a requirement to have "corrective lenses" when driving. A CDL license may

---

[66] However, there are two national indices maintained by the National Driver Registry; one for commercial drivers (CDLIS) and one for problem drivers (PDPS).

[67] 18 USC Section 2721.

have an endorsement that regulates if hazardous material can be hauled.

3. If the license is valid or under suspension or revocation.

A handful of states offer online status checks. Some are free, some are for a fee. For employers, sometimes obtaining a license status is an inexpensive and quick substitute for obtaining the full and more expensive driving record.

Safe Hiring Considerations and Driving Occupations

For a person who is driving a company vehicle or is in a 'driving position' for the company, a MVR check is a necessity. However, in most jurisdictions, 'driving for work' is very broadly defined. The question is, when is an employee driving for work? The term 'driving for work' can cover any employee behind the wheel of a vehicle for the employer's benefit.

For example, an employee who drives to the office supply store during lunch or between branches of the same firm, or attends classes that are paid for by the company, can be considered 'driving for work.' If an accident occurs in any of those situations, an employer may be sued.

The one time an employer likely has no responsibility for an employee's driving is for an employee who only drives to work and drives home. This is referred to as the *Going and Coming Rule* – a worker driving to work and driving home does not drive for the employer in between work and home.

For positions that involve driving, an employer can review the applicant's driving history and verify a license's status. A check of the driving record also may give insight into the applicant's level of responsibility. Just having moving violations may not relate to the ability to perform the job, but if an applicant has a history of failing to appear in court or pay fines, that can be a telling indicator about his level of responsibility.

Statewide driving records databases may be the first place where difficulties with drugs or alcohol are revealed; there may be 'driving-while-impaired' violations. However, there are restrictions on the use of this information under the Americans with Disabilities Act, plus anti-discrimination law in certain states.

The bottom line is the employer must determine whether the MVR information is job-related. The employer should exercise discretion when using it to the detriment of the applicant.[68]

---

[68] Readers interested in extensive, detailed information about state driving records, access restrictions and procedures, and violation codes, may refer to BRB Publications' *The MVR Book* and the *MVR Decoder Digest,* see www.brbpub.com/books/.

Drug Testing

More job applicants are finding that part of the application process involves a pre-employment drug test. Many Fortune 500 companies and an increasing number of smaller firms now require drug testing for new employees.

The U.S. Department of Labor estimates that drug use in the workplace costs employers $75 billion to $100 billion annually in lost time, accidents, health care, and workers' compensation costs. Also, it is reported that 65% of all accidents on the job are related to drug or alcohol issues.

Tests can be performed either pre-hire or post-hire, but the most common type of testing program is during the pre-employment process. Courts have consistently upheld the legality of requiring a pre-employment drug test as a condition of employment.

An Overview on How Testing Is Performed

The majority of drug testing is done by sending an applicant to a
The majority of drug testing is done by sending an applicant to a
collection site where a urine sample is obtained, and then sent to a certified laboratory for analysis. Negative results are normally available within 24 hours. Some employers use instant test kits that are similar in operation to a home pregnancy test. Newer testing methods, such as hair testing and saliva testing, also are being used.

Most employers utilize the standard five-panel test of 'street drugs,' consisting of marijuana (THC), cocaine, PCP, opiates (such as codeine and morphine), and amphetamines (including methamphetamine). Some employers use a ten-panel test that includes testing for prescription drugs if prescribed for use. Employers also can test for blood-alcohol levels.

Although each drug and each person is different, most drugs will stay in the system about two to four days. For chronic users of certain drugs such as marijuana or PCP, results can be detected for up to 14 days, and sometimes much longer. Sedatives such as Valium may stay in the system for up to 30 days.

To avoid the complications from 'second-hand marijuana smoke,' most labs will set a higher threshold before reporting THC in the system.

Most employers will require an applicant to give the urine sample within a specific period of time so that a drug user does not wait until the drugs leave the system.

Laboratories and collection sites also have methods to determine if the applicant has attempted to alter the test sample by drinking excessive water, contaminating the sample, or by using some sort of product that is sold in the hope it will mask drug use.

Testing labs have extensive procedures to reconfirm a positive test before reporting it to an employer. Most drug testing programs use the services of an independent physician – called a medical review officer – to review all test results. In the case of a positive result, the officer will normally contact the applicant to determine if there is a medical explanation.

Employer Considerations For Drug Testing

If a firm plans to test current employees, then the employer should have policies and procedures in place as part of an SHP. The procedures should include supervisory training and what steps to take if and when positive results of a drug test occur. If the positive test is confirmed, the job applicant can usually pay for a retesting of the sample at a laboratory of his choice. Urine samples for all positive tests are retained for that purpose. But merely taking a new test is not helpful since the drugs may have left the person's system. Certified laboratories will stand behind their results and make expert witnesses available. All drug-testing results should be maintained on a confidential basis.

Post-employment testing can include random testing (for safety-sensitive positions), individualized suspicion testing, post-accident testing, and testing that is legally required in certain industries, such as Department of Transportation (DOT) requirements for truck drivers.

Internet and Social Networking Sites

Should an employer utilize social networking sites such as Facebook or MySpace to screen potential applicants? What about searching a name on Google or other web search engines?

Many employers have discovered what appears to be a treasure trove on the web for recruiting and hiring. By using search engines and social networking sites, recruiters often are able to find good candidates for positions. In addition, many employers use the Internet to pre-screen applicants. One employer tells the story of recruiting for a high profile consulting firm. The recruiter ran the applicant's phone number on a search engine, only to discover that the applicant had a business on the side – an adult service of a mature nature, complete with revealing photos. That particular candidate was not hired. Another employer found out that a summer intern had bashed him on the intern's social networking site webpage.

However, there are some issues to consider if you decide to incorporate Internet sites and search engines within a firm's screening program—

- A major problem is often referred to as **TMI** – too much information. What if an Internet search reveals prohibited information such as ethnicity, national origin, sexual orientation, religious preference, or other factors that cannot be considered for employment?

- Another issue is that the search of Facebook or MySpace may contain a photo, revealing personal characteristics or physical problems. This can raise questions of discrimination.

- Privacy is also a concern. There is an assumption that just because something is online, it is fair game for any use. However, sites such as Facebook or MySpace have "terms of use policies" that appear to limit the use of such sites to personal social networking. Only Facebook or MySpace users can argue that they had a reasonable expectation of privacy, in that only others who were interested in social networking would view their materials. That is an issue yet to be decided by courts but can still represent a risk to employers.

- Using private behavior for employment decisions can be problematic since some states have statutory protections in place for workers to limit consideration of off-duty conduct.

- Finally, how can an employer know for sure the online entry item actually belongs to the applicant and is not fake or a sham? **Cyberslamming** – the placing of anonymous and defamatory statements in chat rooms or online discussion boards – does happen and can ruin reputations.

As a result of these issues, job applicants are well advised to monitor their online identity in the event an employer looks them up. There are now websites dedicated to helping applicants protect themselves. Some schools have even required that employers reveal if they do such online searches as a condition for recruiting at the school.

This is a developing new frontier for employers. Employers may want to think through their policies before doing random web searches. One alternative that works in a Safe Hiring Program is to get a specific consent from an applicant for an online search and only do the search after a conditional job offer has been made.

Civil Lawsuits

Another screening tool for employers involves using civil court records. A civil case occurs when one party sues another. Unlike a criminal case, which is brought by the government and a defendant can face jail time, a civil case is typically about money.[69] Civil cases can be for torts or contracts.

A contract case is when one party sues another for a violation or enforcement of an agreement. A tort case is when one party sues another for an injury for actions other than breech of contract. Tort cases can involve both intentional conduct and unintentional conduct. An unintentional tort is typically a negligence action such as an auto accident. An intentional tort can be such causes of action as assault, intentional infliction of emotional distress, or some intentional wrong. Although the same conduct also could form the basis of a criminal case as well, a criminal case is only brought by the government. Tort cases can involve injury to the person (assault and battery or infliction of emotional distress), injury to property (trespass, theft, conversion), injury to reputation, or some business advantage (slander, liable).

A Familiar Illustration of Civil and Criminal Cases—

When O.J. Simpson was prosecuted for murder, the case was brought in the criminal courts by a prosecuting attorney. That case was called, "The People vs. Simpson." However, Simpson also was sued in civil court by private attorneys hired by the family members of the victims. That case had the title of the parties to the case – Sharon Ruffo, et al. vs. Simpson.

The fact that Simpson was found not guilty in the criminal case but guilty in the civil court also illustrated the difference between civil and criminal cases. In a criminal case, a prosecutor must convince all 12 jurors unanimously, beyond a reasonable doubt, the defendant is guilty. On the other hand, in a civil case, a plaintiff only needs to prove the case by a preponderance of the evidence, which is a much lesser standard. That standard means that it is more likely than not the plaintiff proved the case. Sometimes the standard is when the plaintiff must prove the case by 51%. In civil cases, a plaintiff only needs 9 jurors to agree, not all 12.

---

[69] There are some lawsuits that seek remedies other than money, such as a request for an injunction, which is where a party seeks to have another party ordered to do or not do some physical act.

Utilizing Civil Court Records in Employment Decisions

The issue employers must determine is: does the civil lawsuit have any relevance to the position? Many civil lawsuits are clearly not job-related. For example, if an applicant is a plaintiff (the person bringing the action against the defendant) in a personal injury lawsuit, this would not likely have bearing on job performance, unless the applicant was suing a past employer and had a custom and practice of doing that. A civil search may uncover a case of dissolution of marriage. Often such lawsuits will have a detailed description where the parties are bringing out all the dirty laundry. As interesting as that might be to read from a human-interest point of view, it likely to have little bearing upon employment.

Examples of lawsuits that have some rational relationship to workplace performance or be directly job-related include a harassment suit by a former employee or lawsuits for violence or dishonest behavior. These indicate character traits that may be involved in workplace behavior.

Nothing is as simple as it seems when it comes to searching public records. Every lawsuit has some sort of caption that indicates the court where it is filed, the parties involved, and the type of lawsuit. However, lawsuits in state or federal courts usually only have a rather cursory description of the nature of the action in the caption. The lawsuit may be described only as a "Suit for Damages." That tells a researcher almost nothing at all. In order to determine the underlying nature of the litigation, it is again necessary for a court researcher to request that the court clerk copy the first few pages of the file where the essential thrust of the allegations of the lawsuit are usually recounted. The file could indicate, for example, a person was being sued for harassment in the workplace or if the defendant was the employer or manager.

Obtaining Civil Case Records Can be Difficult

Obtaining civil court records is similar to obtaining criminal records, but with many more complications. Researchers locate records for civil lawsuits in the same fashion they search for criminal records. However, unlike criminal records that have a connection to where a defendant has lived or worked, civil records can be more diverse geographically. The rules for jurisdictions are somewhat broader for civil cases. For example, in a lawsuit for breach of contract, the suit can be brought where the contract was formed or breached. A job applicant may not have lived in any of those places. Therefore, civil record searches can take on a needle-in-a-haystack quality.

Another problem is that civil records have very few identifiers. The initial search is by name match only, a similar problem to searching for federal criminal records, as explained previously. For example, if an Adam Smith is involved in a civil lawsuit as either a defendant or a plaintiff, there are no reasons that any identifiers necessarily be present in the file.

In order to determine if a civil record belongs to the job applicant, it is necessary to look for clues in the files to identify the parties, such as information on a summons or proof of service of the lawsuit, reference to employment, or data found in exhibits attached to the civil complaint. Employment screening companies can be expected to know experienced researchers who can properly search civil case records.

Judgments, Liens, and Bankruptcies

Other sources of data about job applicants are judgments, liens, and bankruptcy record databases.

Judgments

A judgment is typically a final decision in a court case where the judge or jury awards monetary damages against the defendant. Often, the party who wins the judgment will record the judgment with the county records clerk. Database vendors have assembled national databases consisting of these judgments.

The purpose of using judgment information as part of a background screen is to allow employers to know if an applicant has been sued. As with civil records, when using judgment records for employment purposes, employers must approach this type of information with caution. First, the employer must make sure the judgment is valid. Next, the employer needs sufficient identifying data to conclude that the judgment pertains to the applicant. Third, the employer must determine if the judgment is relevant to a job. Each of these determinations should be backed by documentation.

Employers also must be aware that judgment databases can have errors and be missing judgment records. In addition, the great majority of civil lawsuits are settled out-of-court, so there may not be a judgment entered on the public record.

Tax Liens

Some employers search to see if an applicant has a recorded tax lien. When a person or business owes delinquent, unpaid taxes to a government agency, the agency can record a tax lien that gives the government priority to collect upon the proceeds from the sale of real property. When performed at the local level, tax lien searches are often combined with a judgment database search. However, there are many tax liens also recorded at the state level in the same state database that records Uniform Commercial Code (UCC) filings.

Like judgments, tax liens must be taken with a grain of salt. An employer must determine 1) if that tax lien data applies to the applicant, 2) if the data is accurate, and 3) if used for employment purposes, is it relevant and fair?

Bankruptcy

All bankruptcy cases are heard in a federal bankruptcy court and the information is easily accessible.

Federal law makes it very clear that using a bankruptcy against a job applicant can be a form of discrimination. Employers should exercise extreme caution in attempting to utilize these records. A private employer may not discriminate with respect to employment if the discrimination is based solely upon the bankruptcy filing.[70] A person cannot be penalized for the lawful exercise of a legal right. Under the "fresh start rule," a consumer is entitled to start over again; if a person went into bankruptcy to re-arrange a life, but cannot get a job because of the bankruptcy, then that person could never get ahead. He would be placed in a new form of debtors' prison, unable to break the debt cycle.

If for any reason an employer feels that bankruptcy is relevant to the job, then the employer should consult an attorney to determine if there is a bona fide occupational reason to justify consideration of a bankruptcy search.

Military Records

Applicants with military service provide critical, trained skills that are extremely valuable in the workforce. Employers may need or wish to verify that on a military service record.

Some Advice on How to Obtain

The standard way to verify military records is to ask an applicant for a copy of his DD-214. This is the common term for the document given to all members of the military who are discharged from the U.S. Navy, Army, Air Force, Marine Corp, or Coast Guard. The "DD" stand for Department of Defense. The short name is "discharge papers."

For employers who want more than a cursory confirmation of military service, the story goes much deeper. There are actually a

---

[70] See 11 USC 525 regarding bankruptcy record use

number of different copies of the DD-214 with different pieces of information. A discharged service person receives Copy 1, which has the least information. The copy with the codes that gives the nature of the discharge, i.e. general, honorable, dishonorable, etc. Details of service are actually on Copy 4. The codes characterize the service record of a veteran. The codes are known as SPD (Separation Program Designator), SPN (Separation Program Number) and RE (Re-Entry) codes. Other issues with access and use of DD-214s are as follows—

- For a discharged service person to get Copy 4, the person must actually ask for it.

- If a person did not ask for the Copy 4, or wants to hide some embarrassing fact, then the person may only present Copy 1 to an employer.

- If the employer wants Copy 4 and the applicant does not have it, then there can be a problem acquiring and understanding the copy. The employer can have the applicant sign a Form 180 and send it to the National Personnel Records Center (NPRC) in St. Louis, Missouri. However, there can be a wait – up to six months. And, some records are no longer available due to a very destructive fire at the St. Louis facility in 1973.[71]

A note of caution is in order. Even after getting a Copy 4, there is the issue of translating the military codes. There are websites that provide a complete list of the codes and definitions. However, should civilian employers use these codes for hiring decisions, since the codes were meant for internal military use only? The various codes may represent items that have no foundation or were the result of clerical errors, or are simply not related to job performance.

Considerations When Using Military Records

When making hiring decisions, employers should be very careful before attempting to draw conclusions from various codes on the DD-214. Using the codes on the DD-214 to infer conduct in order to make hiring decisions could result in claims of discrimination, or decisions being made based upon irrelevant or unsubstantiated criteria. The situation can be further complicated if an employer insists that an applicant first obtains a complete DD-214 and then later rejects the applicant. That record request could potentially be viewed as evidence of discrimination.

---

[71] However the government has reconstructed some of the records by use of other military documents. For details about these military records, see www.archives.gov/research_room/obtain_copies/veterans_service_records.html

An employer also should exercise caution in using a discharge as a basis of an employment decision. There are four common types of military discharges: honorable, general, undesirable, and dishonorable. Of these, only a dishonorable discharge is given as a result of a factual adjudication equivalent to a criminal trial. In order to avoid potential EEOC claims, an employer should treat a dishonorable discharge in the same fashion as a criminal conviction, taking into account the various factors reviewed in the previous chapter. A general discharge or undesirable discharge may or may not have any bearing on employment and generally should not be the basis of an employment decision.

The best advice may be to use the basic DD-214 to confirm a person was in fact in the military, and then ask for the names of references from his military service to obtain job-related information that would be relevant to an employment decision.

Security Clearances

An employer may want to verify that a person had a security clearance in the past. This will occur when an employer receives a resume from an applicant indicating, as part of past qualifications, that he had a security clearance. The employer wants to confirm that the person is being truthful. Some employers will ask if a person has ever had a security clearance, if he had been refused one, and details about the last clearance held, including granting agent, level, date granted, and date expired.

If the current job requires a security clearance, then there is already an established process in place. Entities that have security clearance needs, such as private employers used by government, will have an authorized designee in charge of a process called the Special Security Officer (SSO). Security clearances stay with the entity and do not travel with the individual. If the SSO individual leaves a position, this person no longer has a clearance. When a person leaves one employer that requires a clearance to go to another position that also requires a clearance, then the SSO at each entity arranges for the appropriate transfers.

If an applicant is applying for a job that does not require a security clearance, and the employer wants to verify the past claim, then the best procedure is for the employer or screening firm to contact the past employer and request the name and mailing address of the SSO. If a copy of a release is provided, then the SSO may verify that there was some level of clearance, but may not go into detail.

Another source of information is searching the various sanctions and disbarment databases. These are typically lists of governmental actions or sanctions relating to some sort of license, qualifications, governmental sanctions, or the allowing the subject to do business with the government. See your employment screening company for ways to check these databases.

Sexual Offender Registries

Another tool available to employers is the use of sexual offender databases. The registration requirements were signed into law, popularly known as Megan's Law, by President Clinton on May 17, 1996. The law has two primary goals. The first goal requires each state and the federal government to register sexual predators. The state registry is a compilation of records of offenses that are sexual in nature, or involve harm to children, are accumulated statewide. The second goal provides for community notifications by the local police.

The most accurate sources are the registries lists directly maintained by states and counties. However, not all jurisdictions provide sufficient detail to identify or locate an offender.

Many of the information provider firms that have assembled large national databases composed of criminal record related data include sexual offender data. These national sexual offender databases are an excellent secondary or supplemental tool to perform a broader search that is national in nature.

Finally, the U.S. Department of Justice announced its searchable website in 2005 at www.nsopr.gov. The database supplies what each state reports to it.[72]

In theory, a sexual offender search includes the entire state, so that it is less subject to the limitations of a county search. A person may have been convicted of a sexual offense in a county where an employer or background firm may not know to look. For example, a person may not list the county where the sexual offense occurred, and it may not come up on a SSN Trace.

Use by Employers

There are a number of problems with the accuracy and completeness of the sexual offender data, similar to the issues described previously about criminal databases. For example, some of the national database providers are unable to produce a date of birth or other identifier for all states, so an employer can be stuck with a name match only, which would have to be confirmed by

---

[72] The use notes for each state should be carefully reviewed. In addition, unlike commercial databases, the state lists that are reported through the U.S. Department of Justice database may drop an offender's name when the registration period is over.

going to a more specific state database or pulling a court record. Thus one of the biggest problems is there can be both false positives and false negatives. A false positive is where there is a match, but upon further research it is not the same person as the job candidate. A false negative is where a sexual offender is not located, but in fact the person is a sexual offender. That is one reason why searchable websites, including those maintained by states, have disclaimers warning that records can be missed.

Also, news stories and studies are easily found that indicate a high number of sexual offenders did not register or keep registrations current.

The manner in which records are kept by the state can also contribute to an error rate. Each state's central repository must collect data from local courts. If a county is late or inaccurate, then there can be errors. Also, not every state makes its central repository available to the public – if so a researcher would need to check county by county in order to perform a complete sex offender record search.

Overall, a sexual offender database search, both nationwide and using state and local websites, is an extremely valuable tool. It is especially valuable when the position involves access to a group-at-risk such as children or the elderly. However, employers and volunteer groups need to understand that these databases are not primary tools, but supplemental tools subject to some degree of error and should be utilized with some caution and in conjunction with other safe hiring procedures.

These reasons underscore the basic message – sex offender registry searches, although valuable, are far from perfect and should just be one element among many in the background screening process.

Workers' Compensation Records

Considering the cost related to fraud and compensation claims, many employers want to know whether a job applicant has a history of filing workers' compensation claims. But there are numerous legal restrictions that must be observed closely that prohibit this type of check. An employer cannot view these records in order to not hire anyone who has made a claim.

The federal Americans with Disabilities Act (ADA) as well as numerous state laws protect job seekers from discrimination in hiring as a result of filing valid claims. The ADA also seeks to prevent the discrimination against workers who, although suffering from a disability, are nevertheless able to perform essential job functions as long as there are reasonable accommodations. It is discriminatory to penalize a person who has exercised a lawful right and filed a valid claim.

Safe Hiring Considerations and Workers' Compensation Records

If a firm wishes to use workers' compensation records, then the following procedures should be part of the written SHP policy.

- Under the ADA, an employer may not inquire about an applicant's medical condition or past workers' compensation claims until a conditional job offer has been extended. A conditional job offer means that a person had been made an offer of employment, subject to certain conditions such as a job-related medical review. The conditions must be fulfilled prior to coming on-site for employment.

- Any questioning in a job interview must be restricted to whether the person can perform the essential job functions with or without reasonable accommodation.

- If a candidate discloses a disability, then there should not be any follow-up. Questioning should be limited to whether that applicant can perform the job.

- Only after a conditional job offer has been extended may an employer inquire about past medical history, require a medical exam, or inquire about workers' compensation claims.

- The better practice is to have an applicant fill out a written medical review form that reviews his medical condition and workers' compensation claims history, and provides consent as well. Firms that utilize medical examinations as part of their procedures should have a written medical review policy.

- The procedure should be administered uniformly. If one worker in a job category is the subject of such an investigation, then all applicants must be treated the same. However, an employer may treat different job categories differently. Not all employees must be sent for a medical exam.

- If a history of filing workers' compensation claims is found, then the offer may be rescinded only under very limited circumstances:

    a. The applicant has lied about a workers' compensation history or medical condition, usually during a medical examination;

b. The applicant has a history of filing false claims;

c. The past claims demonstrate the applicant is a safety or health threat to himself or others, in the opinion of a medical expert.

d. The past claims demonstrate the applicant is unable to perform the essential functions of the job even with a reasonable accommodation.

- If the applicant has lied on the medical questionnaire, then the employer may be justified in rescinding the job offer based upon dishonesty. If an applicant has a history of multiple claims that have been denied, then an employer may be justified in rescinding the offer. The recession is based upon an inference of fraud, not disability. However, even individuals with false claims will usually not have multiple false claims. Rescinding the job offer based upon reasons (b) and (c), however, does require a medical opinion.

Some firms contend that a workers' compensation record history also may be used to determine the truthfulness of information on a job application on the theory that an applicant may try to hide a past employer where a claim was filed. However, even with this justification, if used, the best practice may be to review the records post-hire only.

Employers are well-advised to contact their employment screening company or a labor lawyer before seeking to obtain workers' compensation records history. A labor law expert or a screening company can assist an employer in preparing company policies, job descriptions, forms, and procedures necessary to comply with the ADA, including a conditional job offer and medical review form.

International Screening

International background screening is often perceived as difficult, but this mere fact does not relieve an employer from the obligation of due diligence. Nor can employers simply assume that the U.S. government has conducted background checks if the worker was issued a visa. After the events of 9/11, the U.S. has increased checks on foreign visitors and on workers on government *watch lists*. However, the government checks are generally not aimed at verifying a credential or checking for criminal records for employment purposes.

Two terms are commonly used by employment screening companies. The term *International Screening* typically refers to the efforts of a U.S. employer to screen a candidate, who has spent time outside of the U.S., for a job in the U.S. The term *Global Screening* refers to employers who set up an office or operations outside of the U.S. and is screening employees in that foreign country.

To exercise proper due diligence in an SHP, employers should consider screening internationally for—

- Criminal Records
- Prior Employment
- Education Credentials
- Publicly Available Terrorist Lists

About International Criminal Records

The procedures used to access criminal records vary widely by country. The availability of public records that is taken for granted here in the U.S. is often times not available abroad. Although some countries have records available at the courthouse, similar to how criminal records are obtained in the U.S., in other countries records must be obtained from a police agency. And in some countries, the best course of action is to require applicants to obtain their own certificate of good conduct from their local police station.

Keep in mind several key factors when ordering searches from a screening company, or if you are coordinating a search yourself. First, it is important to know *exactly* where the person has lived to ensure you are searching the appropriate court. Different countries also have different rules on the level of searches, but in most countries it is possible to obtain information of offenses that are at the felony level. Keep in mind also that the turnaround time for international criminal searches takes longer than domestic searches.

Another concern is name variations. Many countries have naming conventions that are different than the U.S., such as the use of the mother's name. Complications can also arise for applicants whose name is based on a non-English alphabet, such as Chinese, Arabic, or Japanese. There are numerous ways that such names can be translated into English.

Privacy and data protection is another crucial issue. For example, the European Union (EU) has passed strong privacy rules affecting how personal data can be obtained and utilized. U.S. background firms that do international searches should be a member of the U.S. Department of Commerce Safe Harbor Program, which demonstrates a commitment to the EU privacy and data protection rules.

About International Education Records

Verification of an educational degree earned abroad is a critical step to proper due diligence and to avoid hiring someone with fraudulent credentials. An employer needs to determine if an applicant in fact attended the school claimed and received the degree claimed and also determine if the school is accredited and authentic. The world is awash with phony schools and worthless diplomas. If the employer is not familiar with a school, then an employment screening firm should be hired or the verification research should be conducted in-house. A legitimate school will often have an email address or phone number so that it can be contacted to verify a degree and answer accreditation questions.

About International Employment Histories

Foreign employment also can be verified by contacting the employer even though he is in a foreign country. Be prepared to make such calls in the middle of the night due to time differences. The critical step is to obtain as much information about the past employer as possible from the applicant. If the employer does not speak English, an interpreter may be needed.

Using Terrorist Lists

Other due diligence tools available to search are the various terrorist databases available to the public, such as the Office of Foreign Assets Control (OFAC) list maintained by the U.S. Department of the Treasury. Such lists are readily available but there are limitations as well, such as working with name matches only when no additional identifying details are available.

Legal Implications for Employers Doing International Background Checks

The legal implications of international background screening can be very complex and involve the intersection of U.S. domestic law and the operation of foreign law. Furthermore, international screening and the flow of information across borders is a relativity new and developing area of law. There are three essential considerations – employers must be aware of regarding how the data is obtained, transmitted, and utilized.

Obtaining Foreign Data

The essential rule for any employer in the U.S. is that information should be obtained in a manner consistent with the laws of the country where the data originated. If it is not legal in a particular country to obtain a criminal record from the police, then a U.S.

employer should not do so either and possibly exposing himself to liabilities. If a lawsuit arises, an applicant can claim an invasion of privacy or other violation of rights based upon the illegally obtained records. A complaint could be filed in the foreign country and the U.S. employer could face a lawsuit in the U.S. or the foreign country.

A key element in legally obtaining data is, of course, the applicant's written consent. In the context of pre-employment screening, the assumption is made that the applicant not only has consented, but also wants to assist the employer in obtaining records in order to facilitate the employment decision.

Transmitting Foreign Records

The concept of data transmittal has to do with data privacy protection rules in effect for many countries. Data that may be obtained legally from a source may become improper to use if privacy rules are not followed.

Utilization of Foreign Records

Utilization refers to rules that determine whether an U.S. employer may legally consider information obtained from a foreign country for employment, especially in the context of criminal records.

If the job and the applicant are both in a foreign country, then it is likely the rule of the foreign country applies. As the old saying goes, "When in Rome, do as the Romans do." In this situation the employer is best advised to consult legal counsel in the host country and follow the rules used in that country for any type of pre-employment screening.

If the job and the applicant are in the U.S., then the best practice for the U.S. employer is to apply at the minimum, the same rules he would to information obtained in the U.S., including FCRA and EEOC.

Privacy, Data Protection, and the European Union

Important privacy laws that concern U.S. employers are laws dealing with the EU. These rules went into effect in 1998. The European privacy rules impact the transmissions of "personally identifiable data" from offices in EU countries to businesses in the U.S. The European Commission maintains a website that lists all current members of the European Union; see http://europa.eu.int/abc/governments/index_en.htm.

In addition to the EU privacy rules, other countries are in various stages of dealing with similar issues concerning personal and identifiable consumer information. Canada has privacy rules in effect, see below. A website called Privacy International outlines privacy rights and current status in countries around the world, see www.privacyinternational.org/index.shtml.

The Safe Harbor

Firms that acquire data on individuals from EU member nations without compliance with the EU rules can be in violation of EU law. However, American firms that develop a privacy policy may enter what is called the "Safe Harbor" by certifying a privacy policy that includes adequate mechanisms to protect confidential personal data. The program is administered by the U.S. Department of Commerce.

According to the U.S. Department of Commerce—

"The European Commission's Directive on Data Protection went into effect in October, 1998, and prohibits the transfer of personal data to non-European Union nations that do not meet the European 'adequacy standard' for privacy protection. While the United States and the European Union share the goal of enhancing privacy protection for their citizens, the United States takes a different approach to privacy from the approach of the European Union. The United States uses a sectoral approach that relies on a mix of legislation, regulation, and self-regulation. The European Union, however, relies on comprehensive legislation that requires creation of government data protection agencies, registration of databases with those agencies and, in some instances, prior approval before personal data processing may begin. As a result of these different privacy approaches, the Directive could have significantly hampered the ability of U.S. companies to engage in many trans-Atlantic transactions.

"In order to bridge these different privacy approaches and provide a streamlined means for U.S. organizations to comply with the Directive, the U.S. Department of Commerce, in consultation with the European Commission, developed a 'safe harbor' framework. The safe harbor — approved by the EU in July of 2000 — is an important way for U.S. companies to avoid experiencing interruptions in their business dealings with the EU or facing prosecution by European authorities under European privacy laws. Certifying to the safe harbor will assure that EU organizations know that your company provides 'adequate privacy protection,' as defined by the Directive."

Chapter Summary

This Chapter provides information for **Audit Question 20**.

Audit Question #20: Does the firm use other screening tools and, if so, is the information used in accordance with safe hiring guidelines?

Best Practices #20:

- The firm completes a Form I-9 for each new hire.

- The firm completes a Social Security Verification or Social Security Trace for each new hire.

- The firm requests a credit report only if appropriate and if policies are in place to ensure that use of credit information is recent, relevant, and fair.

- The firm takes these additional steps as necessary – if related to a job or position and if applicable only per guidelines of the ADA, EEOC, or FCRA —

  o Civil court records if relevant

  o Driving record

  o Drug testing

  o International searches of criminal, education, and employment records

  o Military records

  o Workers' compensation claim records

  o Others as needed

Chapter 10

Implementing the Screening Process

Now that you know the core components and tools used when performing in-depth screening of applicants, this chapter puts these pieces together into an overall, comprehensive plan.

A key decision in the implementation of the screening process is deciding if the company wishes to do the screening itself or to outsource to a pre-employment screening firm. This chapter also examines the process and outlines the necessary steps involved when working with a screening company.

Audit Question # 21:

Are the mechanics of your screening program documented?

Audit Question # 22:

If screening is outsourced to a third-party firm, can the employer demonstrate due diligence and show procedures are being used per FCRA?

Audit Question # 23:

Are procedures in place if a person with negative information is hired?

Audit Question # 24:

Are procedures in place if employment is offered before a background check is completed?

The First Steps in the Screening Process

Pre-employment screening is the process of assessing applicants for an employer's particular job or category of job. To reveal fully qualified applicants, the employer or an outside professional firm assembles information such as credentials verifications, criminal record searches, SSN Traces, driving records, and more. The screening assessment is performed according to employer policies, which are based upon the nature of the job category and applicable laws.

When implementing screening into an SHP, an employer must make several key decisions upfront—

1. What level of screening will be done?

2. Who will perform the search?

After these decisions are made, the next step is to—

3. Document the mechanics of the screening program.

Choosing the Screening Level

The level or degree of screening should increase in depth as the job responsibility and risk involved in a bad hire increases. Certainly an employer is not held to the standard of an FBI-level check for each hire. However, given the relatively modest cost of screening compared to the protection afforded, a firm should probably error on the side of more screening than less.

Consider the following factors—

- Does the position involve access to money or assets?

- Does the position carry significant authority, or fiduciary responsibility?

- Does the position have access to members of the public or co-workers where any propensity to violence would cause harm?

- Does the position require the worker to go into someone's home?

- Does the person work with a vulnerable group such as children, the elderly, or people with disabilities?

- Would the position be difficult to replace in terms of recruitment, hiring, and training?

- Would the applicant's falsification of skills, experience, or background put the firm at risk, or lower the firm's productivity?

- Would a bad hire expose the firm to litigation or financial claims from the applicant, co-workers, customers, or the public?
- What degree of supervision will the worker be under?
- Is the position full-time, part-time, seasonal, temporary, or a volunteer?

Using the above factors, an employer should create a table showing each position, including the amount of supervision monitoring and review of the position needs. This becomes a *risk matrix.* The following are suggested screening levels that can be modified to create a documented, customized matrix—

Basic Screening:

Typical job position: For entry-level employees, retail, or manufacturing positions, or positions where the employer internally checks references.

Recommended searches: A full seven-year, onsite criminal records check for felonies and misdemeanors, credit report or Social Security and identity check, and driver's license check. The number of counties searched depends upon the risk factors listed above. For maximum protection, an employer may consider doing *all* counties where a person has lived, worked, or studied.

Standard Screening:

Typical job position: For more responsible non-management positions and permanent hire.

Recommended searches: The aforementioned Basic Screening plus verification of the last three employers and of the highest post-high school education. Check references if given.

Extended Screening:

Typical job position: For positions involving increased responsibility or supervision of others.

Recommended searches: The Basic and Standard Screenings plus checking superior court civil cases for litigation matters that may be job-related.

The Integrity Check:

Typical job position: For any type of position involving significant responsibility, or access to cash or assets.

Recommended searches: Includes everything previously mentioned plus 10-year searches 1) of federal court for criminal and civil cases, 2) of employment history, 3) to verify all college degrees and professional licenses, and 4) for superior court civil lawsuits in the last two counties of residence.

Other Options to Consider

For any position, the employer may wish to consider checking sexual offender registries if a worker will have access to children or vulnerable groups at risk. For positions involving access to money or assets, an employer may consider a credit report, subject to the limitations described in the last chapter. In addition, an employer may consider a supplemental criminal record search of a multi-jurisdictional records database.

International searches also may be considered for applicants who have spent time outside of the U.S.

Background Check or Pre-employment Screening?

Unfortunately, some employers are conducting low cost, instant online background checks on new hires and feel they have performed a pre-employment screen. There are no such shortcuts in an SHP.

Do a Google search on the words "background check" and you will get a plethora of sites touting the *most comprehensive and instant criminal record checks available.* (Some people would call that an oxymoron.) The term "background checks" has become a popular topic among various non-profit organizations and charities including churches, little leagues, Scouts, etc. Even the online dating industry sites offer "background checks" before you meet that dream date.

Herein lies the problem: employers and consumers can be mislead into making an assumption that the applicant must be safe or qualified because he passed a "background check." Nothing may be further from the truth. Unless the business or individual relying on the background check knows exactly what was checked and when and knows the limitations and value of the checking that was done, a "background check" is NOT the same as an in-depth, pre-employment screen, especially the screening as mandated by the FCRA.

Screening: In-house or Outsource?

An important decision an employer faces is whether to perform the pre-employment screening in-house or to outsource. There are some tasks an employer could certainly perform in-house such as local criminal record checks. But in today's world, background screening is not a commodity product – it is a professional, affordable service. As a result, the growing trend among profitable and efficient employers is outsourcing screening tasks to a quality, pre-employment screening company.

There are six points to consider when deciding what part of the screening program an employer should perform in-house and what should be outsourced—

1. Is it a better use of time and energy to outsource?

There are only so many functions an in-house department can provide; it makes sense to identify those tasks that can be efficiently and cost-effectively outsourced to a third party.

2. Does the employer have the required expertise to perform background screening in-house?

An employer would be required to have highly specialized staff and knowledge of the resources available. The employer would have to know the many complicated state and federal laws governing what information he can and cannot access. The employer would need to know the most cost-effective sources for information such as criminal record checks.

3. Is outsourcing more cost-effective than in-house processing?

Consider the real in-house screening costs, including all "soft-costs" and overhead. This can involve training, supervision, infrastructure, the administrative cost of maintaining employees, and the cost of other tasks not being done. The cost of staff time and resources, the physical management of the process, including computers and a software solution to manage and track all applicants being screened also must be considered.

Safe Hiring Tip ➤ Here is a rule of thumb: A typical report from a screening firm should cost less than the first day's salary paid to the new employee. Considering what a bad hire may cost you later, this is a very minimal investment.

---

4. Can the employer effectively manage the outsource process for high quality and performance levels?

There must be appropriate and prioritized controls in place. If outsourcing, the employer should have a high degree of control as possible over the process. Employers have expectations about timeliness and quality. The systems usually used by screening firms allow the employer to privately monitor in real time the exact status of all reports.

5. Are there legal advantages to outsourcing?

When outsourcing screening tasks and following FCRA law, both employers and job applicants enjoy significant legal protection of the FCRA. Employers must take care to not unduly invade applicants' privacy or open the door to discrimination actions. Not all employers are cognizant of special state laws involving use of criminal record information, but screening firms are.

6. Are there organizational advantages to outsourcing?

As a matter of corporate culture, many organizations do not want new applicants to feel as though other company employees are conducting an investigation into their background. By outsourcing the task to an independent third party, there is a greater perception of privacy. HR managers have found there is a substantial advantage to advising applicants that a professional outside agency will be conducting the screening.

Other Benefits of Using a Screening Service

Below are additional reasons why employers outsource some or all of the background screening process to a qualified screening company.[73]

Customer Service, Consulting and Training

Typically, a CRA provides a helpful array of customer support services to the employer. Having a specific account manager who knows an employer's need is certainly a benefit. Having an internal trouble-ticket system is a best practice to make sure nothing falls through the cracks. Often employers will find CRAs that are knowledgeable about special needs of a firm's industry. A CRA can work directly with security or HR departments to provide whatever training and orientation is necessary.

Inquire about the CRAs Internal Quality Assurance processes. This also should include how a CRA trains and updates its own staff.

---

[73] One way to verify if a screening company is qualified is to see if the firm is a member of the National Association of Professional Background Screeners (NAPBS). See www.napbs.com

Software and Internet Options

A CRA should provide technology solutions that fit well with the employer's hiring practices. Most CRAs have online systems for moving data electronically. Many options are available for online consent and seamless business-to-business integrations with hiring and HR systems, including *applicant-tracking systems.*

Data Security and Privacy; References

Background reports have sensitive, personal information that is confidential and access to reports should be restricted to those individuals directly involved in the hiring process. A screening firm has policies and procedures in place to ensure confidentiality and should provide a privacy and data protection statement.

As with any provider of a professional service, an employer would want to check the provider's references. Just as a screening company should advise an employer to carefully screen each applicant before he is hired, an employer should exercise the same due diligence when selecting a screening company.

Document the Mechanics of the Screening Program

This section outlines necessary steps from start to finish for the employer's SHP. The best practices outlined include all necessary procedures if the employer is working with a pre-employment screening firm. Use this outline when documenting for your screening process.

Employer to Sign the Certification Form

Initially, an employer needs to sign a Certification Form with the CRA as required by the FCRA. A signed Certification means the employer has agreed to utilize the information provided according to law. A typical certification form indicates; 1) the employer understands the information can be used for employment purposes only, 2) that all information must remain confidential, 3) that information will not be used to discriminate unlawfully, and 4) the employer will follow the rules contained in the FCRA for the use of consumer reports.

Under the FCRA, a background firm is required to provide two documents to an employer. Document one is the "Notice to Users of Consumer Reports: Obligations of Users under the FCRA." The second document is "A Summary of Your Rights Under the Fair Credit Reporting Act," directed at job applicants.[74]

---

[74] Both documents are available in the Appendix.

Note that California has additional special certification rules that must be followed. Those rules are contained in the California Investigative Consumers Reporting Agencies Act.[75] Any background firm or employer doing business in California, hiring in California, or using the consumer report in connection with a California resident or California employment location must be familiar with and follow these special California requirements.

When to Start the Screening Process

Employers typically utilize pre-employment screening toward the end of the selection process – after the field has been narrowed down. Because of time and expenses involved, firms do not typically request screening on all applicants. Screening normally occurs when a company has decided that an applicant is a good prospect.

There are two directions that firms typically take. The more common approach is to have a CRA perform its screening function on a finalist or after a conditional job offer has been tendered. The purpose of pre-screening at that point is to demonstrate due diligence and to eliminate uncertainties about the applicant.

Alternatively, a firm will ask the CRA to screen the two or three finalists, and then use the results in the selection process. The advantage is that a firm can make a selection with more facts. The disadvantages are time and costs, and possible FCRA and EEOC implications that can be triggered. An argument can be made that the initial selection should be based upon the applicant's job qualifications and job fit only; a pre-employment report is used only to eliminate an applicant with a job-related criminal history, falsified credentials, or other negative history that may be uncovered.[76]

In addition, if any part of the selection process involves consideration of the pre-employment background report, then the "adverse action" rules apply. This means the applicant has the right to receive a copy of the report and the FCRA-compliant statement of his rights. Even if the information relied upon was not negative, the rejected applicant still has these rights under the FCRA.

---

[75] California Investigative Consumers Reporting Agencies Act - Civil Code section 1786 et. seq.

[76] Under a recent federal case from the Ninth Circuit, the timing of the background screening also may impact ADA. If a background report is necessary before a person becomes a finalist, then a firm may need to complete the background check before obtaining medical information or performing pre-employment physicals. The idea is that medical information should be requested only after there has been a real job offer, which means all relevant non-medical information has been evaluated. This enables an applicant to determine if there was a medical basis to a rejection, and to maintain medical privacy until later in the hiring process. See *Leonel v. American Airlines*, 400 F.3d 702 (9th Cir. 2005)

For these reasons, pre-employment screening reports are most often utilized at the very end of the selection procedure, after the company has selected a finalist.

Prepare the Necessary Forms the Applicant Signs or Receives

Employers must utilize forms that are legally compliant under both federal and state law. Although a CRA may provide an employer with forms, it is still the employer's responsibility to ensure the forms are legal and follow any additional state requirements.

Disclosure Form

The FCRA says a separate stand-alone disclosure form document is required be signed by the subject before a background can be performed. An employer must..."make a clear and conspicuous written disclosure to the consumer before the report is obtained, in a document that consists solely of the disclosure, that a consumer report may be obtained." Under the FCRA, applicants do not necessarily sign the form, but that would be a best practice in order to show your compliance.

Release and Authorization Form

The Release and Authorization Form serves several purposes. First, this form allows the release of information so a CRA may obtain background information per the FCRA. Second, this is how the job applicant provides the necessary identifying information to the CRA who will obtain public records. Third, this release may be needed when a former employer or school requests a release before information is given. Also, the form can be used to reassure a job applicant that all of his rights are protected, and that screening is a sound business practice that is not to be taken personally. Whether or not a release form is combined with the disclosure form depends upon how much information an employer wants to be shown on the release form.

The Release and Authorization Form typically asks for the date of birth, which is needed for positive identification.[77] If an employer does not want to have date of birth on the release form, then arrangements need to be made with the CRA to obtain it separately.

There is currently no nationally accepted set of forms for employment screening. A CRA can provide an employer with all the necessary forms for pre-employment screening. If an employer's attorney or legal department already has forms, use those –

---

[77] See Chapter 3 for a discussion of the "date-of-birth issue" and see Chapter 3 on the FCRA for additional issues surrounding these forms and the exception for truck drivers.

assuming those forms fully comply with the FCRA requirements as well as applicable state rules.

Other Issues of Note

Employers need to be knowledgeable about two other issues involving these forms—

1. Disclosure forms may not have excessive language that detracts from a clear understanding of the form.
2. The forms may not include language stating that an applicant waives his rights to sue the employer or CRA.

Per the FTC staff, an applicant cannot be required to waive his rights under the FCRA.[78] However, a form may ask that an applicant waive his rights to the extent permitted by law. It is not clear that such waiver language gives a screening firm or the employer a great deal of protection against state torts such as defamation or invasion of privacy. Even if there is such a waiver, there is a problem of putting it on the disclosure form. For those reasons, some employers and CRAs use two separate forms in this manner: 1) the release form that contains the identifying information along with the waiver language, if utilized; 2) the disclosure form contains only the required language.

As discussed in the Application Process Chapter, employers' disclaimers should have recommended language related to criminal convictions, and truthfulness and honesty on their application forms. Many states have their own requirements as well; an employer should consult legal counsel on these issues.

When the Applicant Signs the Screening Forms

Typically, the actual screening begins after a company has decided 1) an applicant is a good prospect and 2) wants to verify that the hiring assessment is correct. However, the employer may wish to have all forms signed ahead of time even if an applicant is not going to be submitted for screening.

Employers can take one of several approaches. One approach is to have all applicants sign the screening forms as part of the initial application process. There are several advantages. First, by having background forms in the standard application packet, it discourages applicants with something to hide. Applicants with a minor infraction in their past still may wish to apply and tend to self-disclose any negative information. That helps contribute to a very open interview. Employers find it much easier to administer the screening program if the candidate's necessary forms have already been signed.

---

[78] View the 1998 letter to Richard Hauxwell at www.ftc.gov/os/statutes/fcra/hauxwell.htm.

Some firms wait until an offer has been made first. It will cut down on the initial paperwork. Firms use this approach if they feel a background screening may interfere with effective recruiting. Then the HR, Security Department or the hiring manager will give the finalist the forms at a second interview. Even if forms are not filled out as part of the initial application, it is suggested that applicants still be informed there will be a pre-employment background screening as a standard procedure of the hiring process.

Using Electronic Signatures

A developing procedure is the use of electronic consents. In October, 2000, the Electronic Signatures in Global and National Commence Act (ESIGN) was passed into law.[79] Section 101(a) of the act provides that—

"(a) . . . Notwithstanding any statute, regulation, or other rule of law (other than this title and title II), with respect to any transaction in or affecting interstate or foreign commerce -(1) a signature, contract, or other record relating to such transaction may not be denied legal effect, validity, or enforceability solely because it is in electronic form."

The FTC issued an opinion on the issue of electronic authorization in the Zalenski letter issued May 24, 2001.[80] The FTC concluded that in view of the ESIGN Act, it was possible to use electronic signatures for authorization for a background check. The FTC indicated that whether or not the electronic signature is valid depends on the specific facts of each situation. Specifically, the electronic signature must clearly convey the consumer's instructions.

The FTC stated that as specified by Section 101(e) of the ESIGN Act, that a consumer's electronic authorization "must be in a form that can be retained and retrieved in perceivable form." In other words there must be a clear and reproducible record showing the electronic consent.

There are no approved or accepted standards on what type of procedure satisfies this requirement. In legal terms, the concept of authorization or consent means "an agreement to do something" or to "allow something to happen," and made with complete knowledge of all relevant facts such as the risks involved or any available alternatives.

---

[79] See 15USC Sec. 7001 et. seq.

[80] View the 2001 Zalenski letter at www.ftc.gov/os/statutes/fcra/zalenski.htm

> At a minimum, any firm attempting to obtain electronic compliance online should go through a series of screens, each one giving the applicant the chance to continue or to exit.

How the Employer Places a Screening Order

How an order to perform a screening task makes it from the employer to the screening firm depends on the screening firm's methodology. If the screening firm has a web system, then the employer has the ability to key in orders online. If the employer is connected in a seamless interface, then the order's detail and data will automatically transmit without additional key-in. When paper documentation is used, employers and screening companies may prefer the use of fax machines for order communications.

Via Fax or Email

If the employer is faxing an order to a CRA, then an Employee Order Form is typically sent with each order. The form tells the CRA what is being requested, who requested it, and further instructions if necessary. The CRA often customizes a form to reflect the type of screening program the employer requires including the employer's name, contact person, and contact information. To ensure accuracy and avoid delays, the employer needs to confirm that the applicant's name, SSN, driver's license number, and any other data needed to fulfill the order are all accurate and legible.

The form should include the names of past employers and provide the city and state whenever relevant to a reference. The applicant's telephone number could be included so the CRA may contact an applicant directly to clarify anything that is not clear on the form; however, having a screening firm contact the applicant is not always a good practice. An applicant may become concerned or confused, especially if the screening firm is calling to obtain the applicant's SSN or other confidential data.

Electronic, Self-entry System

If an employer utilizes an online system to enter screening orders, the employer needs to first carefully review the application materials before data entry. To save time and avoid data error, if any material is illegible or incomplete, the employer should contact the applicant to clarify.

Some CRAs offer an integrated solution where the data comes seamlessly from the applicant, usually through what is known as an Applicant Tracking System (ATS).

Regardless if the employer uses an online order-entry system, reference resources such as schools and past employers may require a copy of the subject's signed release before providing information.

Even when electronic methods are used, there still may be an occasion when a physical piece of paper must be handled. This occurs when a past employer, school, or DMV requires a written release from the subject. The screening company may need to contact the employer to obtain a physical copy of the subject's release form.

When the Employer Receives the Completed Report

Screening firms using state-of-the-art web-based systems can make reports available to their clients in real time over the Internet. Also, Internet retrieval allows employers to have real-time access to the exact status of the report at anytime. An online system can advise the employer about delays and estimated times of delivery.

Reports also can be faxed or emailed to the employer. A CRA will generally require the fax machine be private and secured. A faxed report should have a cover sheet to warn the unauthorized against seeing confidential information.

When a California, Oklahoma, or Minnesota applicant requests to receive a copy of his credit report, the CRA must provide a copy to the applicant at the same time the employer receives the report.

Probable Turnaround Time

A question often asked of a CRA is "how soon will a report be completed?" A CRA will normally return reports within three to four full business days after receiving the order. For reports involving credential checks on employment or education, extra time may be required. Occasionally there is a delay in obtaining information in a situation where a CRA has no control. For example, it can take longer than three days if there is a potential name match in a criminal case and the court clerk must obtain records from storage. In addition, schools may be closed during the summer or holidays, or employers may not call back or may have merged, moved, or closed. A report can be delayed if a request form is unreadable.

How the Employer Processes the Completed Report

Because the report contains sensitive and confidential information all efforts must be made to keep the contents private and available only to decision-makers directly involved in the hiring process.

The following are recommended best practices; if used, they must be documented in the procedures manual.

- The report itself, along with the Release and Authorization Forms signed by the applicant, should be maintained separately from the employee's personnel file. They should be kept in a relatively secured area, in the same fashion that medical files or sensitive employee matters are kept.

- These reports definitely should not be made available to supervisors or managers other than those in the hiring approval process. For example, during periodic performance appraisals, an employer would not want a supervisor to have access to a non-performance-related confidential background report.

- For employers using screening firms with advanced Internet systems that make a report viewable online, there is in fact no need to physically download the report and keep as a paper file. However, an employer needs to be assured of Internet security, and the employer needs to maintain a system of strong password protections. It is important that authorized users do not share passwords with those not authorized, nor reveal the password in any manner. Some screening firms require the user to change passwords every 30 days as a security measure.

In larger companies, reports are typically returned to either HR or Security Departments. Reports are reviewed for any negative information. If the report is clear, then the hiring manager is notified and the hiring proceeds. If there is a red flag or derogatory information, then the information itself is shared with the appropriate decision-makers. The physical report, however, normally stays with HR or Security. This protects against confidential information wrongfully being made known generally within the company.

Some CRAs carefully monitor their reports to ensure that no information is given to an employer that violates the various rules concerning limitations on what employers can and cannot use in making employment decisions. However, this is a tricky area. A CRA is not acting as an attorney and cannot make legal decisions. On the other hand, there are clear industry-accepted practices about what an employer cannot have.

Some CRAs take the position they are primarily data conduits to the employer, and it is the employer's obligation to not utilize any information an employer should not have. An employer should carefully discuss this issue with a service provider.

Q & A on Other Screening Issues

Can an Employer Screen Some Finalists But Not Others?

No. An important consideration in administering a screening program is that once a decision is made to screen for a particular opening, **all finalists** being considered for that opening should be screened. Selective screenings could raise an inference of discriminatory practice, particularly if the subject is a member of a legally protected group. Furthermore, all screened individuals should be evaluated using the same criteria – for each position, the screening level must be the same for all candidates.

An employer may certainly have different screening requirements for different positions, as described earlier. If there are different screening standards for different positions, then an employer should be able to articulate a rational basis as to why some positions are screened differently. However, all maintenance workers should be screened the same way, and all bookkeepers screened the same way. In addition, not all positions in a firm must be screened. A firm could even decide to stop pre-employment screening in the future. However, for any particular opening, all candidates must be treated the same.

What About Conditional Hiring Based Upon Receipt of the Background Report?

An employer can proceed to hire an applicant with a contingency upon the receipt of an acceptable background report. This may occur when an employer has a difficult position to fill and does not want to risk losing a good candidate.

It is recommended that the offer letter contain the following language—

"This offer of employment is conditioned upon the employer's receipt of a pre-employment background screening investigation that is acceptable to the employer at the employer's sole discretion."

The suggested language specifies that the report must meet the employer's satisfaction so there can be no debate on what constitutes a satisfactory report.

How Long Should Signed Forms and Applicant Records be Kept?

Record-keeping requirements for employers can vary in accordance to the type of document in question. As outlined, the applicable statute of limitations for claims under the FCRA is up to five years. An employer and consumer reporting agency should maintain records concerning pre-employment screening by a CRA for at least six years following a screening, based upon the five-year statute, and an extra year to reflect the amount of time states generally allow to serve a lawsuit.

For employers who utilize the services of a CRA with an advanced Iinternet system, that online system may be set up to archive reports permanently.

There are two reasons why employers also should maintain the background screening authorization forms and disclosure forms as well as any other forms related to ordering a screening report for the same period of time. First, proof may be needed later that the employer had consent for a screening report and a permissible purpose under the FCRA. Second, if a screening firm is audited by a data provider (such as a state motor vehicle department), the applicant's consent may be needed by both the background firm and the employer to demonstrate that the request for information was legal. Many background firms require in their contracts with employers that all such documents will be maintained by the employer and provided to the CRA if necessary for an audit. The data needs to be preserved as well if there is an electronic signature.

General Employment Records

It is generally advisable for an employer to maintain all paperwork concerning the formation of an employment relationship for a period of at least three years from the termination of any relationship. That means if a person is hired, the report and all related screening documentation should be kept during the entire employment relationship and for three years after it terminates. If an applicant is screened and an employment relationship does not occur, then the reports and documents should be maintained for three years from the date of the report. The three-year period should cover any statute of limitations in the event of a claim or lawsuit.

When the Employer Decides Not to Hire the Applicant

An employer does *not* need to specify exactly why an applicant was rejected.

If an employer decides to take any type of adverse action regarding an application for employment, based in any way upon information contained in a screening report, the provisions of the FCRA come into play. The procedures set forth in the FCRA only require the applicant have an opportunity to review the background report prior to an adverse action being taken and be given a statement of his rights. At that point, it is the employer's responsibility to first provide the applicant with a copy of the report and a statement of the consumer's rights. If the applicant does not contest the report and the decision stands, then the employer must send a second notice to the applicant under Section 615 of the FCRA notifying the applicant of a number of specific rights.[81]

If the negative decision is made final, the applicant then receives a letter indicating the action has been made final and was based in part upon the consumer report.

Some CRAs will provide all the necessary notices to the applicant. Although it is the employer's responsibility to provide the pre-adverse and post-adverse action notices, under the rules of the FCRA that duty can be delegated to an agent such as a screening firm. If the applicant disagrees with any of the information contained in the report, then the applicant communicates directly to the CRA. The CRA has a duty under the FCRA to re-investigate within 30 days, and up to 45 days under certain circumstances. The employer, however, has no obligation to keep the position open during the re-investigation period.

The Possibilities of Legal Liabilities

When an employer follows the procedures in the FCRA, and also makes all hiring decisions utilizing legal and job-related reasons, the chances of a lawsuit from a rejected applicant are minimized. If an employer intends to take adverse action based upon a background report, then an applicant must first be provided with a copy of the report and a statement of his rights. Because of this procedure, an applicant has the chance to review the report for accuracy. If the information is inaccurate, then the applicant has the opportunity to object and to offer a correction. At that point, the employer can proceed with the hire. Under the previous system where applicants did not have to be told their reports contained negative or derogatory information and were not given the chance to correct errors, employers ran a greater risk of making hiring decisions based upon incorrect information.

However, no employer can ever make himself immune from a lawsuit. Anyone with enough money to cover the court's filing fee can go to the court and file a lawsuit. There are no court cases where an employer has successfully argued he did not exercise due diligence in his hiring because he was concerned about possible litigation from rejected applicants. Conversely, there are a large number of lawsuits stemming from lack of pre-employment screening and due diligence.

---

[81] This is covered in detail in Chapter 3 and copies of these notices appear in the Appendix.

Screening Current Employees

When setting or reviewing background-checking policies, a question often arises about whether current employees should be screened, or whether the background-check policy should apply to new applicants only.

The need to screen current employees can be necessitated by a new contract with a customer who requires all workers performing the contract have a background check. It can also occur when a firm acquires another workforce through a merger or acquisition. There also can be need-to-screen situations where an employer is concerned about some type of workplace misconduct such as theft or harassment.

There are two factors to consider in screening current employees – legal and practical.

It is perfectly **legal** to screen current employees as long as all their rights are respected. A current employee is entitled to the same legal rights as a new applicant, and if there is a union involved, perhaps even more rights. Under the FCRA, if the background check is performed by a third-party service provider, then current employees are entitled to the same rights as new applicants, which includes a disclosure of rights and written consent. Some states have additional rules that employers must be mindful to follow. If an existing employee is screened for allegations of wrongdoing or misconduct, then his consent may not be needed per the 2003 amendment to the FCRA.

The **practical consideration** is whether the employer wants to ask existing employees to consent to a background check. The issue is one of corporate culture – alienating employees who have been hardworking and loyal by performing background checks.

If an employer decides it is necessary to screen current employees, then it is recommended that HR explain that screening is "a business necessity for the good of the entire organization" and not directed at any employee. This will increase employee buy-in. Equally critical is for employees to understand all their rights are being respected and nothing will occur as a result of a background check until the employee has an opportunity to discuss any negative findings with the employer. Problems can arise if an employee feels powerless in the process or concerned about an adverse action without an opportunity to be heard. It is crucial to tell all employees they may come to HR to privately discuss the procedure. An employee may start off talking about privacy concerns, when in fact there is something of concern in the person's background.

Another consideration: an existing employee may not sign a consent form. That has not proved to be an issue of a practical matter. If employees have a clear understanding of how this policy helps both the employer and the employee, then there is typically good employee buy-in. However, in a worst-case scenario where an employee absolutely refuses to consent, an employer can take the following tack – let the employee know that he has the right not to consent. On the other hand, just as the employee has a right not to consent, the next time the employee is up for a pay raise or promotion, the employer equally has the right not to promote or give a raise. This tactic may be considered if a current employee refuses to sign a consent form before the employer takes the more difficult track of termination.

Kelchner v. Sycamore Manor Health Center

In the first court case to address the issue of an employee not consenting, a Federal District Court in Pennsylvania decided that an employer can terminate a current employee who refused to sign a consent for a background check. In Kelchner v. Sycamore Manor Health Center, 2004 U.S. Dist. Lexis 2942 (M.D. Pa. 2004), the employer required all employees to sign a consent to a consumer report. A worker with 19 years on the job refused to sign and was terminated. The Court held that the plain language of the statute as well as Congressional intent demonstrated that employers had the right to require such a consent and could terminate if an employee refused, just as an employer could refuse to hire an applicant who did not consent in the first place.

If Screening Results Lead to Possible Termination Issues

What if the screening of a current employee results in a decision to terminate? If the screening reveals the applicant had a criminal conviction not indicated on the application, then an employer could choose to terminate for dishonesty. However, keep in mind that the exact wording of the criminal question on the employment application is critical. If the employer only asked about felonies, then an undisclosed misdemeanor – even a serious misdemeanor – may not be grounds to terminate for dishonesty. An employee may give other reasons why failure to disclose was not an act of dishonesty. An employee may claim that he did not realize it was a conviction or claim he did not understand what the judge or his lawyer told them. Some defendants enter a plea of *nolo contendere* or "no contest." Although that may give a criminal defendant some protection if he is later sued in a civil court, a "no contest" plea has the same effect as pleading guilty.

Suppose the screening of existing employees reveals a criminal record that was not mentioned in the application or interview process. This is potential grounds for termination, providing the employer's application form put applicants on notice that any material misstatement or omission is grounds for termination no matter when discovered. The situation becomes difficult when the employee claims he did inform the manager of past difficulties, but the manager failed to inform HR. The solution is to ensure that all pre-hire procedures are followed and documented, and all managers are trained in the hiring procedures.

In addition, if the screening discloses an offense that occurs *after* the hiring, the employer may decide to take action. However, the EEOC rules previously outlined take affect. The employer must take into account the nature and gravity of the offense, how long ago it occurred, and whether it is job-related in order to determine if there is a business necessity to deny continued employment.

An employer also should document any decision *not* to terminate in case the employer has to defend a decision to terminate some employees with criminal records and not others. If the employer has a written policy that requires employees to inform the employer if a criminal conviction occurs after employment begins, then an employer can take the position that the termination is a result of a violation of a written company policy. As a practical matter, an employer would likely be aware of any serious criminal matter after employment commences, since an employee may not show up to work or need time off for court appearances. If an employee is arrested and not able to come to work, then an employer should examine the employee manual to determine the company's rule for unexcused absences.

If termination is considered, then the employer needs to be mindful of the FCRA requirements for pre-adverse action. An employee cannot simply be brought into the office and given his final paycheck. The FCRA requires a **pre-adverse action notice**, giving the employee a meaningful opportunity to review, reflect, and respond to the consumer report if the employee feels it is inaccurate or incomplete. One method is to meet with the employee, explain that a matter of concern came up in the screening report, and to provide the employee with a copy of the report and a statement of his rights prepared by the FTC, which the employer can acquire from a screening firm. The employee also should be provided a letter advising him to respond to the employer or the screening firm as soon as possible, if there is anything the employee wishes to challenge or explain.

Since, by definition, the employer notice is pre-adverse action, an employer may consider placing the employee on three days paid administrative leave with instructions to either contact the employer in three days, if the employee plans to contest the consumer report, or the leave will turn into a termination. If the employer does not hear back, then the employee is terminated.

If the applicant notifies the employer of plans to contest the report, then the employer can make a case-by-case judgment to either continue the employment, or continue the unpaid leave, or terminate pending a resolution of the re-investigation with a right to reapply. The FCRA does not require the employer keep a job open or keep an employee on paid leave during the re-investigation period, but only requires a meaningful opportunity to receive notice of pre-adverse action and to deal with the report before the adverse action is taken. If the decision to terminate becomes final, then the employee is entitled to the second FCRA post-adverse action letter. The decision to place on leave also can be affected by the provisions of the employee manual or the existence of union contracts.

Employee Misconduct Issues

Another situation where a background check may be warranted involves workplace misconduct, such as theft, harassment, or threats of violence. The investigation of current employees by employer may take place without FCRA consents, subject to some requirements, such as if an adverse action was taken that there be disclosure.

Continuous Screening

A new, evolving screening practice for existing employees is called continuous screening. The concept is this: although a background screening is typically conducted at the point of hire, it is possible that after a person is hired, an offense can be committed. A continuous-screening program is aimed at running periodic criminal records checks. These periodic checks have the potential to identify criminal cases, but there are a number of factors to consider—

- **False Sense of Security.** Since private employers generally do not have access to the FBI national criminal database, such ongoing screening programs are based upon running various proprietary criminal databases, and not by sending researchers to actual courthouses. As discussed previously, these proprietary databases are subject to a number of potential error factors.

- **Consent Issue.** Employers must ensure that such searches are done with consent. In California for example, it is arguable that such continuous searches require a new consent each and every time it is done in order to comply with California state law. Another issue is whether an employer can legally not hire someone, or terminate someone, because he refuses to consent to ongoing criminal record checks.

- **What to do if a Record is Found and EEOC Considerations.** If HR conducts continuous criminal checking and finds a record, then the employer needs a written policy and procedure on how to respond to the information legally. Under the EEOC rules, a criminal record cannot be utilized to automatically terminate an employee without some business justification. There are also restrictions on the use of arrests. Employers need to exercise caution in how such records are utilized, and to determine what type of record may be relevant to employment.

- **Impact on Workforce:** Another issue is the impact on the workforce for checking on a bi-weekly or monthly basis to see if current employees have become crooks. There may be some industries where the risk factor justifies continuous checking.

Although such continuous searches can be a valuable risk-management tool, an employer needs to understand the limitation to the searches and the issues surrounding the legal use of such data. Remember, too, if an employee commits an offense that is serious, an employer will be made aware an issue exists by the employee's absence from work. One possible solution for employers considering continuous screening – use a random pool similar to drug testing, and perform your searches at the actual courthouse.

The Importance of Consistency and Scope

Critical in nearly every area of employee screening, similarly situated people should be treated in a similar fashion. Proper pre-employment screening does not mean all applicants must be screened exactly the same. What it does mean is that all applicants who are finalists for a particular job should receive the same level of scrutiny. A firm may choose to screen in more detail those candidates for a vice president's position than those applying to be on the maintenance crew. All vice presidential applicants should be screened in the same way, while a maintenance worker candidate should be screened like all other maintenance worker candidates.

All applicants do not have to be submitted to an outside agency performing background screening. An employer might elect to utilize only those services for a finalist or finalists. Regardless, each similarly situated finalist should be screened in the same fashion. Similarly, if background checks are handled in-house, it is acceptable only to perform the courthouse searches for those individuals who you have narrowed down to be potential new hires, as long as it is done consistently.

The degree of scrutiny for any particular category of jobs is determined by a number of factors, such as access to money or assets, the level of authority over others, or access to the public or co-workers. Also, employers should take into account the difficulty faced in replacing the new hire if he or she does not work out, or the damage that could be done to the organization's productivity if an incompetent person is hired in that position.

Once an employer has determined how intensively the position should be researched, then all finalists for this job level should receive consistent treatment. There are laws working against you if you don't.

Chapter Summary

This Chapter provides information for **Audit Questions 21-24**.

Audit Question #21:   Are the mechanics of your screening program documented?

Best Practices #21:

- At the point or stage in the hiring process, e.g. only the finalists are subject to screening.

- There is a matrix showing the degree of screening for each position.

- The documentation shows there are uniform screening procedures; similarly situated applicants are treated in the same non-discriminatory manner; when screening begins it is documented.

- Storage and retention of reports are separate from personnel files.

- Each step in working with a screening company is pre-determined, documented, and then implemented.

Audit Question #22: If screening is outsourced to a third-party firm, can the employer demonstrate due diligence and show procedures are being used per FCRA?

Best Practices #22:

- Employer agrees and certifies that laws will be followed, e.g. not discriminate; use for employment purposes only.

- The employer obtains the applicant's written release/disclosure on a stand-alone document.

- If adverse information is found, the employer prepares a pre-adverse action copy of report and statement of rights and gives to applicant so applicant can object the information is inaccurate or incomplete.

- A second letter is sent to applicant if a non-hiring decision, based on the adverse information, is made final.

- All forms, including those provided by a screening firm, are reviewed for legal compliance.

- Employer is aware many states have their own rules on screening and obeys these rules.

Audit Question #23: Are procedures in place if a person with negative information is hired?

Best Practices #23:

- Firm has examined the support, supervision, and structure needed to improve the chances of the applicant's success.

- Firm has considered the nature of the job and the circumstances of the past offense and takes appropriate measures to protect the firm, co-workers, and the public from harm.

- Firm has documented all decision-making related factors.

Audit Question #24: Are procedures in place if employment is offered before a background check is completed?

Best Practices #24:

- If employment begins before completion of a background check, there is a written statement that employment is conditioned upon receiving a background report that is satisfactory to the employer.

- The policy eliminates a possible debate over what is an acceptable background report.

Chapter 11

Screening Essential Non-Employees

Employers know the goal of safe hiring is to find individuals who are qualified and fit for their position in the organization. The same due diligence should be applied to the vendors, independent contractors, volunteers, or temporary employees hired by the organization.

This chapter gives instructional guidelines on how to lessen the liability issues when hiring these individuals.

Audit Question # 25:

Does your organization have written policies, practices, and procedures for screening essential non-employees?

What Are the Employer's Screening Duties?

Up to this point, *The Safe Hiring Audit* has emphasized that employers are sitting ducks for expensive litigation, workplace violence, negative national publicity, and economic loss if they do not take measures to conduct pre-employment screening and exercise due diligence in hiring.

Many employers do not realize they potentially face the same exposure from vendors, independent contractors, volunteers, or temporary employees from staffing firms. Employers' risk management controls often do not take into account the 'need to know' about these workers who are not on their payroll but are on their premises or job sites, with access to computer systems, clients, co-workers, and assets.

The practical issue for employers is how they ensure that vendors or workers hired by third parties are safe and qualified. Fortunately, there are a number of cost-effective avenues available to employers to protect their businesses, their workers, and the public. Employers can insist in any contract for any service that any time a worker comes on premises, that worker has been the subject of a background screening. This has become a practice which is gaining widespread acceptance by American businesses. An employer *must* have a hard and fast rule – no worker supplied by a third party is allowed to work unless the worker has a background check.

Suggested Best Practices

The following steps can help in administering the process—

- Make it clear to all current service providers and independent contractors that the business has a background-checking policy for its own employees, and the same policies apply to all workers supplied by a vendor, or to work performed by third-party vendors.

- Subject independent contractors to the same screening and safe hiring practices as would be done with a W-2 employee. Some employers may wish to alter the consent form in order to clarify that the individual being screened is an "independent contractor," and that "the screening procedure does not alter the nature of the relationship."

- When using a temporary worker from a staffing firm, require the staffing agency or Professional Employer Organization (PEO) to conduct a background check. As an extra precaution, an employer can request that the FCRA release extend to the employer's workplace. Under the FCRA, as long as the applicant consents to this, it is perfectly acceptable for both the staffing firm and the employer at the workplace to review the background report.

- A vendor must certify there has been a background check that is acceptable under the employer's criteria.

- The vendor must provide the employer with the name and identity of the firm performing the background check, and a statement that the firm performing the background checks is experienced and suitable for the assignment.

- For extra precaution, require the vendor to provide the employer with a "Certification of Compliance." This certification should indicate the following—

  o The name, identity, and qualifications of the firm that provided the vendor's background checks.

  o A statement that the vendor has advised his background service of the criteria required.

  o Only workers who pass the background check are allowed on your premises.

  o In the event there is something negative in the worker's background, the vendor has thoroughly investigated the issue and has determined the matter does not otherwise disqualify the worker from going onto your premises.

  o In the event there is negative material, then the business may ask to review it to determine if the worker meets the business's criteria. The best practice is to require the vendor to have the worker sign a release permitting that process.

Employers often ask if these policies are illegal and will the policies make it more difficult to find vendors and suppliers of services. The answer is a resounding *no* to both questions. An employer has an absolute right to exercise the same due diligence in selecting vendors that he would use in selecting his own employees. As long as the screening requirements are fair, non-discriminatory, and validly job-related, there is no legal reason why an employer cannot take protective action.

In this way, vendors and suppliers also demonstrate that safe hiring and due diligence are critical parts of their business. Any vendor not willing to engage in pre-employment screening is not likely to be a good choice anyway. Although there may be a slight increase to the vendor in terms of expenses, a vendor should be willing to pay necessary costs to obtain good workers and to satisfy the needs of employer-clients.

Safe Hiring Tip ➤ Employers must be careful. Make sure the vendor, staffing firm, or PEO does more than go through the motions. Reports must be ordered, tracked, and documented. The employer must require the vendor to certify that he has reviewed the screening reports looking for any red flags, and has taken appropriate steps. Although this may seem obvious, it is worth clarifying who has the responsibility to review background reports and determine eligibility to work. [82]

The bottom line is there is no reason for employers not to require that vendors and independent contractors undergo background checks.

Let's look at several categories of essential non-employees and the particular practices and policies that an employer may want to implement when hiring.

Screening Vendors and Independent Contractors

The law is absolutely clear that if a vendor or independent contractor harms a member of the public or a co-worker, the employer can be just as liable as if the person were on the employer's payroll. All of the rules of due diligence in hiring apply with equal force to vendors, temporary workers, or independent contractors. A business can be liable if, in the exercise of reasonable care, the business should have known that a vendor, temporary worker, or independent contractor was dangerous, unqualified, or otherwise unfit for employment. An employer has an absolute obligation to exercise due diligence not only in whom he hires on payroll, but also in whom he allows on the premises to perform work.[83]

In addition, many employers have found out the hard way that unscreened workers from a vendor or staffing firm or hired as an independent contractor can cause damage. When an employer is the victim of theft, embezzlement, or resume fraud, the harm is just as bad regardless of whether the worker is on his payroll or someone else's. No employer would dream of walking down the street and handing the keys to the business to a total stranger, yet many employers across America essentially do exactly that everyday when engaging the services of vendors and temporary workers.

---

[82] See e.g. a compilation of cases throughout the U.S. annotated in 78 ALR3d 910

[83] See e.g. a compilation of cases throughout the U.S. annotated in 78 ALR3d 910.

For example, firms routinely hire nighttime janitorial services without appropriate due diligence. Employers in the fast food industry routinely hire suppliers and service firms that come into their restaurants to clean or deliver supplies. Without knowing who has the keys to facilities, an employer is giving total strangers unfettered access to his business, and is totally exposed to the risk of theft of property, trade secrets, or other damages.

Case law from courts throughout the U.S. makes it clear that businesses have liability for acts of independent contractors. The duty of care must be exercised in all aspects of hiring, and it applies to retaining the services of a vendor or independent contractor.

Employment-Like Nature of the Relationship

Another issue for an employer is that an independent contractor may be misclassified and is, in fact, an employee. A business may have an incentive to classify a worker as an independent contactor rather than an employee in order to avoid paying benefits, overtime, employer taxes like withholding, workers' compensation, or unemployment insurance. The IRS along with state agencies and courts look closely at the true nature of the labor relationship, and not what the parties choose to call it. IRS' 20-point guideline is the most-often used determiner of the true nature of the relationship. As example guidelines, true independent contractors may have business cards, insurance, and yellow page advertising. True independent contractors would probably provide their services to multiple businesses. However, a firm that hires a so-called independent contractor who works under the firm's direction and control – and the so-called contractor does not provide the same services to other firms, and does not have insurance, a business license, or other typical attributes of a true independent business – is likely to be considered an employee in disguise. Proper employee classification is an important issue for a business, especially if an event occurs that triggers an audit such as an "independent contractor" filing a workers' compensation claim, or seeking unemployment insurance payments. If an employer is found to have misclassified workers as independent contractors instead of payroll employees, the business can be held accountable for back taxes and all payments to state programs that should have been made, as well as fines and penalties.

In addition, the FTC has suggested that the FCRA applies to situations where a consumer has an employment like relationship regardless of the label. FTC staff-issued letters of opinion following the 1997 amendment to the FCRA – although the letters do not have the force of law – are considered highly persuasive. In the

Herman L. Allison letter dated February 23, 1998, the FTC staff was asked if the FCRA rules concerning disclosures and releases applied in the case of a certain trucking company that employed independent owner-operators. The truck drivers were not on the payroll as employees, but "owned and operated their own vehicles." The FTC rejected the position that there was not an employment relationship. The FTC cited a Fourth Circuit Court of Appeals case[84] that the broad purposes of the FCRA required that "employment" not be strictly defined in traditional terms, but would include independent contractor relationships. As a result, the application of the FCRA does not depend upon whether a worker receives a W-2 tax form as an employee *or* a 1099 as an independent contractor. The essential factor is the employment-like nature of the relationship. Keep in mind, if an employer has classified a worker as an independent contractor, it is critical to adjust the background screening consent form to take out any reference to employment. An employer can utilize wording referring to an "engagement" instead.

Staffing Firms and Temporary Workers

Employers would not intentionally bring people on the premises with criminal records, unsuitable for a particular job, yet they consistently hire temporary workers and independent contractors from staffing agencies with no idea who these people are. Employers hire temporary workers from agencies often without any assurance as to their backgrounds or qualifications. Consider this: given the sensitive information found on business computer systems, even one bad temp could do substantial damage.

Most staffing firms do not routinely perform due diligence checks before supplying workers. Staffing firms often do not want to incur the costs associated with doing background checks on workers they place. That reluctance is for two reasons. First, staffing firms are exceptionally cost conscious and given the large volume of workers they handle, the cost of background checks, such as criminal checks, has a significant impact on their bottom line. Second, staffing firms must work on an extremely tight time line. Staffing firms need to place workers as soon as possible. Every hour of delay is lost revenue to a staffing firm. If a potential worker is told to wait a day or two for a background check, that worker may go down the street to another staffing firm.

---

[84] *Hoke v. Retail Credit Corporation,* 521 F.2d 1079, 1082 (4th Cir. 1975), *cert. denied,* 423 U.S. 1087 (1976).

Staffing firms often advertise "we carefully screen all applicants," but without stating the extent of the screening. A business utilizing staffing services needs to be very specific when asking exactly what screening is done. Unless the staffing firm specifically tells the employer a criminal check is being done, an employer should assume that no criminal check is being conducted. An employer is well advised to require some of the steps suggested in the previous pages in order to confirm exactly what is being done in terms of a criminal background check. Issues regarding screening and criteria should be specifically addressed in any contract between a business and the staffing vendor.

A staffing firm and employer can have a "co-employment relationship" with temporary workers. Co-employment has been defined as a legal relationship in which more than one employer has legal rights and obligations with respect to the same employee or group of employees. Both the IRS and various courts have found that a temporary worker of a supplier working at the customer's work site – even though paid and treated as an employee of the supplier – may still be considered an employee of both the supplier and the customer for legal purposes. The employer sets the specific duties, the duration of the assignment, and the level and types of skills required even though the staffing firm is responsible for recruitment, placement, and pay rates.

From the Staffing Firm's Prospective

Staffing firms and recruiters need to be very clear with a client on the issue of background checks, including if they are performed, who pays for them, what criteria are used, and who reviews the reports. If a business wants to review the background report, the staffing firm should ensure that the worker has signed an appropriate release.

Consider implementing the following best practices—

- Carefully review any marketing materials and sales presentation to ensure that clients are accurately informed about your practices. Do not imply that your firm "carefully screens" or only "sends the best" if in fact you are not doing adequate background checks.
- Make sure your contracts with clients accurately describe what if any background checks you will be doing. Consider—
  - Depth and level of screening
  - Who reviews reports, what criteria are used, and who makes decisions on eligibility
  - Who selects the screening firms

  o Adequacy of consent issue – consent forms need to release information to both the staffing firm and employer.

Remember: even though workers may be on the payroll of a staffing agency, since the workers perform duties at an employer's place of business, the employer can certainly be liable for harm a worker causes.

Screening Volunteers

Over the past few years, there has been a substantial increase in volunteer groups, youth organizations, and churches performing background checks. Criminal record checks have become standard procedures for organizations like the Little League or Scouts. The increased emphasis on these checks has been fueled by numerous news stories and lawsuits about children being the victims of criminal conduct, especially sexual abuse. Unfortunately, in today's world, the fact remains that sex offenders and deviants exploit volunteer, youth, and faith-based organizations to gain access to potential victims. Doing background checks will help protect children and the vulnerable from criminals.

Certain states have legislation permitting organizations to take advantage of state fingerprinting or criminal record programs. On October 9, 1998, President Clinton signed the **Volunteers for Children Act** into law – Public Law 105-251 – amending the National Child Protection Act of 1993. Organizations and businesses involving children, elderly, or the disabled now may use national fingerprint-based criminal history checks to screen out volunteers and employees with relevant criminal records.

The Wisconsin Attorney General's Office has produced an excellent brochure describing not only its state program, but also the federal act and how to obtain FBI background checks; see www.doj.state.wi.us/dles/cib/forms/brochures/vol_children.pdf

The same office also provides a website listing state sites where volunteer organizations can obtain fingerprint information. See www.doj.state.wi.us/dles/cib/sclist.asp.

Safe Hiring Tip ➤ A question that often arises is whether a screening of a volunteer needs to be conducted under the FCRA, since the volunteer is not paid. The best practice is still to operate under the FCRA. There is no requirement under the FCRA that a person is only considered to be *employed* if he is paid in *monetary form*. Also, as noted earlier, the FTC takes the position that the FCRA is given broad interpretation to protect consumer's rights. Therefore, you should not assume the FCRA does not apply because a person is a volunteer.

One beneficial idea for volunteer organizations is to use the services of private firms for fast, low-cost background checks. Also, using the criminal offender databases described earlier provides low-cost and instant searches of some sexual offender database information. Although a very valuable tool, these "offender databases" should be used with caution since they do not cover all states and they are not exhaustive, meaning that volunteers and individuals with criminal records can escape detection. Any organization planning to perform background checks must very carefully review its own situation, including resources available in its state, to develop a cost-effective program. In addition, organizations should consider no-cost tools, such as reference checking, to weed out potential problems.

Workers in the Home

There are horror stories about innocent and unsuspecting people who opened their doors to home service providers or workers, and became the victims of serious crimes, including murder, in their own homes. Routinely, home owners casually allow workers in to deliver appliances or furniture, act as nannies or caregivers, clean carpets, perform household repairs such as plumbing or electrical, kill pests, and a multitude of other tasks.

Unfortunately, people are particularly vulnerable in their homes. Good help is harder to get, and if there are children, senior citizens, or a disabled person at home, the risks are greater. Yet, no state except Texas currently requires background checks on workers who enter homes. Results are tragic.

U.S. courts have held employers liable for negligence when their workers were found to have committed crimes in the home. An employer obviously does not send a worker into the home to steal, murder, or sexually assault, and certainly, criminal action is not in the scope and course of the employee's duties. However, employers are held to a higher standard of care in view of the inherent risks involved in sending workers into homes. Employers can be found negligent for not only hiring someone who they should have known was dangerous, unqualified or unfit, but also for failure to supervise, train, or properly assign workers. If an employer was on notice that a current worker was unsafe, and retained the person anyway, then that employer can be sued for negligent retention.[85]

The $9 Million Service Call

According to a news article by the *Daytona Beach News-Journal Online*, a civil case was settled for $9 million when a well-know air conditioner repair firm sent a worker who was a twice convicted sex offender to a home and he killed the home owner. According to the June 1, 2004 article, the repairman cleaned the air ducts and then returned six months later and raped and murdered the victim. According to the news study, a criminal background check would have revealed the repairman's criminal past. The victim's family has started an organization called the Sue Weaver CAUSE (Consumer Awareness of Unsafe Service Employment) to raise awareness that not all contractors can be trusted.

Hiring Seasonal or Temporary Contract Personnel

Industries with large hourly, seasonal, or temporary contract workforces typically include hospitality and tourism, manufacturing, service, retail, food and restaurants, drug and groceries stores, and call centers. Compounding their hiring problems are multiple locations and large turnovers.

Unicru is an employment assistance firm that specializes in total workforce acquisitions solutions for specific industries, usually with large hourly workforces. According to a 2002 special report by Unicru—

"In the United States, over 90 million workers – more than 80 percent of the labor pool – are hourly or front-line employees. On an annual basis, large companies will hire far more hourly workers than salaried or professional staff.

The mechanics of hiring from these two segments are vastly different. Hiring cycles for salaried personnel are longer than for hourly workers. The former tend to apply to positions and/or organizations in large numbers, while the latter tend to apply in much smaller numbers to locations within five miles of their homes. Psychologically, hourly workers feel

---

[85] See ALR5th 21 for an article entitled, *Employer's Liability for Assaults, Theft or Similar Intentional Wrong Committed by Employee at Home or Business of Customer.*

much more pressure to find work quickly and tend to be on the market for only a few days, while a salaried candidate's shelf life is measured in months. A manager of salaried staff will typically interview only three candidates for a position and hire one person or less per year, but a location or store manager will hire more than 15 people per year, interviewing an average of five applicants per position. In the salaried workforce, turnover is less than 10 percent; it is 6 to 10 times that among hourly employees."[86]

The challenge is greater if the firm is engaged in providing services that have a greater degree of risk to third parties. For example, resorts hiring seasonally have greater exposure because of the fact children are present during their peak seasons. If temporary or seasonal employees are involved in higher risk activities in roles as lifeguards, ski instructors, or other similar jobs, then the stakes are higher.

So, how do industries with significant turnover – or with large numbers of hourly, seasonal, temporary, or contract workers – protect themselves in a cost-effective and efficient manner? Employers are under pressure to reduce the time and cost per hire by minimizing those costs and delays associated with pre-employment screening. A cost-effective solution is to devise a mechanism that incorporates the elements of the SHP along with reasonable and appropriate background checks. A key element is to emphasize tools that discourage applicants with something to hide in the first place, and encourage early self-disclosure of negative information while using AIR Process described in previous chapters in an assembly-line fashion.

At a minimum, run a basic public records search. It is essential to run a Social Security Trace, and at least one county criminal record check. If any driving is involved, then a driving record also should be run. Of course, if it is a driving position regulated by the Department of Transportation, or for any other position that is regulated by federal or state rules, then all applicable laws must be followed.

About Hiring Juveniles

Hiring juveniles presents special problems. Juvenile records are typically not public and criminal records are difficult to acquire unless the juvenile was tried as an adult. Juvenile workers and young workers usually do not have a significant employment

---

[86] See www.unicru.com/literature/whitepapers/SalariedVsHourlyHiring.pdf. Unicru main website is www.unicru.com

history. Employers, however, can require that youths provide at least two letters of recommendation from non-family members or teachers who know them. This procedure helps eliminate those applicants without the initiative to obtain such letters, and helps an employer show *some* due diligence in hiring.

Parental consent and state child labor laws are issues; if an employer is only obtaining public records, verifying past employment information or school attendance, parental consent is probably not required, in the absence of a specific state law. Consents are not intrusive and there are FCRA protections. If parental consent is available, it does add extra protection.

In Conclusion—

Although the cost of background checks can add up for large hiring programs, employers are still held to a standard of due diligence when hiring for hourly, temporary, or seasonal employees, or volunteers. If sued, an employer might assert the defense that imposing the requirement of doing background checks was too costly of a burden to place on employers, but such a defense is not likely to succeed. Courts have taught employers that the cost of safe hiring is minor when compared to the possible harm not performing the check could cause.

CEOs, hiring mangers, and business owners who take the position that safe hiring and pre-employment screening are not important or are too expensive need to carefully review the true economics of their firms and the risk factors involved from a single bad hire.

Chapter Summary

This Chapter provides information for **Audit Question 25**.

Audit Question #25: Does the organization have written policies, practices, and procedures for screening essential non-employees?

Best Practices #25:

- The company's safe hiring commitment covers the extended workforce – temporary workforce, independent contractors, and vendors.

- An organization should not assume the FCRA does not apply just because a person is a volunteer.

- Employers need to be careful to make sure the vendor, staffing firm, or Professional Employer Organization (PEO) certify that they have reviewed the screening reports looking for any red flags, and that they took appropriate steps.

The Appendix

The Appendix contains legal notices, forms, charts, and other tools to assist employers. The Appendix is divided into 6 sections as follows—

Appendix 1: FCRA Summaries

Appendix F to Part 698 - General Summary of Consumer Rights

The prescribed form for this summary is a disclosure that it substantially similar to the Commission's model summary with all information clearly and prominently displayed. The list of federal regulators that is included in the Commission's prescribed summary may be provided separately so long as this is done in a clear and conspicuous way. A summary should accurately reflect changes to those items that may change over time (e.g., dollars amounts, or telephone numbers and addresses of federal agencies) to remain in compliance. Translation of this summary will be in compliance with the Commission's prescribed model, provided that the translation is accurate and that it is provided in a language used by the recipient consumer.

Para informatcion en espanol, visite www.ftc.gov/credit o escribe a la FTC Consumer Response Center, Room 130-A 600 Pennsylvania Ave. N.W., Washington, DC 20580.

A Summary of Your Rights Under the Fair Credit Reporting Act

The federal Fair Credit Reporting Act (FCRA) promotes promote accuracy, fairness and privacy of information in the files of consumer reporting agencies. There are many varieties of consumer reporting agencies, including credit bureaus and specialty agencies (such as agencies that sell information about check writing histories, medical records, and rental history records). Here is a summary of your major rights under the FCRA For more information, including information about additional rights, go to www.ftc.gov/credit or write to: Consumer Response Center, Room 130-A, Federal Trade Commission, 600 Pennsylvania Ave. N.W., Washington, DC 20580.

- **You must be told if information in your file has been used against you.** Anyone who uses a credit report or another type of consumer report to deny your application for credit, insurance, or employment – or to take another adverse action against you – must tell you, and must give you the name, address and phone number of the CRA that provided the information.

- **You have the right to know what is in your file.** You may request and obtain all the information about you in the files of a consumer reporting agency (your "file disclosure"). You will be required to provide proper identification, which may include your Social Security number. In many cases, the disclosure will be free. You are entitled to a free file disclosure if:

- o   a person has taken adverse action against you because of information in your credit report;

- o   you are a victim of identity theft and place a fraud alert in your file; your file contains inaccurate information as a result of fraud;

- o   you are on public assistance;

- o   you are unemployed but expect to apply for employment within 60 days.

- In addition, by September 2005 all consumers will be entitled to one free disclosure every 12 months upon request from each nationwide credit bureau and from nationwide specialty consumer reporting agencies. See www.ftc.gov/credit for additional information.

- **You have the right to ask for a credit score.** Credit scores are numerical summaries of your credit worthiness based on information from credit bureaus. You may request a credit score from consumer reporting agencies that create scores or distribute scores used in residential real property loans, but you will have to pay for it. In some mortgage transactions, you will receive credit score information for free from the mortgage lender.

- **You have the right to dispute incomplete or inaccurate information.** If you identify information in your file that is incomplete or inaccurate and report it to the consumer reporting agency, the agency must investigate unless your dispute is frivolous. See www.ftc.gov/credit for an explanation of dispute procedures.

- **Consumer reporting agencies must correct or delete inaccurate, incomplete, or unverifiable information.** Inaccurate, incomplete or unverifiable information must be removed or corrected, usually within 30 days. However, a consumer reporting agency may continue to report information it has verified as accurate.

- **Consumer reporting agencies may not report outdated negative information.** In most cases, a consumer reporting agency may not report negative information that is more than seven years old, or bankruptcies that are more than 10 years old.

- **Access to your file is limited.** A credit reporting agency may provide information about you only to people with a valid need -- usually to consider an application with a creditor, insurer, employer, landlord, or other business. The FCRA specifies those with a valid need for access.

- **You must give your consent for reports to be provided to employers.** A consumer reporting agency may not give out information about you to your employer, or a potential employer, without your written consent given to the employer. Written consent generally is not required in the trucking industry. For more, go to www.ftc.gov/credit.

- **You may limit "prescreened" offers of credit and insurance you get based on information in your credit report.** Unsolicited "prescreened" offers for credit and insurance must include a toll-free phone number you can call if you choose to remove your name and address from the lists these offers are based on. You may opt-out with the nationwide credit bureaus at 1-800-XXX-XXXX.

- **You may seek damages from violators.** If a consumer reporting agency, or, in some cases, a user of consumer reports or a furnisher of information to a consumer reporting agency violates the FCRA, you may be able to sue in state or federal court.

- **Identity Theft victims and active duty military personnel have additional right.** For more information, visit www.ftc.gov.credit.

State may enforce the FCRA, and many states have their own consumer reporting laws. In some cases, you may have more rights under state law. For more information, contact your state or local consumer protection agency or your state Attorney General. Federal enforcers are:

TYPE OF BUSINESS:	CONTACT:
Consumer reporting agencies, creditors and others not listed below	**Federal Trade Commission: Consumer Response Ctr - FCRA**, Washington, DC 20580; 877-382-4357
National banks, federal branches/agencies of foreign banks (word "National" or initials "N.A." appear in or after bank's name)	**Office of the Comptroller of the Currency** Compliance Management, Mail Stop 6-6, Washington, DC 20219; 1-800-613-6743
Federal Reserve System member banks (except national banks and federal branches/agencies of foreign banks)	**Federal Reserve Board Division of Consumer & Community Affairs**, Washington, DC 205551 202-452-3693
Savings associations and federally chartered savings banks (word "Federal" or initials "F.S.B." appear in the federal institution's name)	**Office of Thrift Supervision** Consumer Complaints, Washington, DC 20552; 800-842-6929
Federal credit unions (words "Federal Credit Union" appear in institution's name)	**National Credit Union Administration** 1775 Duke St, Alexandria, VA 22314; 703-519-4600
State-chartered banks that are not members of the Federal Reserve System	**Federal Deposit Insurance Corporation,** Consumer Response Center, 2345 Grand Ave, Suite 100, Kansas City, MO 64108-2638; 1-877-275-3342
Air, surface, or rail common carriers regulated by former Civil Aeronautics Board of Interstate Commerce Commission	**Department of Transportation,** Office of Financial Management, Washington, DC 20590; 202-366-1306
Activities subject to the Packers and Stockyards Act of 1921	**Department of Agriculture,** Office of Deputy Admin. - GIPSA, Washington, DC 20590; 202-720-7051

Appendix G to Part 698 – Notice of Furnisher Responsibilities

The prescribed form for this disclosure is a separate document that is substantially similar to the Commission's model notice with all information clearly and prominently displayed. Consumer reporting agencies may limit the disclosure to only those items that they know are relevant to the furnisher that will receive notice.

All furnishers subject to the Federal Trade Commission's jurisdiction must comply with all applicable regulations, including regulation promulgated after this notice was prescribed in 2004. Information about applicable regulations currently in effect can be found at the Commission's website, www.ftc.gov/credit. Furnishers who are not subject to the Commission's jurisdiction should consult with their regulators to find any relevant regulations.

Notices to Furnishers of Information: Obligations of Furnishers Under The FCRA

The federal Fair Credit Reporting Act (FCRA), 15 U.S.C. 1681-1681y, imposes responsibilities on all persons who furnish information to consumer reporting agencies (CRAs). These responsibilities are found in Section 623 of the FCRA, 15 U.S.C. 1681s-2. State law may impose additional requirements on furnishers. All furnishers of information to CRAs should become familiar with the law and may want to consult with their counsel to ensure that they are in compliance. The text of the FCRA is set forth in full at the website of the Federal Trade Commission (FTC): **www.ftc.gov/credit**.

Section 623 imposes the following duties upon furnishers:

Accuracy Guidelines

The banking and credit union regulators and the FTC will promulgate guidelines and regulations dealing with the accuracy of information provided to CRAs by furnishers. The regulations and guidelines issued by the FTC will be available at www.ftc.gov/credit when they are issued. **Sections 623(e)**.

General Prohibition on Reporting Inaccurate Information

The FCRA prohibits information furnishers from providing information to a CRA that they know or have reasonable cause to believe is inaccurate. However, the furnisher is not subject to this general prohibition if it clearly and conspicuously specifies an address to which consumers may write to notify the furnisher that certain information is inaccurate. **Sections 623(a)(1)(A) and (a)(1)(C)**.

Duty to Correct and Update Information

If at any time a person who regularly and in the ordinary course of business furnishes information to one or more CRAs determines that the information provided is not complete or accurate, the furnisher must promptly provide complete and accurate information to the CRA. In addition, the furnisher must notify all CRAs that received the information of any corrections, and must thereafter report only the complete and accurate information. **Section 623(a)(2)**.

Duties After Notice of Dispute from Consumer

If a consumer notifies a furnisher, at an address specified by the furnisher for such notices, that specific information is inaccurate, and the information is, in fact, inaccurate, the furnisher must thereafter report the correct information to CRAs. *Section 623(a)(1)(B)*

If a consumer notifies a furnisher that the consumer disputes the completeness or accuracy of any information reported by the furnisher, the furnisher may not subsequently report that information to a CRA without providing notice of the dispute. *Section 623(a)(3)*

The federal banking and credit union regulators and the FTC will issue regulations that will identify when an information furnisher must investigate a dispute made directly to the furnisher by a consumer. Once these regulations are issued, furnishers must comply with them and complete and investigation within 30 days (or 45 days, if the consumer later provides relevant additional information) unless the disputer is frivolous or irrelevant or comes from a "credit repair organization." The FTC regulations available at www.ftc.gov/credit. Section 623(a)(8).

Duties After Notice of Dispute from Consumer Reporting Agency

If a CRA notifies a furnisher that a consumer disputes the completeness or accuracy of information provided by the furnisher, the furnisher has a duty to follow certain procedures. The furnisher must:

- Conduct an investigation and review all relevant information provided by the CRA, including information given to the CRA by the consumer. **Sections 623(b)(1)(A) and (b)(1)(B)**.

- Report the results to the CRA that referred the dispute, and, if the investigation establishes that the information was, in fact, incomplete or inaccurate, report the results to all CRAs to which the furnisher provided the information that compile and maintain files on a nationwide basis. **Sections 623(b)(1)(C) and (b)(1)(D)**.

- Complete the above steps within 30 days from the date the CRA receives the dispute (or 45 days, if the consumer later provides relevant additional information to the CRA). Section 623(b)(2).

- Promptly modify or delete the information, or block its reporting. Section 623(b)(1)(E).

Duty to Report Voluntary Closing of Credit Accounts

If a consumer voluntarily closes a credit account, any person who regularly and in the ordinary course of business furnishes information to one or more CRAs must report this fact when it provides information to CRAs for the time period which the account was closed. *Sec. 623(a)(4)*

Duty to Report Dates of Delinquencies

If a furnisher reports information concerning a delinquent account placed for collection, charged to profit or loss, or subject to any similar action, the furnisher must, within 90 days after reporting the information, provide the CRA with the month and the year of the commencement of the delinquency that immediately preceded the action, so that the agency will know how long to keep the information in the consumer's file. Section 623(a)(5)

Any person, such as a debt collector, that has acquired or is responsible for collecting delinquent accounts and that reports information to CRAs may comply with the requirements of Section 623(a)(5) (until there is a consumer dispute) by reporting the same delinquency date previously reported by the creditor. If the creditor did not report this date, they may comply with the FCRA by establishing reasonable procedures to obtain and report delinquency dates, or, if a delinquency date cannot be reasonably obtained, by following reasonable procedures to ensure that the date reported precedes the date when the account was place for collection, charged to profit or loss, or subject to any similar action. Section 623(a)(5).

Duty of Financial Institutions When Reporting Negative Information

Financial Institutions that furnish information to "nationwide" consumer reporting agencies, as defined in Section 603(p), must notify consumers in writing if they may furnish or have furnished negative information to a CRA. Section 623(a)(7). The Federal Reserve Board has prescribed model disclosures, 12 CFR Part 222, App. B.

Duty When Furnishing Medical Information

A furnisher whose primary business is providing medical services, products, or devices (and such furnisher's agents or assignees) is a medical information furnisher for the purposes of the FCRA and must notify all CRAs to which it reports of this fact. Section 623(a)(9). This notice will enable CRAs to comply with their duties under Section 604(g) when reporting medical information.

Duties When ID Theft Occurs

All furnishers must have in place reasonable procedures to respond to notifications from CRAs that information furnished is the result of identity theft, and to prevent refurnishing the information in the future. A furnisher may not furnish information that a consumer has identified as resulting from identity theft unless the furnisher subsequently knows or is informed by the consumer that the information is correct. Section 623(a)(6). If a furnisher learns that it has furnished inaccurate information due to identity theft, it must notify each consumer reporting agency of the correct information and must thereafter report only complete and accurate information. Section 623(a)(2). When any furnisher of information is notified pursuant to the procedures set forth in section 605B that a debt has resulted from identity theft, the furnisher may not sell, transfer, or place for collection the debt except in certain limited circumstances. Section 615(f).

The FTC's website, www.ftc.gov/credit, has more information about the FCRA, including publications for business and the full text of the FCRA.

Appendix H to Part 698 - Notice of User Responsibilities

The prescribed form for this disclosure is a separate document that is substantially similar to the Commission's notice with all information clearly and prominently displayed. Consumer reporting agencies may limit the disclosure to only those items that they know are relevant to the furnisher that will receive notice.

All users subject to the Federal Trade Commission's jurisdiction must comply with all applicable regulations, including regulations promulgated after this notice was prescribed in 2004. Information about applicable regulations currently in effect can be found at the Commission's website, www.ftc.gov/credit. Persons not subject to the Commission's jurisdiction should consult with their regulators to find any relevant regulations.

Notice to Users of Consumer Reports: Obligations of Users Under the FCRA

The federal Fair Credit Reporting Act (FCRA), 15 U.S.C. 1681-1691y, requires that this notice be provided to inform users of consumer reports of their legal obligations. State law may impose additional requirements. The text of the FCRA is set forth in full at the Federal Trade Commission website at www.ftc.giv/credit. Other information about user duties is also available at the Commission's website. **Users must consult the relevant provisions of the FCRA for details about their obligations under the FCRA.**

This first section of this summary sets forth the responsibilities imposed by the FCRA on all users of consumer reports. The subsequent sections discuss the duties of users of reports that contain specific types of information, or that are used for certain purposes, and the legal consequences of violations. If you are a furnisher of information to a consumer reporting agency (CRA), you have additional obligations and will receive a separate notice from the CRA describing your duties as a furnisher.

I. OBLIGATIONS OF ALL USERS OF CONSUMER REPORTS

A. Users Must Have a Permissible Purpose

Congress has limited the use of consumer reports to protect consumers' privacy. All users must have a permissible purpose under the FCRA to obtain a consumer report. Section 604 of the FCRA contains a list of the permissible purposes under the law. These are:

- As ordered by a court or a federal grand jury subpoena. **Section 604(a)(1)**.

- As instructed by the consumer in writing. **Section 604(a)(2)**.

- For the extension of credit as a result of an application from a consumer, or the review or collection of a consumer's account. Section 604(a)(3)(A).

- For employment purposes, including hiring and promotion decisions, where the consumer has given written permission. Sections 604(a)(3)(B) and 604(b).

- For the underwriting of insurance as a result of an application from a consumer. Section 604(a)(3)(C).

- When there is a legitimate business need, in connection with a business transaction that is initiated by the consumer. Section 604(a)(3)(F)(i).

- To review a consumer's account to determine whether the consumer continues to meet the terms of the account. Section 604(a)(3)(F)(ii).

- To determine a consumer's eligibility for a license or other benefit granted by a governmental instrumentality required by law to consider an applicant's financial responsibility or status. Section 604(a)(3)(D).

- For use by a potential investor or servicer, or current insurer, in a valuation or assessment of the credit or prepayment risks associated with an existing credit obligation. Section 604(a)(3)(E).

- For use by state and local officials in connection with the determination of child support payments, or modifications and enforcement thereof. Sections 604(a)(4) and 604(a)(5).

In addition, creditors and insurers may obtain certain consumer report information for the purpose of making "prescreened" unsolicited offers of credit or insurance. Section 604(c). The particular obligations of users of "prescreened" information are described in Section VII below.

B. Users Must Provide Certifications

Section 604(f) prohibits any person from obtaining a consumer report from a consumer reporting agency (CRA) unless the person has certified to the CRA the permissible purpose(s) for which the report is being obtained and certifies that the report will not be used for any other purpose.

C. Users Must Notify Consumers When Adverse Actions Are Taken

The term "adverse action" is defined very broadly by Section 603 of the FCRA. "Adverse actions" include all business, credit, and employment actions affecting consumers that can be considered to have a negative impact as defined by Section 603(k) of the FCRA – such as denying or canceling credit or insurance, or denying employment or promotion. No adverse action occurs in a credit transaction where the creditor makes a counteroffer that is accepted by the consumer.

1. Adverse Actions Based on Information Obtained From a CRA

If a user takes any type of adverse action as defined by the FCRA that is based at least in part on information contained in a consumer report, Section 615(a) requires the user to notify the consumer. The notification may be done in writing, orally, or by electronic means. It must include the following:

- The name, address, and telephone number of the CRA (including a toll-free telephone number, if it is a nationwide CRA) that provided the report.
- A statement that the CRA did not make the adverse decision and is not able to explain why the decision was made.
- A statement setting forth the consumer's right to obtain a free disclosure of the consumer's file from the CRA if the consumer requests the report within 60 days.
- A statement setting forth the consumer's right to dispute directly with the CRA the accuracy or completeness of any information provided by the CRA.

2. Adverse Actions Based on Information Obtained From Third Parties Who Are Not Consumer Reporting Agencies

If a person denies (or increases the charge for) credit for personal, family, or household purposes based either wholly or partly upon information from a person other than a CRA, and the information is the type of consumer information covered by the FCRA, Section 615(b)(1) requires that the user clearly and accurately disclose to the consumer his or her right to be told the nature of the information that was relied upon if the consumer makes a written request within 60 days of notification. The user must provide the disclosure within a reasonable period of time following the consumer's written request.

3. Adverse Actions Based on Information Obtained From Affiliates

If a person takes an adverse action involving insurance, employment, or a credit transaction initiated by the consumer, based on information of the type covered by the FCRA, and this information was obtained from an entity affiliated with the user of the information by common ownership or control, Section 615(b)(2) requires the user to notify the consumer of the adverse action. The notice must inform the consumer that he or she may obtain a disclosure of the nature of the information relied upon by making a written request within 60 days of receiving the adverse action notice. If the consumer makes such a request, the user must disclose the nature of the information not later than 30 days after receiving the request. If consumer report information is shared among affiliates and then used for an adverse action, the user must make an adverse action disclosure as set forth in I.C.1 above.

D. Users have Obligations When Fraud and Active Duty Military Alerts are in Files

When a consumer has placed a fraud alert, including one relating to identity theft, or an active duty military alert with a nationwide consumer reporting agency as defined in Section 603(p) and resellers, 605A(h) imposes limitation on users of reports obtained from the consumer reporting agency in certain circumstances, including the establishment of a new credit plan and the issuance of additional credit cards. For the initial fraud alerts and active duty alerts, the user must have reasonable policies and procedures in place to form a belief that the user knows the identity of the applicant or contact the consumer at a telephone number specified by the consumer; in the case of extended fraud alerts, the user must contact the consumer in accordance with the contact information provided in the consumer's alert.

E. Users Have Obligations When Notified of an Address Discrepancy

Section 605(h) requires nationwide CRAs, as defined in Section 603(p), to notify users that request reports when the address for a consumer provided by the user in requesting the report is substantially different from the addresses in the consumer's file. When this occurs, users must comply with regulations specifying the procedures to be followed, which will be issued by the Federal Trade Commission and the banking and credit union regulators. The Federal Trade Commission's regulations will be available at www.ftc.gov/credit.

F. Users Have Obligations When Disposing of Records

Section 628 requires that all users of consumer report information have in place procedures to properly dispose of records containing this information. The Federal Trade Commission, the Securities and Exchange Commission, and the banking and credit union regulators have issued regulations covering disposal. The Federal Trade Commission's regulations may be found at www.ftc.gov/credit.

II. CREDITORS MUST MAKE ADDITIONAL DISCLOSURES

If a person uses a consumer report in connection with an application for, or a grant, extension, or provision of, credit to a consumer on material terms that are materially less favorable than the most favorable terms available to a substantial proportion of consumers from or through that person, based in whole or in part on a consumer report, the person must provide a risk-based pricing notice to the consumer in accordance with regulations to be jointly prescribed by the Federal Trade Commission and the Federal Reserve Board.

Section 609(g) requires a disclosure by all persons that make or arrange loans secured by residential real property (one to four units) and that use credit scores. These persons must provide credit scores and other information about credit scores to applicants, including the disclosure set forth in section 609(g)(1)(D)("Notice to the Home Loan Applicant").

III. OBLIGATIONS OF USERS WHEN CONSUMER REPORTS ARE OBTAINED FOR EMPLOYMENT PURPOSES

A. Employment Other Than in the Trucking Industry

If information from a CRA is used for employment purposes, the user has specific duties set forth in FCRA Section 604(b). The user must:

- Make a clear and conspicuous written disclosure to the consumer before the report is obtained, in a document that consists solely of the disclosure, that a consumer report may be obtained.

- Obtain from the consumer prior written authorization. Authorization to access reports during the term of employment may be obtained at the time of employment.

- Certify to the CRA that the above steps have been followed, that the information being obtained will not be used in violation of any federal or state equal opportunity law or regulation, and that, if any adverse action is to be taken based on the consumer report, a copy of the report and a summary of the consumer's rights will be provided to the consumer.

- **Before** taking an adverse action, the user must provide a copy of the report to the consumer as well as the summary of the consumer's rights. (The user should receive this summary from the CRA.) A Section 615(a) adverse action notice should be sent after the adverse action is taken.

An adverse action notice also is required in employment situations if credit information (other than transactions and experience data) obtained from an affiliate is used to deny employment. Section 615(b)(2).

The procedures for investigative consumer reports and employee misconduct investigations are set forth below.

B. Employment in the Trucking Industry

Special rules apply for truck drivers where the only interaction between the consumer and the potential employer is by mail, telephone, or computer. In this case, the consumer may provide consent orally or electronically, and an adverse action may be made orally, in writing, or electronically. The consumer may obtain a copy of any report relied upon by the trucking company by contacting the company.

IV. OBLIGATIONS OF USERS OF INVESTIGATIVE CONSUMER REPORTS

Investigative consumer reports are a special type of consumer report in which information about a consumer's character, general reputation, personal characteristics, and mode of living is obtained through personal interviews by an entity or person that is a consumer reporting agency. Consumers who are the subjects of such reports are given special rights under the FCRA. If a user intends to obtain an investigative consumer report, Section 606 requires the following:

- The user must disclose to the consumer that an investigative consumer report may be obtained. This must be done in a written disclosure that is mailed, or otherwise delivered, to the consumer at some time before or not later than three days after the date on which the report was first requested. The disclosure must include a statement informing the consumer of his or her right to request additional disclosures of the nature and scope of the investigation as described below, and the summary of consumer rights required by

Section 609 of the FCRA. (The summary of consumer rights will be provided by the CRA that conducts the investigation.)

- The user must certify to the CRA that the disclosures set forth above have been made and that the user will make the disclosure described below.

- Upon the written request of a consumer made within a reasonable period of time after the disclosures required above, the user must make a complete disclosure of the nature and scope of the investigation. This must be made in a written statement that is mailed, or otherwise delivered, to the consumer no later than five days after the date on which the request was received from the consumer or the report was first requested, whichever is later in time.

V. SPECIAL PROCEDURES FOR EMPLOYEE INVESTIGATIONS

Section 603(x) provides special procedures for investigations of suspected misconduct by an employee or for compliance with Federal, state or local laws and regulations or the rules of a self-regulatory organization, and compliance with written policies of the employer. These investigations are not treated as consumer reports so long as the employer or its agent complies with the procedures set forth in Section 603(x), and a summary describing the nature and scope of the inquiry is made to the employee if an adverse action is taken based on the investigation.

VI. OBLIGATIONS OF USERS OF MEDICAL INFORMATION

Section 604(g) limits the use of medical information obtained from consumer reporting agencies (other than payment information that appears in a coded form that does not identify the medical provider). If the report is to be used for an insurance transaction, the consumer must give consent to the user of the report or the information must be coded. If the report is to be used for employment purposes – or in connection with a credit transaction (except as provided in regulations issued by the banking and credit union regulators) – the consumer must provide specific written consent and the medical information must be relevant. Any user who receives medical information shall not disclose the information to any other person (except where necessary to carry out the purpose for which the information was disclosed, or as permitted by statute, regulation, or order.)

VII. OBLIGATIONS OF USERS OF "PRESCREENED LISTS"

The FCRA permits creditors and insurers to obtain limited consumer report information for use in connection with unsolicited offers of credit or insurance under certain circumstances. Sections 603(l), 604(c), 604(e), and 615(d). This practice is known as "prescreening" and typically involves obtaining from a CRA a list of consumers who meet certain pre-established criteria. If any person intends to use prescreened lists, that person must (1) before the offer is made, establish the criteria that will be relied upon to make the offer and to grant credit or insurance, and (2) maintain such criteria on file for a three-year period beginning on the date on which the offer is made to each consumer. In addition, any user must provide with each written solicitation a clear and conspicuous statement that:

- Information contained in a consumer's CRA file was used in connection with the transaction.
- The consumer received the offer because he or she satisfied the criteria for credit worthiness or insurability used to screen for the offer.
- Credit or insurance may not be extended if, after the consumer responds, it is determined that the consumer does not meet the criteria used for screening or any applicable criteria bearing on credit worthiness or insurability, or the consumer does not furnish required collateral.
- The consumer may prohibit the use of information in his or her file in connection with future prescreened offers of credit or insurance by contacting the notification system established by the CRA that provided the report. The statement must include the address and the toll-free telephone number of the appropriate notification system.

In addition, once the Federal Trade Commission by rule has established the format, type size, and manner of the disclosure required by Section 615(d), users must be in compliance with the rule. The FTC's regulations will be at www.ftc.gov/credit.

VIII. OBLIGATIONS OF RESELLERS

A. Disclosure and Certification Requirements

Section 607(e) of the FCRA requires any person who obtains a consumer report for resale to take the following steps:

- Disclose the identity of the end-user to the source CRA.
- Identify to the source CRA each permissible purpose for which the report will be furnished to the end-user.
- Establish and follow reasonable procedures to ensure that reports are resold only for permissible purposes, including procedures to obtain:
  1. the identity of all end-users;
  2. certifications from all users of each purpose for which reports will be used; and
  3. certifications that reports will not be used for any purpose other than the purpose(s) specified to the reseller. Resellers must make reasonable efforts to verify this information before selling the report.

B. Re-investigations by Resellers

Under Section 611(f), if a consumer disputes the accuracy or completeness of information in a report prepared by a reseller, the reseller must determine whether this is a result of an action or omission on its part and, if so, correct or delete the information. If not, the reseller must send the dispute to the source CRA for reinvestigation. When any

CRA notifies the reseller of the results of an investigation, the reseller must immediately convey the information to the consumer.

C. Fraud Alerts and Resellers

Section 605(f) requires resellers who receive fraud alerts or active duty alerts from another consumer reporting agency to include these in their reports.

IX. LIABILITY FOR VIOLATIONS OF THE FCRA

Failure to comply with the FCRA can result in state government or federal government enforcement actions, as well as private lawsuits. Sections 616, 617, and 621. In addition, any person who knowingly and willfully obtains a consumer report under false pretenses may face criminal prosecution. Section 619.

Safe Hiring Tip ➤ The Federal Trade Commission website at www.ftc.gov/os/statutes/fcrajump.htm is a great resource filled with information, including Staff Opinion Letters, Educational Materials, and a complete copy of the act.

Appendix 2: Title VII EEOC Notices

There are four important notices written by the Equal Employment Opportunities Commission (EEOC) that detail what an employer can and cannot do with criminal records and age.

- Notice N-915.043 (July, 1989)
- Notice N-915-061 (9/7/90)
- Notice N-915 (7/29/87)
- Notice N-915 (2/4/87)

For more about the EEOC, visit their website at www.eeoc.gov

Notice N-915.043 (July, 1989)

1. SUBJECT: Job advertising and Pre-Employment Inquiries Under the Age Discrimination In Employment Ace (ADEA).

2. PURPOSE: This policy guidance provides a discussion of job advertising and pre-employment inquiries under the ADEA. Additionally, certain defenses are discussed that may be proffered by respondents when impermissible practices appear to be involved.

3. EXPIRATION DATE: As an exception to EEOC Order 205.001, Appendix B, Attachment 4, § a(5), this Notice will remain in effect until rescinded or superseded.

The ADEA makes it unlawful, unless a specific exemption applies, for an employer to utilize job advertising that discriminates on account of age against persons 40 years of age or older. Specifically, sec. 4(e) of the ADEA provides as follows:

It shall be unlawful for an employer, labor organization, or employment agency to print of publish, or cause to be printed or published, any notice or advertisement relating to employment by such an employer or membership in or any classification or referral for employment by such a labor organization, or relating to any classification or referral for employment by such an employment agency, indicating any preference, limitation, specification, or discrimination, based on age. 29 USC. § 623(e).

The commission interpretative regulation further develops the statutory language by providing the following guidance.

When help wanted notices or advertisements contain terms and phrases such as "age 25 to 35," "young," "college student," "recent college graduate," "boy," "girl," or others of a similar nature, such a term or phrase a violation of the Act, unless one of the exceptions applies. Such phrases as "40 to 50," "age over 65," "retired persons," or "supplement your pension" discriminate against others within the protected group and, therefore, are prohibited unless one of the exceptions applies. 29 C.F.R. S 1625.4(a).

Notice N-915-061 (9/7/90)

1. <u>SUBJECT</u>: Policy Guidance on the Consideration of Arrest Records in Employment Decisions under Title VII of the Civil Rights Act of 1964, as amended, 42 USC. § 2000e <u>et seq.</u> (1982).

2. <u>PURPOSE</u>: This policy guidance sets forth the Commission's procedure for determining whether arrest records may be considered in employment decisions.

3. <u>EFFECTIVE DATE</u>: September 7, 1990.

4. <u>EXPIRATION DATE</u>: As an exception to EEOC Order 205.001, Appendix B, Attachment 4, § a(5), this Notice will remain in effect until rescinded or superseded.

The question addressed in this policy guidance is "to what extent may arrest records be used in making employment decisions?" The Commission concludes that since the use of arrest records as an absolute bar to employment has a disparate impact on some protected groups, such records alone cannot be used to routinely exclude persons from employment. However, conduct which indicates unsuitability for a particular position is a basis for exclusion. Where it appears that the applicant or employee engaged in the conduct for which he was arrested and the conduct is job-related and relatively recent, exclusion is justified.

Notice N-915 (7/29/87)

1. <u>SUBJECT</u>: Policy statement on the use of statistics in charges involving the exclusion of individuals with conviction records from employment

2. <u>PURPOSE</u>: This policy statement sets forth the commission's view as to the appropriate statistics to be used in evaluating an employer's policy of refusing to hire individuals with conviction records.

3. <u>EFFECTIVE DATE</u>: July 29, 1987

4. <u>EXPIRATION DATE</u>: January 29, 1988

5. <u>ORIGINATOR</u>: title VII.EPA Division, Office of Legal Counsel.

<u>Green v. Missouri Pacific Railroad Company</u>, 523 F.2d 1290, 10 EPD 10,314 (8th Cir. 1975), is the leading Title VII case on the issue of conviction records. In <u>Green</u>, the court held that the defendant's policy of refusing employment to any person convicted of a crime other than a minor traffic offense had an adverse impact on Black applicants and was not justified by business necessity. In a second appeal following remand, the court upheld the district court's injunctive order prohibiting the defendant from using an applicant's conviction record as an absolute bar to employment but allowing it to consider a prior criminal record as long as it constituted a business necessity.

Notice N-915 (2/4/87)

1. SUBJECT: Policy Statement on the Issue of Conviction Records under Title VII of the Civil Rights Act of 1964, as amended, 42 U.S.C. § 2000e et seq. (1982).

2. PURPOSE: This policy statement sets forth the Commission's revised procedure for determining the existence of a business necessity justifying, for purposes of Title VII, the exclusion of an individual from employment on the basis of a conviction record.

3. EFFECTIVE DATE: February 27, 1987.

4. EXPIRATION DATE: September 15, 1987.

5. ORIGINATOR: Office of Legal Counsel.

At the Commission meeting of November 26, 1985, the Commission approved a modification of its existing policy with respect to the manner in which a business necessity is established for denying an individual employment because of a conviction record. The modification, which is set forth below, does not alter the Commission's underlying position that an employer's policy or practice of excluding individuals from employment on the basis of their conviction records has an adverse impact on Blacks[1] and Hispanics[2] in light of statistics showing that they are convicted at a rate disproportionately greater than their representation in the population. Consequently, the Commission has held and continues to hold that such a policy or practice is unlawful under Title VII in the absence of a justifying business necessity.

Three factors to determine whether a decision was justified by business necessity:

1. The nature and gravity of the offense or offenses:

2. The time that has passed since the conviction and/or completion of the sentence; and

o The nature of the job held or sought.[6]

The Commission continues to hold that, where there is evidence of adverse impact, an absolute bar to employment based on the mere fact that an individual has a conviction record is unlawful under Title VII.[8] The Commission's position on this issue is supported by the weight of judicial authority [9]

---

[6] See Commission Decision No. 78-03, CCH EEOC Decisions (1983) ¶ 6714.

[8] See, e.g., Commission Decision No. 78-35, CCH EEOC Decisions (1983) ¶ 6720.

[9] See Green, 523 F.2d at 1298; Carter v. Gallagher, 452 F.2d 315, 3 EPD ¶ 8335 (8ᵗʰ Cir. 1971), cert. denied, 406 US 950, 4 EPD ¶ 7818 (1972) (brought under 42 U.S.C. §§ 1981 and 1983); and Richardson v. Hotel Corporation of America, 332 F. Supp. 519, 4 EPD ¶ 7666 (E.D. La. 1971), aff'd mem., 468 F.2d 951, 5 EPD ¶ 8101 (5ᵗʰ Cir. 1972). See also Hill v. United States Postal Service, 522 F. Supp. 1283 (S.D.N.Y. 1981); Craig v. Department of Health, Education, and Welfare, 508 F. Supp. 1055 (W.D. Mo. 1981); and Cross v. United States Postal Service, 483 F. Supp. 1050 (E.D. Mo. 1979), aff'd in relevant part, 639 F.2d 409, 25 EPD ¶ 31,594 (8ᵗʰ Cir. 1981).

Appendix 3: The Application Process Checklist

Task	Yes/No/ NA	Date/ Initials	Notes/Follow-up
Application Process—			
Did applicant sign the consent form?			
Is application complete?			
Did applicant sign and date application?			
Did applicant leave criminal questions blank?			
Did applicant indicate a criminal record?			
Did applicant explain why left past jobs?			
Did applicant explain gaps in job history?			
Any excessive cross-outs or changes seen?			
Interview Process—			
Did applicant explain any excessive cross-outs/changes?			
Leaving past jobs: Did applicant explain?			

Task	Yes/No/ NA	Date/ Initials	Notes/Follow-up
Leaving past jobs: Was verbal reason consistent with reason on app?			
Employment Gaps: Did applicant explain?			
Employment Gaps: Are verbal explanations consistent with app?			
Security Question 1 – "Our firm has a standard policy of background checks and drug tests on all applicants. Do you have any concerns you would like to share with me about our procedures?"			Answer:
Security Question 2 – "If I were to contact the courthouse or Police Dept., would we locate any criminal convictions or pending cases?"			Answer:
Security Question 3 – "If I were to contact past employers pursuant to the release you have signed, what do you think they would tells us about you?"			Answer:
Security Question 4 – "If I were to contact past employers pursuant to the release you have signed, would any of them tell us you were terminated or were disciplined?"			Answer:

Task	Yes/No/ NA	Date/ Initials	Notes/Follow-up
Security Question 5 – "Please explain any gaps in employment."			Answer:

Reference Checks[87]—

Task	Yes/No/ NA	Date/ Initials	Notes/Follow-up
Have references been checked for at least last 5-10 years, regardless of whether past employers will give details?			
Have efforts been documented?			
Discrepancies between information located and what applicant reported in application: a. dates/title salary/ job title b. reason for leaving			

Background Check—

Task	Yes/No/ NA	Date/ Initials	Notes/Follow-up
Submitted for background check?			
Check completed?			
Background check reviewed for discrepancies/issues?			
If not CLEAR or SATISFACTORY, what action is taken per policy and procedures?			Describe:

---

[87] Reference checks can either be performed by employer or by a third party.

Appendix 4: Verification & Reference Worksheet

Name Of Applicant	
Social Security Number	
Previous Employer Name	
City/State	
Phone Number	
Fax Number	
Contact Name	
Relationship To Candidate	
Title And Department	

	Applicant Reported	**Employer Reported**
Start Date		
End Date		
Starting Position		
Ending Position		
Ending Salary		
Reason For Leaving		
Eligible for rehire?		

Will employer give reference? YES NO
If yes, see last page for reference information

Call History...

Date	Time	Who Called	Results	Notes

1. Please record all efforts made to obtain a Verification and Reference for this applicant
2. Please note any changes in phone numbers or special instructions needed to obtain a reference on this applicant
3. If unsuccessful and no response to voice mail, contact the main number and send a fax to the employer. Note time and date fax sent.

EMPLOYMENT REFERENCE for: _____

If given by a source different than above, please note:

Reference Name	
Phone Number	
Relationship To Candidate	
Title And Department	
Current employer (if different)	

1. What were the applicant's job and
   the nature of his/her duties?

2. Is the applicant's resume description
   of their duties accurate and consistent?

3. Can you describe or give examples
   of the applicant's strengths?

4. What could the applicant do to
   improve his/her job performance?

5. How would you describe the quality of his/her work?
   Can you give examples?

6. Can you describe how he/she got along with others?
   (Teamwork, relationship to supervisors, etc.)

7. Can you give examples of times when the applicant
   demonstrated leadership characteristics?

8. How would you describe the applicant's communication skills?
   (If a supervisor, describe how he/she supervised others)

9. How did the applicant show initiative or leadership in his/her job?

10. Were there any problems with attendance or punctuality?

11. Were there any work-related problems with this applicant?

12. On a scale of 1-10 (10 being the highest), overall,
    how would you rate the applicant's performance?

13. If you were responsible for the hiring process,
    would you consider him/her eligible for rehire?

14. Do you have any additional comments regarding this applicant?

Additional Interview Questions of a Past Employer...

1. In what areas did the applicant show the need for improvement?

2. How did the applicant get along with supervisors/managers?

3. Did the applicant exhibit any tendency towards violence or
   inappropriate conduct/behavior that was workplace related?
   (this may include use of drugs, alcohol or dishonesty)

4. How did the candidate compare to the person doing the job now?

5. Can you identify specific jobs this applicant would be better suited for?

6. How did the candidate respond when confronted with an urgent assignment?

7. Do you have any additional comments regarding this applicant?

8. Why didn't you try to rehire or induce him/her to stay?

Appendix 5: The Safe Hiring Timeline

Time	Event/Action	Notes
Pre-need stage (prior to vacancy or creation of new position)	Development of training policy and procedures.	Organizational assessments are made specifically targeting hiring policies and procedures that need to be in place before new hires are made. Necessary managerial/HR/security training is outlined and begun. Methods for auditing system progress and performance are reviewed/agreed upon.
Creation of new Position ~ or ~ **Existing Position becomes open**	Development of announcement of vacancy, employment classifieds, etc.	Method of job advertising is selected (print, electronic media, etc.[88]) Specific screening policy language is included in all announcements and classifieds ads mentioning employment.
Application stage	Applicants respond to job ad, begin to submit resumes/CVs to hiring firm.	Candidates should be asked to fill out and submit an application along with/instead of a resume or CV. Application includes specific language discussing screening policies, also specific questions, releases, and standard statements.
Application Review stage	Sorting and weeding. Applicants are narrowed into candidates.	Hiring manager reviews all applications for red flags, including incomplete or ambiguous answers; reviews and considers applicants' reasons for leaving previous jobs. Hiring manager identifies suitable applicants, makes note of further required areas of questioning, and notifies candidates of their status.

---

[88] Some job board software and application service provider solutions are available that allow a degree of assessment and/or skills testing to take place during the application process. These require the specific needs –education, skills, etc. – be considered and addressed at the time the job advertisement is created.

Time	Event/Action	Notes
Interview stage	More sorting and weeding. Candidates are selected conditional on passing a background check.	Interviewers ask candidates permissible questions designed to ensure honesty and integrity, making sure all candidates are asked the same questions and treated equally. Candidates are again informed of company's screening policies.
Background Investigation stage	Candidate-provided statements and information are verified. Further information on the candidate's past is researched and collected.	References are checked, previous employers are contacted. Wages, credentials, degrees, licenses, etc. are verified. Court records are checked. Credit reports are requested. Workers' Comp claims are researched. All information is gathered in compliance with state/local laws and the FCRA.
Analysis of Information stage	Collected data is reviewed.	Information retrieved is reviewed and compared to candidate statements and claims. Discrepancies are identified. Negative information from a candidate's past is reviewed in the context of its impact on a candidate's ability to perform the required tasks or eligibility for employment. Ineligibility must be in compliance with EEOC, state and regional rules.
Post-hire stage	Policies and procedures are in place to maintain a safe workplace.	Screening is standard procedure for promotion, reassignment, and retention. Investigations are possible where necessary for claims of harassment, theft, violence, or other difficulties.

Appendix 6: Description of Pre-Employment Screening Tools

Criminal Record Search   (County Courts)

What It Will Tell	Reason you need this information	Limits/Notes on using this information
Felony and Misdemeanor convictions and pending cases, usually including date and nature of offense, sentencing date, disposition and current status. Generally goes back seven years. May also search federal court records. It is critical to search both for felonies and misdemeanors in state court, since many serious job-related violations can be classified as misdemeanors.	... Is critical information to protect your business and employees. Protects employer from negligent hiring exposure and helps reduce threat of workplace violence, theft, disruption and other problems. Failure to honestly disclose a prior criminal conviction can be a basis not to hire. For the maximum protection, all jurisdictions where an applicant has lived, worked or studied in the past seven years should be checked.	Some restrictions on having certain information (such as arrests not resulting in convictions), or certain minor offenses.[89] Employment cannot be automatically denied based upon a criminal record, but must show some sound business reason. Criminal records are not available by computer nationwide. Check public records at county courthouses[90] in locations where applicant resided or worked. Be careful in using databases– if there is a "hit" then file must be reviewed for identifiers and details.

Social Security Number Trace / Social Security Number Check

What It Will Tell	Reason you need this information	Limits/Notes on using this information
Provides names and addresses associated with the applicant's Social Security Number and may indicate fraudulent use. Helps verify other applicant information.	Helps verify applicants are who they say they are, critical to ensure employer not the victim of a fraudulent application by someone with something to hide. Can show where to search criminal records.	Where employer does not have a sound business reason to obtain a business credit report, the Social Security trace gives information to help confirm identity and may uncover fraud.

---

[89] For instance, in New York state, misdemeanors cannot be considered — and all misdemeanors could not be found as there are over 1300 courts handling some sort of misdemeanor records in New York.

[90] There can be delays when a court clerk pulls a file. Some courts charge a court search fee, copy fee, certification fee.

Driver's License Search

What It Will Tell	Reason you need this information	Limits/Notes on using this information
Driving history for three years. Verification of driving privilege, and operator restrictions that might indicate the applicant's ability to perform job tasks.	Helps verify identity. Gives insight on level of applicant's responsibility. Determine if applicant keeps commitments to appear in court or pay fines, has a drug/alcohol problem, and current license status. "Driving for work" is broadly defined in most jurisdictions and is not limited to driving jobs.	This information can be accessed by an outside agency on the employer's behalf. Background firms can also help interpret the DMV record. An alternative is having applicants go to the DMV to obtain their records, which is not practical and is subject to fraud. DMV may have a program for firms that would like record updates.

Credit Report

What It Will Tell	Reason you need this information	Limits/Notes on using this information
Credit history and public records such as judgments, liens, and bankruptcies. May include previous employers, addresses, and other names used.[91]	Helps determine whether an employee is suitable for a position involving handling cash or the exercise of financial discretion. A way to gauge trustworthiness and reliability.	A credit report should only be requested when it is specifically relevant to a job function, and the employer has appropriate policies and procedures in place to ensure that the use of credit reports are relevant and fair.

Employment Verification

What It Will Tell	Reason you need this information	Limits/Notes on using this information
Basic verification includes dates of employment, job title, and reason for leaving. Some employers will verify salary. Usually obtained from HR, personnel, or payroll dept. Some employers provide reference information recorded on 900 service.	Past employment information confirms applicant's resume, and verifies their previous job history. Helps eliminate *unexplained gaps* in employment, which ensures that appropriate jurisdictions have been checked for criminal	Employers are often hesitant to give recommendations and may limit prior employment checks to release of basic information only. Limited results *if*— not allowed to contact current employer, employer will not return call, past employer is out of business or cannot be located, or if

---

[91] An employment credit report differs from commercial credit report-employment version. The employment version does not have age, credit scoring, or account numbers of credit cards.

	records, reducing chance of incarceration for a serious offense.	employee was working through an agency.

Employment Reference Check

What It Will Tell	Reason you need this information	Limits/Notes on using this information
This is a more in-depth reference check that seeks job duties, performance, salary history, strengths and weaknesses, eligibility for rehire, and other detailed information.	Allows an employer to have a realistic assessment of a candidate from former employers. It promotes a better "fit," confirms the hiring opinion, and protects the expensive hiring investment.	Although most employers would like references, few past employers give them due to concerns over legal liability. Always attempt to obtain verifications and references in order to demonstrate due diligence.

Personal Reference Check

What It Will Tell	Reason you need this information	Limits/Notes on using this information
Contact personal references to ascertain additional information about your applicant concerning fitness for the job in question.	Personal references can provide valuable information as to a person's character as it relates to the job opening.	Inquire about the applicant's relationship to the reference and how long they have known each other in order to judge the usefulness of the information provided. Contact "developed references" for a better picture of the applicant.

Education Verification

What It Will Tell	Reason you need this information	Limits/Notes on using this information
Will confirm degrees, diplomas or certificates, and dates attended.	Confirms that applicant has educational experience and professional ability to do the job.	Industry sources show that 30% of all job applicants falsify information about educational background. Expect to pay a fee for transcripts, but verifications generally free. Some schools require a verification fee, or only fax back documents to an 800 number.

Professional Licenses

What It Will Tell	Reason you need this information	Limits/Notes on using this information
The type of license, whether currently valid, dates issued, state licensing authority.	Confirms whether an applicant has the required credentials or licenses for the position.	There is a high rate of job applicants making up or falsifying licenses or credentials.

Civil Court Records (includes litigation, judgments, and tax liens)

What It Will Tell	Reason you need this information	Limits/Notes on using this information
Date of filing, case type, case number or file record, jurisdiction, and identity of parties involve, if available.	Discover whether your applicant has sued former employers or has been sued for reasons that are relevant to employment.	An employer should use this information where it is relevant to job performance. Have standard policies and procedures for civil records use.

Workers' Compensation Records

What It Will Tell	Reason you need this information	Limits/Notes on using this information
Information about Workers' Compensation claims and previous injuries.	This information allows the employer to conduct *post-job offer* reviews in compliance with strict standards of the Americans with Disabilities Act.	Federal and state laws regulate the use of these records. Have policies and procedures in place before requesting or utilizing Workers' Comp records.

Index

Meet Author Lester S. Rosen...

Lester S. Rosen is an attorney at law and President of Employment Screening Resources, a national background screening company located in California. He is a consultant, writer and frequent presenter nationwide on pre-employment screening and safe hiring issues.

He is a former deputy District Attorney and defense attorney and has taught criminal law and procedure at the University of California Hastings College of the Law. His jury trials have included murder, death penalty, and federal cases. He graduated UCLA with Phi Beta Kappa honors and received a J.D. degree from the University of California at Davis, serving on the Law Review. He holds the highest attorney rating of A.V. in the national Martindale-Hubbell listing of U.S. Attorneys.

In 2002, he worked with the California legislature to amend AB 655, a law that adversely affected employers in the area of reference checks and hiring in California, and testified before the state legislature. He has qualified and testified in the California and Arkansas Superior Courts as an expert witness on issues surrounding safe hiring and due diligence. His speaking appearances have included numerous national and statewide conferences.

He is also featured as the narrator in a training video by Kantola Productions called "Safe Hiring: How You Can Avoid Bad Hires" which you can learn more about at www.esrcheck.com/safe_hiring_video.php

Mr. Rosen was the chairperson of the steering committee that founded the National Association of Professional Background Screeners (NAPBS), a professional trade organization for the screening industry with over 500 members. He was also elected to the first Board of Directors and served as the Co-chairman in 2004.

Mr. Rosen resides with his wife and daughter in Tiburon, California. To contact Mr. Rosen for speaking or professional consultation for businesses, he may be reached at speaker@esrhire.com.